Maths
in Practice
Year 7 Pupil's Book

3

Author team:
David Bowles, Sophie Goldie,
Andrew Manning, David Pritchard,
Shaun Procter-Green, Alan Smith

DL DYNAMIC LEARNING
Innovate • Motivate • Personalise

HODDER
EDUCATION
PART OF HACHETTE LIVRE UK

The Publishers would like to thank the following for permission to reproduce copyright material:
Photo credits: p 27 2001 Census. Crown copyright material is reproduced with the permission of the Comptroller of HMSO; **p 30** Edward Gooch/Getty Images; **p 104** Loolee/Alamy; **p 142** David Cannon/Getty Images; **p 228 (both)** Visual Arts Library (London)/Alamy

Acknowledgements Every effort has been made to trace all copyright holders, but if any have been inadvertently overlooked the Publishers will be pleased to make the necessary arrangements at the first opportunity.

Although every effort has been made to ensure that website addresses are correct at time of going to press, Hodder Education cannot be held responsible for the content of any website mentioned in this book. It is sometimes possible to find a relocated web page by typing in the address of the home page for a website in the URL window of your browser.

Hachette Livre UK's policy is to use papers that are natural, renewable and recyclable products and made from wood grown in sustainable forests. The logging and manufacturing processes are expected to conform to the environmental regulations of the country of origin.

Orders: please contact Bookpoint Ltd, 130 Milton Park, Abingdon, Oxon OX14 4SB. Telephone: (44) 01235 827720. Fax: (44) 01235 400454. Lines are open from 9 a.m. to 5 p.m., Monday to Saturday, with a 24-hour message-answering service. Visit our website at www.hoddereducation.co.uk.

© Sophie Goldie, Andrew Manning, David Pritchard, Shaun Procter-Green, 2008
First published in 2008 by
Hodder Education,
Part of Hachette Livre UK
338 Euston Road
London NW1 3BH

Impression number   10 9 8 7 6 5 4 3 2 1
Year   2013 2012 2011 2010 2009 2008

Illustrations © Oxford Designers and Illustrators; Barking Dog Art
Cover photo © GK Hart/Vikki Hart/Getty
Typeset in VAG Rounded 11/14pt by Pantek Arts Ltd, Maidstone, Kent
Printed in Italy

A catalogue record for this title is available from the British Library

ISBN: 978 0 340 94850 7

Contents

1 Rules of arithmetic 1

2 Lines and angles 7

3 Sequences 18

4 Collecting data 27

5 Multiples and factors 33

6 Decimals 44

7 Accuracy and rounding 54

8 Multiplying and dividing 63

9 Symmetry 73

10 Triangles and quadrilaterals 79

11 Perimeter and area 85

12 Constructions 97

13 Symbols for numbers 104

14 Expressions 109

15 Functions 114

16 Interpreting data 121

17 Averages and range 131

18 Negative numbers 142

19 Fractions 147

20 Units of measurement 157

21 Transformations 165

22 Solids 173

23 Percentages, fractions and decimals 182

24 Proportion and ratio 194

25 Substitution and formulae 204

26 Equations 211

27 Graphs 217

28 Probability 224

29 Representing data 231

1 Rules of arithmetic

Subject links
- science
- geography

Wanted:	Maths Games Tester
Needed for:	28 days
Pay:	£1000 per day
	or 1p for day 1
	2p for day 2
	4p for day 3
	8p for day 4 and so on

Coming up …

- the order of operations
- brackets
- squares and square roots
- solving word problems
- using a calculator

Chapter starter

An eccentric (and rich!) maths professor places this advert in the local paper.

Wanted:	Maths Games Tester
Needed for:	28 days
Pay:	£1000 per day
	or 1p for day 1
	2p for day 2
	4p for day 3
	8p for day 4 and so on

Investigate both methods of payment.

How would you like to be paid?

Do you remember?

- how to add and subtract whole numbers and decimals
- how to multiply and divide whole numbers by 2
- the multiplication and division facts to 10×10
- how to multiply and divide whole numbers by 10, 100, 1000
- how to multiply and divide whole numbers by 20, 30, …, 90

Key words

addition (+)

subtraction (−)

multiplication (×)

multiply (×)

division (÷)

operation (+, −, × and ÷)

square number

square root

Jess and Su Ling are working out this calculation.

Work out the value of 3 + 2 × 6.

Jess says

You start at the left and work out the calculations in the order they are written.
3 + 2 is 5, so
3 + 2 × 6 = 5 × 6
= 30

Su Ling says

You work out the multiplication first.
2 × 6 is 12, so
3 + 2 × 6 = 3 + 12
= 15

This example shows that you can get two different results, depending on the order in which the operations are carried out.

In mathematics, brackets can be used to indicate the part of the calculation that is done first.

Jess has worked out (3 + 2) × 6 = 5 × 6 = 30.

Su Ling has worked out 3 + (2 × 6) = 3 + 12 = 15.

Mathematicians have agreed that when calculations involve several processes, anything in brackets should be worked out first.

Multiplication and division are done next, with equal priority.

Addition and subtraction are done last, again with equal priority.

Brackets

$\begin{cases} \textbf{M}\text{ultiplication} \\ \textbf{D}\text{ivision} \end{cases}$

$\begin{cases} \textbf{A}\text{ddition} \\ \textbf{S}\text{ubtraction} \end{cases}$

> **Hint**
> Some people like to remember this using the phrase *Bless My Dear Aunt Sally*. Try making up your own phrase to learn B-MD-AS.

So the correct way to work out 3 + 2 × 6 is to do the multiplication first.

3 + 2 × 6 = 3 + 12
= 15

Example

Work out these.

(a) (15 + 3) × 2

(b) 16 − (5 − 3)

(c) 42 ÷ 2 − 5 × 3

Solution

(a) (15 + 3) × 2 = 18 × 2   — Brackets first.
= 36

(b) 16 − (5 − 3) = 16 − 2
= 14

(c) 42 ÷ 2 − 5 × 3 = 21 − 15   — Multiplication and division first.
= 6

Work out these.

① $4 + 8 \times 3$	⑥ $3 + 4 \times 7$	⑪ $60 \div 5 \times 2$	⑯ $121 \div 11 + 9$
② $6 + 10 \div 2$	⑦ $(10 - 3) \times (4 + 6)$	⑫ $10 - 3 + 1$	⑰ $(9 + 3) \times (9 - 3)$
③ $3 + 7 - 4$	⑧ $6 \times (2 + 5)$	⑬ $(5 + 7) \times (3 + 8)$	⑱ $9 + 3 \times 9 - 3$
④ $12 - 2 - 5$	⑨ $20 \div (5 - 3)$	⑭ $12 + 9 \times 8 - 7$	⑲ $64 - (32 - 16)$
⑤ $(3 + 4) \times 7$	⑩ $20 \div 5 - 3$	⑮ $8 + 11 \times 12$	⑳ $12 \div 6 \div 2$

1.2 Word problems

When you have a word problem to solve you have to work out what calculation or calculations you need to do. There is often more than one. It is a good idea to write them down.

Sometimes there are different ways to solve the problem.

Example

A carton of orange juice costs 24p.

A pack of four cartons costs 88p.

Neil buys a four-pack of orange juice instead of four separate cartons.

How much does he save?

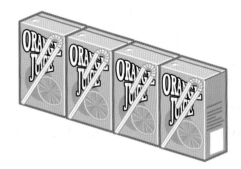

Solution: Method 1

Find the cost of four individual cartons by multiplying.

$4 \times 24p$

To find $4 \times 24p$ double 24p then double the answer.

$$24p \xrightarrow{\text{double}} 48p \xrightarrow{\text{double}} 96p$$

Four separate cartons cost 96p altogether.

Find the difference in price of four cartons by subtraction.

$96p - 88p = 8p$

Write down the answer to the problem.

Neil saves 8p by buying a four-pack of orange juice.

Solution: Method 2

Find the cost of one of the cartons in a four-pack by dividing.

$88p \div 4$

To find $88p \div 4$ halve 88p then halve the answer.

Continued ...

$$88p \xrightarrow{\text{halve}} 44p \xrightarrow{\text{halve}} 22p$$

One carton in a four-pack costs 22p.

Find the difference in price of each carton by subtraction.

24p – 22p = 2p

Find the total saving by multiplying by 4.

4 × 2p = 8p

Write down the answer to the problem.

Neil saves 8p by buying a four-pack of orange juice.

Now try these 1.2

For each of the following questions, write down the calculation or calculations you need to do and then work out the answer.

1 The advert shows the cost of a party at Gino's.

Gino's Pizzas
Children's parties
£7 per person

How much would it cost for a party for Tom and seven friends?

2 Amy is on a cycling holiday.

She cycles 25 miles on the first day, 32 miles on the second day and 39 miles on the third day.

How far does she cycle altogether?

3 Asif is playing at darts.

With three darts he scores 18, 3 and double 17.

How many points does he score altogether?

4 Dan was born on 1st January 2007.

How old will Dan be on 1st January 2050?

5 A minibus takes nine people to the airport.

The cost of the minibus is £63.

The cost is shared equally between the nine people.

How much does each person pay?

6 A hotel has seven sets of stairs.

The number of stairs in each set is shown in the table.

Set	1	2	3	4	5	6	7
Number of stairs	16	17	4	15	5	11	8

(a) How many stairs are there altogether?

When Kurt visits the hotel he decides to exercise by running up and down stairs.

(b) How many steps does he cover if he runs up and down stairs

(i) twice

(ii) four times

(iii) eight times?

1.3 Square numbers

You say '4 squared'.

A short way of writing 4×4 is 4^2. $\qquad 4^2 = 16 \qquad\qquad 10^2 = 10 \times 10 = 100$

This way of writing is called index notation.

$40 \times 40 = 4 \times 10 \times 4 \times 10$

$= 4 \times 4 \times 10 \times 10$

$= 16 \times 100$

$= 1600$

Now try these 1.3

1 Copy and complete this table.

4^2	=	4 × 4	=	16
	=	10 × 10	=	
3^2	=		=	
	=	5 × 5	=	
8^2	=		=	
	=	1 × 1	=	
6^2	=		=	
	=		=	144
11^2	=		=	
	=		=	4
	=	7 × 7	=	
	=		=	81

2 Brain strain

Copy and complete this table.

40^2	=	40 × 40	=	1600
	=	50 × 50	=	
	=		=	900
70^2	=		=	
	=		=	400
	=	60 × 60	=	
80^2	=		=	
	=		=	8100

Techie task

You can use the $\boxed{x^2}$ key on your calculator to find square numbers quickly.

For example to find 11^2 you press these keys.

   $\boxed{=}$

The answer should be 121.

Now check that you can use the $\boxed{x^2}$ key correctly by checking your answers to Now try these 1.3.

1.4 Square roots

You say 'the square root of 9'.

$\sqrt{9} = 3$ because 3×3 or $3^2 = 9$.

If you know that 3 squared is 9, you also know that the square root of 9 is 3.

Now try these 1.4

1 Copy and complete each of the following. The first one has been done for you.

(a) $\sqrt{25} = 5$

(b) $\sqrt{16} =$

(c) $\sqrt{49} =$

(d) $\sqrt{1} =$

(e) $\sqrt{81} =$

(f) $\sqrt{36} =$

(g) $\sqrt{100} =$

(h) $\sqrt{64} =$

2 Brain strain

Copy and complete each of the following. The first one has been done for you.

$\sqrt{900} = 30$ because 30×30 or $30^2 = 900$.

(a) $\sqrt{900} = 30$

(b) $\sqrt{2500} =$

(c) $\sqrt{10000} =$

(d) $\sqrt{8100} =$

Techie task

You can use the $\boxed{\sqrt{}}$ key on your calculator to find square roots quickly.

For example to find $\sqrt{144}$ you press these keys.

The answer should be 12.

Now check that you can use the $\boxed{\sqrt{}}$ key correctly by checking your answers to Now try these 1.4.

2 Lines and angles

Subject links
● design and technology
● geography

Coming up ...

● measuring and drawing angles to the nearest degree
● recognising parallel and perpendicular lines
● using the fact that the angles on a straight line add up to 180°
● using the fact that the angles at a point add up to 360°
● recognising vertically opposite angles
● using the fact that the angles in a triangle add up to 180°
● solving problems involving angle

Do you remember?

● that you can use centimetres and millimetres to measure lines
● that a right angle is 90°
● that angles are measured in degrees (°)

Chapter starter

The clock tower of the Houses of Parliament in London was built in the 1850s.

It is usually called 'Big Ben', which is really the name of the largest bell in the tower.

① **(a)** What is the angle between the hands at 3 o'clock?

(b) At what other times is the angle between the hands 90°?

The hour hand of 'Big Ben' is 2.7 metres long.

The minute hand is 4.3 metres long.

The hour hand of Sarah's watch is 5 millimetres long.

The minute hand is 9 millimetres long.

② Does the length of the hands make any difference to the angle between them at a particular time?

Key words

centimetre	right angle
millimetre	reflex angle
vertex (plural: vertices)	degree (°)
	protractor
angle	anticlockwise
triangle	clockwise
square	intersect
pentagon	parallel
full turn	perpendicular
straight line	vertically opposite angles
acute angle	
obtuse angle	

The mathematical name for a corner is **vertex**.

The plural of vertex is **vertices**.

Vertex

This line is labelled AB or BA.

A ———————— B

This angle is labelled angle ABC or angle CBA.

The letter at the vertex is always in the middle.

You can use the symbol ∠ instead of the word 'angle'. You can write ∠ABC.

To name a shape you start at any vertex and go round either clockwise or anticlockwise.

Write down the letters in order.

This rectangle is labelled rectangle ABCD. Rectangle BCDA, rectangle CDAB, rectangle DABC, rectangle ADCB, rectangle DCBA, rectangle CBAD and rectangle BADC are also correct.

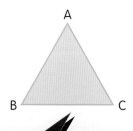

This triangle is labelled as triangle ABC. Triangle BCA, triangle CAB, triangle ACB, triangle CBA and triangle BAC are also correct.

Now try these 2.1

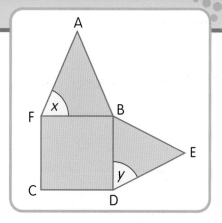

1. **(a)** Write down the labels for the sides of triangle ABF.

   (b) Write down the two possible labels for the angle marked *x*.

   (c) Write down the two possible labels for the angle marked *y*.

   (d) Write down all the possible labels for the square.

2. **(a)** Draw any triangle. Label the vertices ABC.

   (b) On the side AB draw a rectangle ABDE.

   (c) On the side BC draw a triangle BCF.

   (d) Compare your drawing with a friend's drawing.

   Are they both the same?

   Are they both correct?

Continued ...

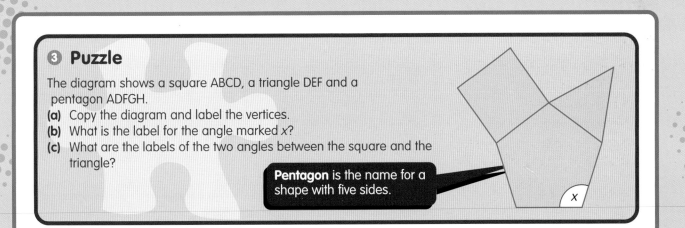

❸ Puzzle

The diagram shows a square ABCD, a triangle DEF and a
pentagon ADFGH.
(a) Copy the diagram and label the vertices.
(b) What is the label for the angle marked x?
(c) What are the labels of the two angles between the square and the
triangle?

Pentagon is the name for a
shape with five sides.

2.2 Types of angle

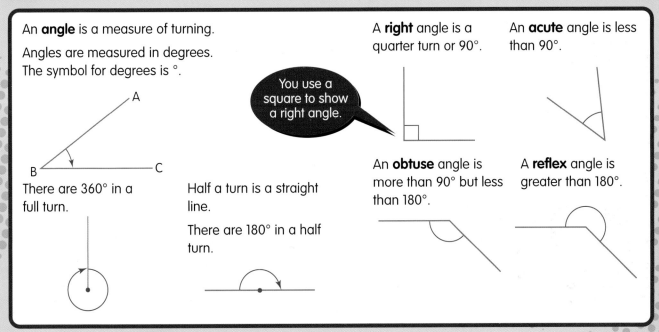

An **angle** is a measure of turning.

Angles are measured in degrees.
The symbol for degrees is °.

There are 360° in a
full turn.

Half a turn is a straight
line.

There are 180° in a half
turn.

You use a
square to show
a right angle.

A **right** angle is a
quarter turn or 90°.

An **acute** angle is less
than 90°.

An **obtuse** angle is
more than 90° but less
than 180°.

A **reflex** angle is
greater than 180°.

Now try these 2.2

❶ For each of these angles say whether it is acute, obtuse, reflex or a right angle.

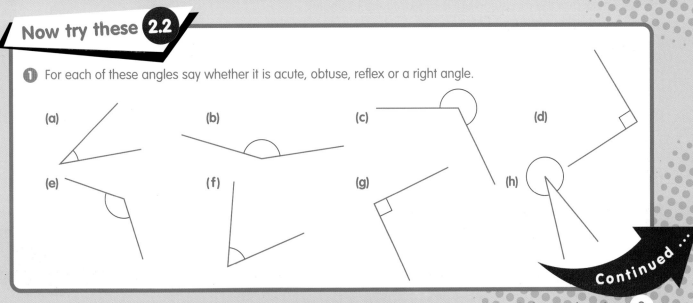

(a) **(b)** **(c)** **(d)**

(e) **(f)** **(g)** **(h)**

Continued ...

2 Look at this pentagon.

Say whether each of the marked angles is acute, obtuse, reflex or a right angle.

(a) Angle TPQ

(b) Angle PQR

(c) Angle QRS

(d) Angle RST

(e) Angle STP

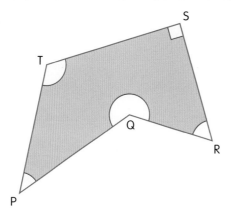

3 **Puzzle**

Three angles meet at B.

Angle ABC is a reflex angle.
Angle CBD is an obtuse angle.

Angle ABD is an acute angle.
Draw a diagram showing these angles.

2.3 Measuring angles

To measure angle LMN, you need a protractor.

1 Begin by estimating the size of the angle.
Angle LMN is less than 90° but more than 45°.
An estimate would be 50°, 60° or 70°.

2 Put the protractor on the angle.
Make sure that
  ● the centre mark of the protractor is exactly on the vertex, M
  ● one of the lines that makes the angle goes through 0° on the protractor.
Protractors have two sets of numbers measuring from 0° to 180°.
One set of numbers goes clockwise and the other goes anticlockwise.
Always start measuring from the line that goes through 0°.

3 For angle LMN the line MN goes through 0° on the anticlockwise scale so the angle is measured using the anticlockwise scale. The line ML goes through 63° so angle LMN = 63°.

4 Check that the measurement is similar to the estimate.

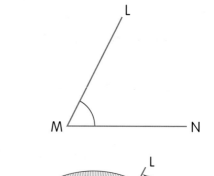

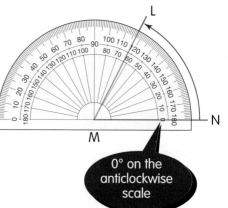

0° on the anticlockwise scale

To measure a reflex angle using a semicircular protractor you have to use your knowledge about angles.

In section 2.2 you learnt that a full turn is 360°.

To measure a reflex angle using a semicircular protractor, measure the acute or obtuse angle and subtract the measurement from 360°.

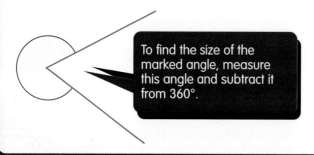

To find the size of the marked angle, measure this angle and subtract it from 360°.

Make sure you use the correct line.
On most protractors it is not the bottom of the protractor

Continued ...

Example

(a) What type of angle is angle x?

(b) Estimate the size of angle x.

(c) Measure angle x.

Solution

(a) Angle x is a reflex angle.

(b) The angle is between 180° and 270°.

An estimate would be 230°, 240° or 250°.

(c) To measure the reflex angle x, first measure the obtuse angle FGH.

Angle FGH is an obtuse angle.

It is between 90° and 180°.

An estimate is 110°, 120° or 130°.

Angle FGH = 120°

> 0° on the clockwise scale

> The line FG goes through 0° on the clockwise scale so the angle is measured on the clockwise scale.

Angle x = 360° − 120°

> Work out the size of the reflex angle by subtracting from 360°.

= 240°

Check your answer makes sense.

If the angle is reflex then make sure your answer is between 180° and 360°.

Now try these 2.3

1. For each of the angles a to j,

   (a) say whether the angle is acute, obtuse or reflex

   (b) estimate the size of the angle in degrees

   (c) measure the angle with a protractor.

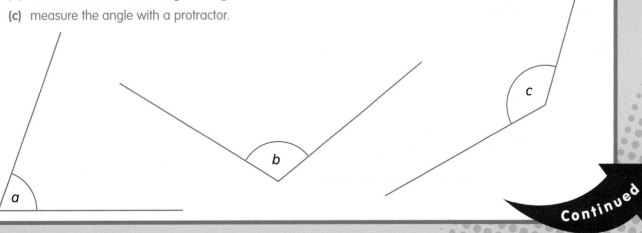

Continued …

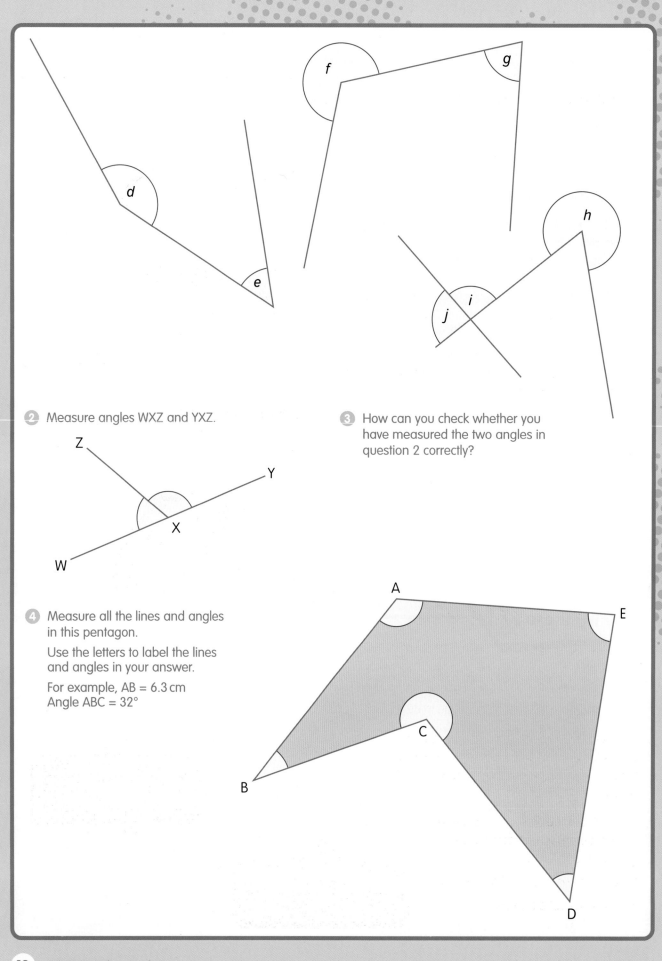

2 Measure angles WXZ and YXZ.

3 How can you check whether you have measured the two angles in question 2 correctly?

4 Measure all the lines and angles in this pentagon.

Use the letters to label the lines and angles in your answer.

For example, AB = 6.3 cm
Angle ABC = 32°

① To draw an angle you must first draw one of the lines.

② Put your protractor on the line.
Make sure that
● the centre mark of the protractor is exactly on the end of the line where the angle will be
● the line points to or goes through 0°.

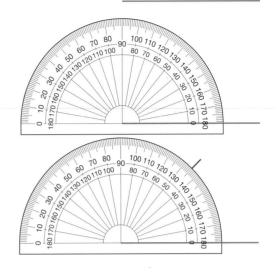

③ Follow the scale round from 0° to the angle you want.
Here the angle is 45°.
Put a small mark on your paper.

 Make sure you use the correct scale.

④ Remove the protractor and join the end of the line that was under the centre mark of the protractor to the mark you have drawn.

⑤ Look at the angle you have drawn and check that it looks the right size.

Example

Draw an angle of 128°.

Solution

128°

To draw a reflex angle using a semicircular protractor you have to use your knowledge about angles in the same way as you did to measure a reflex angle.

① Work out the size of the acute or obtuse angle that completes a full turn of 360°.

② Draw the acute or obtuse angle.

③ Mark the reflex angle.

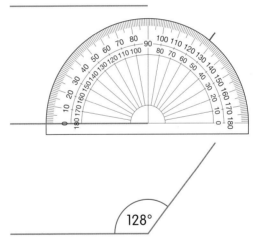

286°

360° − 286° = 74°
Draw an angle of 74°.
Mark the reflex angle 286°.

360° − 232° = 128°
Draw an angle of 128°.
Mark the reflex angle 232°.

232°

① Draw these angles.

   (a) 60°   **(b)** 150°   **(c)** 78°   **(d)** 230°   **(e)** 163°   **(f)** 317°

② Brain strain

Robin is making a small cushion cover in his Technology lesson.

He plans to put a boat made out of material on the cushion cover.

First he needs to make a paper pattern of the boat.

The sizes of the lines and angles are given on the diagram on the right.

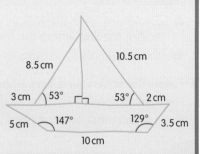

Use the diagram to help you to draw a pattern for the boat to the correct size.

2.5 Using angle facts

In section 2.2 you learnt these facts.

● A right angle is 90°.   ● A straight line is 180°.   ● A full turn is 360°.

You can use this information to help you to work out the sizes of angles when lines intersect.

Example

Angle PRQ is 60°.

Find the size of angle PRS.

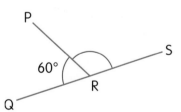

Solution

QS is a straight line so angle PRQ + angle PRS = 180°.

$60° + $ angle PRS $ = 180°$
angle PRS $ = 180° - 60°$
angle PRS $ = 120°$

> **Hint**
> When you answer a question like this, always show your working.

Example

All of the angles marked x in this diagram are the same size.

What is the value of x?

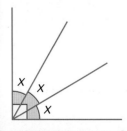

Solution

The angle that is marked as a right angle is 90°.

$$x + x + x = 90° \qquad or \qquad x + x + x = 90°$$

$$30° + 30° + 30° = 90° \qquad\qquad 3x = 90°$$

so $\qquad\qquad x = 30° \qquad\qquad\qquad x = 90° \div 3$

$\qquad\qquad\qquad\qquad$ so $\qquad\qquad x = 30°$

1. Work out the sizes of the angles marked with letters in these diagrams.

   The angles are not drawn accurately, so do not measure them.

   Show your working out.

  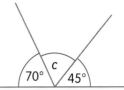

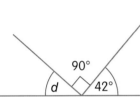 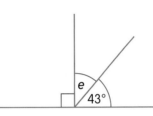 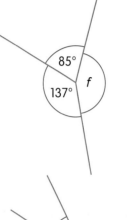

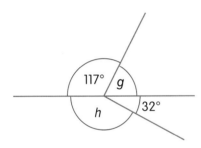 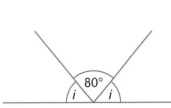 

2. One side of a straight line is divided into two equal angles.

   (a) What is the size of each angle?

   (b) What would the size of each angle be if the line was divided into

      (i) three equal angles?

      (ii) four equal angles?

   (c) How many equal angles would there be if each one was 15°?

   (d) How many equal angles would there be if each one was $\frac{1}{2}$°?

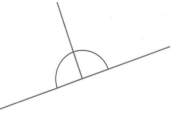

❸ Brain strain

Angles AXB, BXC and CXA meet at a point.

In the diagram, one of the angles is acute, one is obtuse and one is reflex.

Is it possible to draw the three angles so that two are obtuse and one is acute?

What combinations of acute, obtuse and reflex angles are possible?

What if there were four angles at a point?

2.6 Vertically opposite angles

Investigation

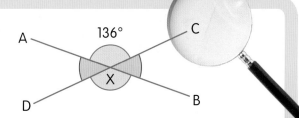

1. In the diagram, AB and CD are straight lines.

   (a) What is the size of angle AXD?

   (b) What is the size of angle CXB?

   (c) What is the size of angle BXD?

   (d) What do you notice about the angles marked in red and the angles marked in blue?

2. Draw two lines that make an X-shape.
   Measure the four angles.
   What do you notice?

With a friend

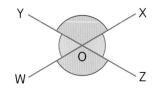

Compare your answer to question 2 of the investigation with a friend's answers.

Have you both got the same answers?

Are both of your answers correct?

When two straight lines intersect, the angles across from each other are always equal.

They are called **vertically opposite** angles.

Angle WOY and angle XOZ are vertically opposite.

Angle WOZ and angle YOX are vertically opposite.

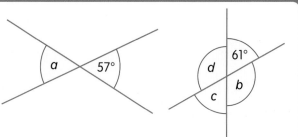

Now try these 2.6

1. Work out the sizes of the angles marked with letters in the diagrams.

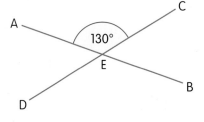

2. Calculate the sizes of these angles in the diagrams below.

   (a) Angle AED

   (b) Angle CEB

   (c) Angle DEB

   (d) Angle GJI

   (e) Angle GJF

   (f) Angle IJH

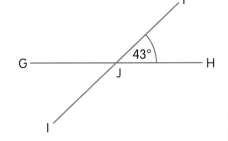

When you have worked out the answers check that the vertically opposite angles are equal.

Continued ...

③ Dan is talking about the angles made by two intersecting lines.

> If you know one of the four angles you only need to do one calculation to know the other three angles.

Is Dan right?
How do you know?

2.7 Angles in a triangle

In any triangle the angles always add up to 180°.

$a + b + c = 180°$

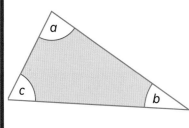

Hint
When you answer a question like this, always show your working.

Example

Work out the size of angle x in this diagram.

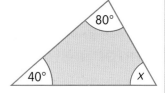

Solution

The three angles of the triangle add up to 180°.

$40° + 80° + x = 180°$
$120° + x = 180°$
$x = 180° - 120°$
$x = 60°$

Now try these 2.7

Calculate the sizes of the angles marked with letters in the diagrams below. Show your working out.

①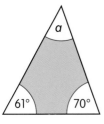

②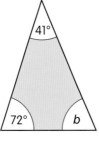

③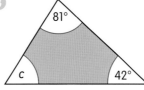

④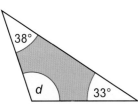

⑤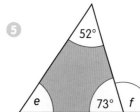

Sequences

Coming up ...

- continuing sequences of numbers
- generating sequences using term-to-term rules
- generating sequences using position-to-term rules
- finding the rule for the *n*th term of an arithmetic sequence
- special sequences

Do you remember?
- your multiplication tables
- what odd and even numbers are

Chapter starter

Have you ever tried to build a house of cards?

No glue is allowed and the cards have to be stacked very carefully to make sure that the house does not collapse.

In 1999 Bryan Berg broke his own world record for the tallest house of cards.

He built a house that was over 7.7 metres high.

The tower had 131 storeys and was made from over 1700 packs of cards.

The picture shows a simple house of cards.

The more storeys you build the more cards you need.

Key word

sequence
term
rule
term-to-term
increasing sequence
position-to-term
infinite sequence
decreasing sequence
consecutive
even number
odd number
square number
cube number
triangular number

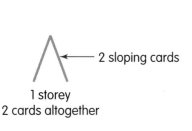

1 storey
2 cards altogether

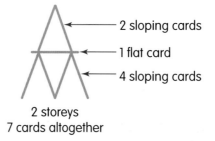

2 sloping cards
1 flat card
4 sloping cards

2 storeys
7 cards altogether

1. Find how many flat cards do you need for

    (a) three storeys **(b)** four storeys **(c)** five storeys.

2. Without drawing work out how many flat cards you need for eight storeys.

A **sequence** is an ordered set of numbers, letters or shapes which follow a rule.

The sequence 2, 4, 6, 8, 10, …

is the sequence of **even numbers**.

This sequence is also called **multiples** of 2.

The three dots show that the sequence continues in the same way.

A **term** is a particular number in a sequence.

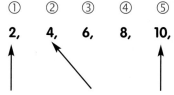

Term number ① ② ③ ④ ⑤

2, 4, 6, 8, 10, …

A sequence that goes on forever is called an **infinite** sequence.

first term   second term   fifth term

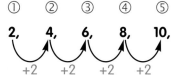

Term number ① ② ③ ④ ⑤

2, 4, 6, 8, 10, …

+2 +2 +2 +2

This is called an **increasing** sequence because each term is greater than the term before.

The **rule** that takes you from one term to the next in this sequence is add 2.

Example

(a) For the sequence of even numbers find these terms.

  (i) seventh term   **(ii)** eighth term   **(iii)** tenth term

(b) How could you find the 100th term without working out every term up to the 100th term?

(c) What is the 100th term?

Solution

Continue the sequence.

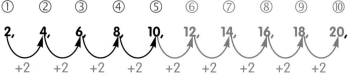

Term number ① ② ③ ④ ⑤ ⑥ ⑦ ⑧ ⑨ ⑩

2, 4, 6, 8, 10, 12, 14, 16, 18, 20, …

+2 +2 +2 +2 +2 +2 +2 +2 +2

(a) (i) The seventh term is 14.

  (ii) The eighth term is 16.

  (iii) The tenth term is 20.

Continued …

(b) You could start with the first term and add 2 ninety-nine times to get the 100th term.

So the 100th term is 2 + 99 × 2.

or You could say that each term is 2 times the term number.

So the 100th term 2 × 100.

(c) The 100th term is 200.

Sequences can be made by adding, subtracting, multiplying or dividing.

Example

The rule that takes you from one term to the next in a sequence is divide by 2. The first term is 256.

(a) What are the first ten terms?

(b) Is this an infinite sequence? Explain your answer.

Solution

(a) Term number ① ② ③ ④ ⑤ ⑥ ⑦ ⑧ ⑨ ⑩

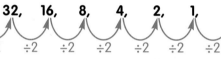

256, 128, 64, 32, 16, 8, 4, 2, 1, $\frac{1}{2}$

÷2 ÷2 ÷2 ÷2 ÷2 ÷2 ÷2 ÷2 ÷2

This is an example of a **decreasing** sequence. Each term is smaller than the term before.

(b) The sequence is an infinite sequence.
The numbers will keep getting smaller, but the sequence will go on forever.

Now try these 3.1

1 The rules in the table show how to get from one term to the next in these sequences.
Copy and complete the table.

	Rule	First term	Second term	Third term	Fourth term
(a)	Add 6	3	9		
(b)	Subtract 2	12			
(c)	Multiply by 5	2			
(d)	Divide by 2 then add 10	8			

2 Puzzle

Copy the table and fill in the missing values.

	Rule	First term	Second term	Third term	Fourth term
(a)	Add 12		18	30	
(b)	Subtract 6				40
(c)	Divide by 2		10		
(d)			20	100	500

3 The rules show how to get from one number to the next in some sequences.

For each sequence the first term is 10.

Write down the next three terms.

(a) Rule: multiply by 2 then subtract 5
(b) Rule: add 6 then divide by 2
(c) Rule: subtract 8 then multiply by 10

Continued ...

④ Puzzle

Copy each of the following sequences and fill in the missing numbers.
Then write down the rule for each sequence.

Example

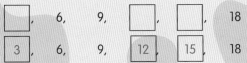
☐, 6, 9, ☐, ☐, 18

3, 6, 9, 12, 15, 18

Rule: Add 3

(a) 11, ☐, ☐, ☐, 63, 76

(b) 6, $7\frac{1}{2}$, ☐, ☐, 12, $13\frac{1}{2}$

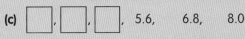
(c) ☐, ☐, ☐, 5.6, 6.8, 8.0

(d) ☐, 20, ☐, 12, ☐, 4

⑤ Another way to show a sequence is as a number chain.

(a) Here is a number chain.

3 → 5 → 7 → 9 → 11 →

What is the rule for this number chain?

(b) Here is another number chain.

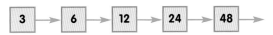
3 → 6 → 12 → 24 → 48 →

What is the rule for this number chain?

(c) Here is another number chain.

1 → 4 → ☐ → ☐ → ☐ →

Show three different ways to continue this number chain.
For each chain say what your rule is.

⑥ This is the rule to get from one number to the next number in a chain.

Divide by 2 then add 4

Find the first and last numbers in the chain.

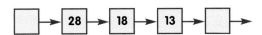
☐ → 28 → 18 → 13 → ☐ →

⑦ For each of these sequences

(i) write down the rule for getting from one term to the next

(ii) write down the tenth term

(iii) explain how you can find the 100th term without writing down all the terms up to the 100th term

(iv) write down the 100th term.

(a) 3, 6, 9, 12, …

(b) 5, 10, 15, 20, …

(c) 8, 16, 24, 32, …

With a friend

Copy the table.

	Rule	First term	Second term	Third term	Fourth term
(a)					
(b)					
(c)					
(d)					

Make up some rules and first terms and write them in your table.

Give your rules and first terms to a friend.

Ask your friend to write down the next three terms of each sequence.

Do you both have the same answers?

Techie task

You can use a spreadsheet to generate sequences.

❶ Open a new spreadsheet and type in the first row as shown below.

Remember that in a spreadsheet
- every formula must start with =
- on a computer * means ×, and - means –, and / means ÷
- when you have entered the formula you will see the result *not* the formula in the cell.

❷ Type the first term in cell B2 and the formulae shown below into cells C2 to F2.

	A	B	C	D	E	F
1	Term number	1	2	3	4	5
2		2	=B2+2	=C2+2	=D2+2	=E2+2

❸ You should now have the first five terms of a sequence in row two of your spreadsheet. Write the name of this sequence of numbers in cell A2.

❹ Type the first term and the formulae shown below into the cells in row three.

	A	B	C	D	E	F
1	Term number	1	2	3	4	5
2						
3		1	=B3+2	=C3+2	=D3+2	=E3+2

❺ Write the name of the sequence of numbers in row three in cell A3.

❻ Write formulae in the cells so that you get the sequences of numbers shown below. Write the rule for each sequence in the cell at the beginning of the row.

	A	B	C	D	E	F
1	Term number	1	2	3	4	5
2						
3						
4		1	3	9	27	81
5		64	32	16	8	4
6		47	37	27	17	7

❼ Now write first terms and formulae in the cells to make some sequences of your own. Write the rule for each sequence in the cell at the beginning of the row.

Another way to describe a sequence is the position-to-term rule. This is usually a simple piece of algebra. It allows you to work out each term directly from its position in the sequence; you do not need to know the previous term.

Example

The nth term of a sequence is given by the rule $3n + 1$.

(a) Work out the first three terms.

(b) Find the 12th term.

Solution

(a) The nth term is given by $3n + 1$.

1st term:	$3 \times 1 + 1 = 3 + 1 = 4$
2nd term:	$3 \times 2 + 1 = 6 + 1 = 7$
3rd term:	$3 \times 3 + 1 = 9 + 1 = 10$

So the first three terms are 4, 7, 10.

(b) 12th term: $3 \times 12 + 1 = 36 + 1 = 37$

> This means multiply 3 by the value of n, then add 1.

Sometimes a sequence consists of numbers going down in size, not up.

Example

The nth term of a sequence is given by the rule $40 - 5n$.

(a) Work out the first three terms.

(b) Which term will be 0?

Solution

(a) The nth term is given by $40 - 5n$.

1st term:	$40 - 5 \times 1 = 40 - 5 = 35$
2nd term:	$40 - 5 \times 2 = 40 - 10 = 30$
3rd term:	$40 - 5 \times 3 = 40 - 15 = 25$

So the first three terms are 35, 30, 25.

(b) The nth term is given by $40 - 5n$.

So, when one of the terms becomes zero, $5 \times n$ would have to be 40.

So, $n = 40 \div 5 = 8$.

The eighth term is zero.

Now try these 3.2

1 Work out the first five terms of the sequences with nth terms given by these rules.

(a) $5n + 1$ **(b)** $4n - 3$ **(c)** $2n + 2$ **(d)** $30 - 2n$

(e) $3 \times (n + 1)$ **(f)** $4 + 10n$ **(g)** $n^2 + 1$ **(h)** $n \times (n + 1)$

2 The nth term of a sequence is given by the rule $6n + 2$.

(a) Work out the first five terms of the sequence.

(b) Work out the tenth term of the sequence.

3 The nth term of a sequence is given by the rule $60 - 5n$.

(a) Work out the first four terms of the sequence.

(b) Work out the 20th term of the sequence.

4 Brain strain

The nth term of a sequence is given by the rule $1 + 7n - n^2$.

(a) Work out the first five terms of the sequence.

(b) Find the value of the first negative term in the sequence.

5 Brain strain

The nth term of a sequence is given by the rule $n^2 - n$.

(a) Work out the first five terms of the sequence.

(b) Explain carefully why all the terms are even numbers.

Square numbers

Pattern number ① ② ③ ④

  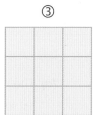

Square numbers	**1**	**4**	**9**	**16**
	1×1	2×2	3×3	4×4
	1^2	2^2	3^2	4^2

> 4^2 is a short way of writing 4×4.
> You say '4 squared'.

How can you continue the sequence of square numbers without drawing the diagrams?

How can you find a square number if you know its pattern number?

Cube numbers

Pattern number ① ② ③ ④

  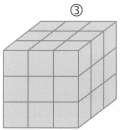 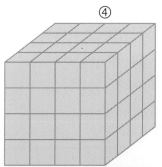

Cube numbers	**1**	**8**	**27**	**64**
	$1 \times 1 \times 1$	$2 \times 2 \times 2$	$3 \times 3 \times 3$	$4 \times 4 \times 4$
	1^3	2^3	3^3	4^3

> 4^3 is a short way of writing $4 \times 4 \times 4$.
> You say '4 cubed'.

How can you continue the sequence of cube numbers without drawing the diagrams?

How can you find a cube number if you know its pattern number?

Techie task

You can use the $\boxed{x^3}$ key on your calculator to find cube numbers quickly.

For example to find **15^3** press these keys.

$\boxed{1}\ \boxed{5}\ \boxed{x^3}\ \boxed{=}$

The answer should be 3375.

Check that you can use the $\boxed{x^3}$ key correctly by using your calculator to find some cube numbers you already know.

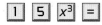

Continued ...

Triangular numbers

Pattern number

        ①   ②   ③   ④

   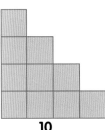

Triangular numbers   1   3   6   10

How can you continue the sequence of triangular numbers without drawing the diagrams?

Triangular numbers are important in several games, for example ten-pin bowling and snooker.

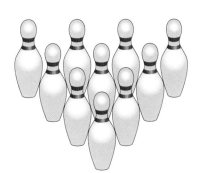 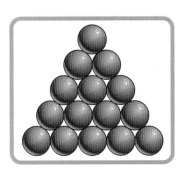

Now try these 3.3

1. **(a)** Draw the next two patterns in this sequence.

   (b) How many squares are there in the fifth pattern?

   (c) How many squares are there in the sixth pattern?

   (d) How can you work out how many squares there are in the tenth pattern without drawing all of the patterns?

   (e) How many squares are there in the tenth pattern?

Pattern number

    ①   ②   ③

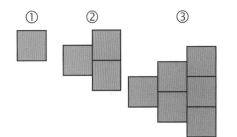

2. **(a)** Write down the first ten square numbers.

   (b) Write down the first ten cube numbers.

   (c) Write down the first ten triangular numbers.

3. From the numbers in the box write down

   (a) five square numbers

   (b) five cube numbers

   (c) five triangular numbers.

21	9	6	64	15
49	1	8	100	
27	36	16	125	90

Continued ...

4 Look at these patterns.

Pattern number   ①   ②   ③

(a) Draw the next two patterns in this sequence.

(b) Copy and complete this table.

Pattern number	1	2	3	4	5
Number of red squares					
Number of blue squares					
Total number of squares					

(c) Write down how many red squares you need to make the 12th pattern. Explain how you know.

(d) Work out how many blue squares you need to make the 12th pattern. Explain how you know.

5 The patterns below are made with green and purple tiles.

Pattern number   ①   ②   ③

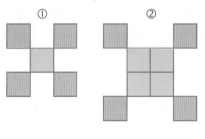 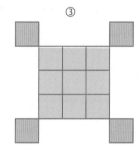

(a) **(i)** How many purple tiles do you need for the sixth pattern?

    (ii) How many green tiles do you need for the sixth pattern?

    (iii) How many tiles do you need altogether for the sixth pattern?

(b) **(i)** How many purple tiles do you need for the tenth pattern? How do you know?

    (ii) How many green tiles do you need for the tenth pattern? How do you know?

    (iii) How many tiles do you need altogether for the tenth pattern? How do you know?

6 Brain strain

Here are some unusual sequences.

They *do not* follow patterns like the ones you have come across in this chapter.

Try to find the next three terms in each sequence.

(a) 2, 3, 5, 7, 11, 13, 17, ...
(b) J, F, M, A, M, J, ...
(c) B, C, D, F, G, H, J, ...
(d) 3, 3, 5, 4, 4, 3, ...

Investigation

How many squares are there on a chessboard?

4 Collecting data

Subject links
● science
● geography
● PHSE

count me in
Census2001

Coming up ...

● collecting and organising data
● designing data collection sheets and questionnaires
● constructing frequency tables for discrete data

Chapter starter

A census is a survey of all people and households in a country.

There has been a census in the UK every ten years since 1801 (excluding 1941).

The most recent census in the UK was on 29 April 2001.

The next census in the UK will take place in 2011.

The census provides essential information for government, business and the community.

It is compulsory to complete the census form.

If you refuse you can be fined.

> **Census 2001**
>
> **England and Wales**
>
> **England Household Form**

❶ What types of questions do you think the census asks?

❷ What questions do you think are not asked in the census?

❸ How long do you think it takes to collect all of the census information?

Do you remember?
● how to use tally marks
● how to interpret bar charts

Key words
statistics
data
grouped data
survey
census
data collection sheet
questionnaire
category
tally
frequency

The word **statistics** was first used in the 18th century. Statistics means the study of **data.** Data is a collection of facts and information. Data is often collected by using a **survey**.

It is important to make sure that

● the right data is collected
● the data is reliable.

Surveys can be carried out in different ways.

Data collection sheets are often used to record the information collected in the survey.

A data collection sheet could be a questionnaire or a table.

A **questionnaire** has one or more questions about a topic.

It is very important to think carefully about how you write a questionnaire.

Questions need to be carefully written to make sure that the data needed is collected.

You need to make sure your questions are easy to understand and that it is easy for people to answer.

Also, completing the census is compulsory but filling in a questionnaire is not.

When you write a questionnaire you have to write the questions in a way that does not make people stop answering truthfully or stop answering altogether.

For example, many people do not like saying how old they are.

The census asks for your date of birth.

Questionnaires usually give ranges of ages, such as under 16, or 35 to 44, and asks you to tick the correct range.

Example

Here are some questions from a questionnaire about recycling.

What is wrong with the questions?

How can they be improved?

(a) Don't you agree that recycling is a fantastic idea?

(b) What do you think about recycling? Is it

☐ an excellent idea

☐ a good idea

☐ it is neither good nor bad.

(c) Is it reasonable that in this day and age it is not beyond the realms of reason that people should be willing to participate in recycling for the benefit of the world in the future?

(d) How far is it to your nearest recycling facility?

☐ 0–1 miles

☐ 1–2 miles

☐ 3–5 miles

Solution

(a) This is a **leading question**.

You can tell that the person asking the question wants you to say yes!

Question **(b)** is a better way to ask for an opinion about recycling.

(b) The range of choices does not allow for all possible responses.

There are two positive options and a neutral option but no negative options.

There should be an equal number of positive and negative options.

Continued ...

You could ask:

What is your opinion of recycling?

☐ Very positive

☐ Positive

☐ Neutral

☐ Negative

☐ Very negative

(c) This is too difficult to understand!

It is also quite similar to the first two questions.

In addition it asks whether you should be willing to, not whether you actually do recycle.

A better question might be whether or not you recycle or what proportion of various types of waste you recycle.

For example,

How often do you recycle waste glass?

☐ Usually

☐ Often

☐ Sometimes

☐ Never

(d) It would be difficult to decide which box to tick for some answers, for example if your nearest facility is 1 mile away or 2.5 miles away.

Also, what if your nearest facility is more than 5 miles away?

Here are some ways the options could be improved.

● By using symbols, for example
0 miles < distance ⩽ 1 mile,
1 mile < distance ⩽ 2 miles, etc.

● By asking for the distance to the nearest mile and using the categories 0 miles, 1 mile, 2 miles, etc. or 0–2 miles, 3–4 miles, etc.

● By asking people to tick the first box that applies and using the categories less than 1 mile, less than 2 miles, etc.

There should also be a category to cover distances greater than 5 miles, or whatever is the greatest distance you specify.

Now try these 4.1

1. David wants to find out whether

   Boys in Year 7 do more homework than girls.

   He produces this questionnaire.

   There are at least three things wrong with David's questionnaire.

   (a) Make a list of three things that are wrong with the questionnaire.

   (b) Write the questionnaire again correcting the mistakes.

   Year 7 Homework Questionnaire

   1 Name …………………………………………………

   2 About how much homework did you do on the last week night? (Monday, Tuesday, Wednesday or Thursday)

   ☐ 0–15 minutes

   ☐ 30–45 minutes

   ☐ 1 hour or more

   3 About how much homework did you do altogether last weekend? (Friday, Saturday and Sunday)

   ☐ $0-\frac{1}{2}$ hours   ☐ $1\frac{1}{2}-2$ hours

   ☐ $\frac{1}{2}-1$ hour   ☐ Over 2 hours

   ☐ $1-1\frac{1}{2}$ hours

   ---

2. Judi is doing a Year 7 Healthy Eating project.

   She wants to find out how much pupils eat and drink between meals and what they eat and drink.

   Write three questions she could include on a questionnaire.

   Remember to give a choice of answers.

3. Write a questionnaire that could be used to investigate what people think about recycling and what they recycle.

Continued …

Research

This is an extract from the Domesday Book.
What was the Domesday Book?

Who ordered its writing and when?
What information does it contain?
In your own words write a magazine article about the Domesday Book.

4.2 Tables

Tables are often used on data collection sheets to record the data that are collected.

In a table information is arranged in rows and columns.

The number of times each item appears is often recorded using **tally marks**.

| means one.

You write a stroke each time an item appears.

|||| means four.

卌 means five.

You write the fifth stroke across the previous four to show a group of five. This makes it easier to find the total.

The number of times each item appears is called the **frequency** of the item.

Now try these 4.2

① In a food technology lesson the class use a data collection sheet to compare four different types of chocolate muffin.

Ten pupils put one tally mark next to each type of flour in the table showing how much they liked each muffin.

(a) Copy the table and replace the tally marks in each box with a number showing the frequency.

(b) Use your frequency table to write the muffins in order from most popular to least popular.

Chocolate muffin comparison			
Type of flour used	☺	😐	☹
Plain flour			||||	卌
Self-raising flour	卌 ||||			
Wholemeal flour	||||	||||	||
Gluten-free flour	||	||||	||||

Continued ...

2 The table shows the results of the first matches in the English Premiership in a season.

Anna plans to keep a record of the goals scored by these teams during this season.

She also wants to record the goals scored against the teams on the same table so that she only needs to write down the team names once.

Draw a table that Anna could use and fill in the data for the first matches of the season.

Home team	Goals scored	Away team	Goals scored
Manchester United	0	Reading	0
Chelsea	3	Birmingham City	2
Arsenal	2	Fulham	1
Aston Villa	1	Liverpool	2
Bolton Wanderers	1	Newcastle United	3
Derby County	2	Portsmouth	2
Everton	2	Wigan	1
Middlesbrough	1	Blackburn Rovers	2
West Ham	0	Manchester City	2
Sunderland	1	Tottenham Hotspur	0

4.3 Grouped data

When the data covers a large range of values it is sometimes best to put the data into classes or groups.

For example, Aisha collects this information about the number of trading cards her friends have to swap.

12	14	28	9	14	7	11	7
4	17	19	30	3	27	14	2
19	22	15	12	8	3	16	6

She records this information in a table using groups.

> Choose four to six groups. The groups should not overlap. It is easier if the groups are all the same size.

Number of cards	Tally	Frequency
0–5	||||	4
6–10	卌	5
11–15	卌 ||	7
16–20	||||	4
21–25	|	1
26–30	|||	3
		24

> Check that the total is the same as the total number of items.

Now try these 4.3

1 This grouped frequency table is used to record the marks of the pupils in a test.

Exam mark	Tally	Frequency
0–10		
11–20		
21–30		
31–40		
41–50		

(a) Copy the table and use tally marks to record each of the results from the list below in the table.

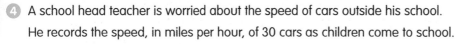

27	32	19	35	21	50	6	32	46	34
11	30	39	38	35	24	32	41	33	26

(b) Count the tally marks and fill in the frequency column.

2 A bus company wants to find out how many passengers are on each of the buses that leave a bus station on a particular day.

Draw a grouped frequency table that can be used to record the information. You will need columns for the number of passengers, tally marks and frequency.

Use the groups 0–5, 6–10, 11–15, ... for the number of passengers.

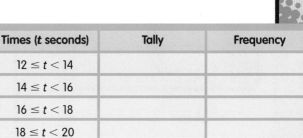

3 Year 7 pupils are asked how far they travel to school to the nearest mile.

Draw a grouped frequency table which could be used to record this infomation for your class.

4 A school head teacher is worried about the speed of cars outside his school.

He records the speed, in miles per hour, of 30 cars as children come to school.

27.5	31.2	37.5	33.4	42.3	29.7	34.7
38.5	45.8	30.4	32.9	37.6	31.8	42.5
39.6	40.0	32.2	25.6	34.9	22.8	27.6
22.8	37.8	23.2	29.9	31.3	30.7	28.6
26.5	27.0					

Speed (s mph)	Tally	Frequency
$25 \leq s < 30$		
$30 \leq s < 35$		
$35 \leq s < 40$		
$40 \leq s < 45$		
$45 \leq s < 50$		

(a) Copy and complete this frequency table for the data.

(b) The speed limit is 30 miles per hour.
Do you think the head teacher is right to be worried? Explain your answer.

5 There are 20 pupils trying to get into the school running team.

These are their times to run 100 metres.

14.3	15.8	17.3	14.3	15.2	16.9	15.0
15.7	14.8	13.8	14.9	15.4	16.3	16.9
14.7	18.3	14.7	13.9	16.8	14.6	

Times (t seconds)	Tally	Frequency
$12 \leq t < 14$		
$14 \leq t < 16$		
$16 \leq t < 18$		
$18 \leq t < 20$		

(a) Copy and complete this frequency table for the data.

(b) Pupils who run 100 metres in under 16 seconds can join the team.

How many pupils get into the team?

6 There are 25 pupils trying to get into the long jump team.

These are the lengths, in metres, of their best jumps.

3.78	4.03	3.88	4.23	4.51	3.29	4.87	4.02	3.68	3.99
4.12	4.35	4.65	4.99	5.02	3.75	4.04	4.75	3.96	4.00
3.75	3.86	4.44	4.29	4.78					

Display this data in a grouped frequency table.

5

Multiples and factors

Coming up...

● finding multiples of a number
● finding factors of a number
● the prime numbers between 1 and 100
● why a number is not prime
● finding the lowest common multiple of a set of numbers
● finding the highest common factor of a set of numbers
● working with prime factors
● solving problems involving the lowest common multiple and the highest common factor

Do you remember?
● multiplication tables up to 10×10
● sequences
● inverse operations
● square numbers

Chapter starter

A Christmas tree has flashing lights.

The red lights flash every 4 seconds.
The blue lights flash every 6 seconds.
The green lights flash every 8 seconds.

The red, blue and green lights all flash at the same time.
How long will it be before they all flash at the same time again?

Key words

integer
digit
multiple
sequence
term
factor
factor pair
prime
common multiple
lowest common multiple
common factor
highest common factor

Note
All the numbers in this chapter are positive integers.

A **multiple** of a number is found by multiplying that number by any integer.

Here are some multiples of 3.

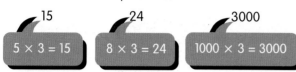

15   24   3000

| $5 \times 3 = 15$ | $8 \times 3 = 24$ | $1000 \times 3 = 3000$ |

These are the multiples of 3.

3, 6, 9, 12, 15, 18, 21, 24, 27, ...

The three dots show that the sequence continues in the same way.

A sequence that goes on forever is called an **infinite** sequence.

Here are some multiples of 7.

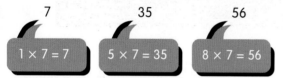

7   35   56

| $1 \times 7 = 7$ | $5 \times 7 = 35$ | $8 \times 7 = 56$ |

These are the multiples of 7.

7, 14, 21, 28, 35, 42, 49, 56, ...

You can often use divisibility tests to answer questions on multiples.

Example

Is 65 348 a multiple of 9?

Solution

If 65 348 is a multiple of 9 then 65 348 will be exactly divisible by 9.

A number is divisible by 9 if the sum of the digits is divisible by 9.

$6 + 5 + 3 + 4 + 8 = 26$ which is not exactly divisible by 9.

So 65 348 is not a multiple of 9.

Now try these 5.1

1 Write down

   (a) the multiples of 4 that are less than 10
   (b) the multiples of 9 that are less than 40
   (c) the multiples of 6 that are between 15 and 35
   (d) the multiples of 3 that are between 10 and 25
   (e) the smallest multiple of 17
   (f) the multiples of 10 that are between 105 and 205
   (g) the smallest multiple of 5 that has exactly three digits
   (h) the largest multiple of 2 that has exactly four digits.

2 In each part, give a reason for your answer.

   (a) Is 562 336 a multiple of 4?
   (b) Is 25 556 a multiple of 5?
   (c) Is 36 822 a multiple of 6?
   (d) Is 825 867 a multiple of 9?

5.2 Factors

A **factor** of a number is an integer that will divide exactly into that number.

These are all the factors of 8.

1   2   4   8

| because $8 \div 1 = 8$ | because $8 \div 2 = 4$ | because $8 \div 4 = 2$ | because $8 \div 8 = 1$ |

Continued

The factors of 8 are 1, 2, 4 and 8.

Factors come in pairs.

Using factor pairs is an easy way to find factors.

| 1 and 8 are a factor pair because 1 × 8 = 8. |
| 2 and 4 are a factor pair because 2 × 4 = 8. |

Example

Find all of the factors of 24.

Make sure you don't confuse factors and multiples.
Multiples are always greater than or equal to the number itself.
Factors are always less than or equal to the number itself.

Solution

Try 1   1 × 24 = 24   — So 1 and 24 are factors.

Try 2   2 × 12 = 24   — So 2 and 12 are factors.

Try 3   3 × 8 = 24   — So 3 and 8 are factors.

Try 4   4 × 6 = 24   — So 4 and 6 are factors.

Try 5   ✗   — 5 is not a factor.

Try 6   6 × 4 = 24   — So 6 and 4 are factors.

But you already have this factor pair. 6 × 4 is the same as 4 × 6. So you have now finished finding factor pairs.

The factors of 24 are 1, 24, 2, 12, 3, 8, 4, 6.

In order they are 1, 2, 3, 4, 6, 8, 12, 24.

1, 2, 3, 4, 6, 8, 12, 24

Now try these 5.2

1   Write down all the factors of each of these numbers.

(a) 10   (b) 7   (c) 15   (d) 20
(e) 16   (f) 11   (g) 28   (h) 12
(i) 40   (j) 2   (k) 35   (l) 25
(m) 42   (n) 50   (o) 3   (p) 49
(q) 6   (r) 54   (s) 32

2   Write down the factor pairs of these numbers.

(a) 64   (b) 72   (c) 100   (d) 75

3   Charlie has 36 plants.

He wants to plant them out so that they grow in a rectangle shape.

Draw diagrams to show all the ways he can arrange them.

All the rows must contain the same number of plants.

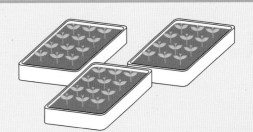

Continued ...

4 (a) How many different ways can you make £1?

List the ways using just one type of coin.

(b) Using the same type or different types of coins, how can you make £1 using

   (i) one coin

   (ii) two coins

   (iii) three coins

   (iv) four coins

   (v) five coins

   (vi) six coins

   (vii) seven coins

   (viii) eight coins

   (ix) nine coins?

> **Hint**
> Not all of these are possible.

Investigation

Find all the numbers between 1 and 100 that have an odd number of factors.

What is special about these numbers?

5.3 Prime numbers

A **prime number** has exactly two factors.

> The factors of a prime number are 1 and itself.

5 is a prime number because it has exactly two factors.

> The factors of 5 are 1 and 5.

13 is a prime number because it has exactly two factors.

1 is *not* a prime number because it only has one factor.

> The factors of 13 are 1 and 13.

You can explain why a number is not prime by showing that it is divisible by a number that is not 1 or itself.

> **Hint**
> A number that has more than two factors cannot be prime.

Example

Explain why 49 is not a prime number.

Solution

49 is a multiple of 7 so 7 is a factor of 49.

So 49 is not a prime number.

> The factors of 49 are 1, 7 and 49.

Example

Explain why these numbers cannot be prime numbers.

(a) 4 333 792

(b) 98 765

(c) 111 111 111

Solution

(a) 4 333 792 is divisible by 2 because the last digit is an even number.

So 4 333 792 is not a prime number.

> It has at least 3 factors: 1, 2 and 4 333 792.

Continued

(b) 98 765 is divisible by 5 because the last digit is 5.

So 98 765 is not a prime number.

It has at least 3 factors: 1, 5 and 98 765.

Adding the digits: 1+1+1+1+1+1+1+1+1 = 9.

(c) 111 111 111 is divisible by 9 because the sum of the digits is divisible by 9.

So 111 111 111 is not a prime number.

It has at least 3 factors: 1, 9 and 111 111 111.

Now try these 5.3

❶ Puzzle

Here is a way to find all the prime numbers up to 100.

(a) Draw a hundred square.
Colour the square containing the number 1.

(b) Colour all the squares containing a multiple of 2 except 1 × 2. The first few have been done for you.

You don't have to use different colours.

(c) Colour all the white squares containing a multiple of 3 except 1 × 3. The first few have been done for you.

(d) What do you notice about the squares containing a multiple of 4? Which other numbers will this be true for?

(e) Colour all the white squares containing a multiple of 5 except 1 × 5.

(f) Colour all the white squares containing a multiple of 7 except 1 × 7.

The white squares that remain show all the prime numbers up to 100.

(g) What do you notice about the numbers you coloured multiples of?

(h) Why don't you need to colour multiples of 11?

1	2	3	4	5	6	7	8	9	10
11	12	13	14	15	16	17	18	19	20
21	22	23	24	25	26	27	28	29	30
31	32	33	34	35	36	37	38	39	40
41	42	43	44	45	46	47	48	49	50
51	52	53	54	55	56	57	58	59	60
61	62	63	64	65	66	67	68	69	70
71	72	73	74	75	76	77	78	79	80
81	82	83	84	85	86	87	88	89	90
91	92	93	94	95	96	97	98	99	100

❷ Explain why 266 is not a prime number.

❸ Show that 477 is not a prime number.

❹ Karen says that 34 895 is a prime number. Explain why she must be wrong to say this.

❺ Explain why 235 568 321 607 cannot be prime.

❻ Is your home telephone number a prime number? Is your mobile number a prime number?

❼ Explain why the only even prime number is 2.

Continued ...

Research

Mathematicians like prime numbers.

① Look at the puzzle in question 1.
Find the name of this method of finding prime numbers.
Is it a new method?

② What work has been done to try to find the largest prime number?

❽ Brain strain

Which prime numbers less than 100 can be written as the sum of two square numbers?

The first sum of two square numbers that is a prime number is 5.

$1^2 + 2^2 = 1 + 4 = 5$

Hint
There are ten more prime numbers to find.
Work systematically to find them all.

5.4   Prime factorisation

Here is a reminder of the first few prime numbers.

2,   3,   5,   7,   11,   13,   17,   19,   23,   …

Other numbers can be written as a product of two or more prime numbers.

These prime numbers are called the **prime factors**.

For example, $6 = 2 \times 3$ and $20 = 2 \times 2 \times 5$.

One way of writing a large number as a **product of its prime factors** is a factor tree.

Example

Write 60 as a product of its prime factors.

Solution

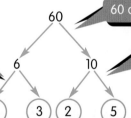

60 decomposes into 6 times 10.

6 is 2 times 3 and these are both prime. Circle the prime numbers.

10 is 2 times 5. Again these are both prime so you circle them.

The process stops when all the factors are circled to indicate that they are prime.

So $60 = 2 \times 3 \times 2 \times 5$
$= 2 \times 2 \times 3 \times 5$
$= 2^2 \times 3 \times 5$

The neatest way to write a number as a product of its prime factors is using index notation, which you learnt about in Chapter 1.

There are other ways of setting out the steps, but the end result will be the same.

Continued

For example, if you split 60 into 2 times 30 at the first stage then the factor tree might look like this.

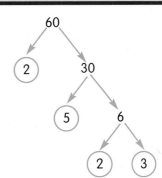

Another way to find the **prime factor decomposition** of a number is to use systematic division by the prime numbers.

Example

Find the prime factor decomposition of 126.

Solution

Try 2 first.

```
2 | 1  2  6
3 |    6  3
3 |    2  1
7 |       7
  |       1
```

62 is not divisible by 2 so try 3.

You can divide by 3 again.

7 is prime. You must continue until you get to 1 so divide by 7.

These are the prime factors of 126.

So $126 = 2 \times 3 \times 3 \times 7$
$= 2 \times 3^2 \times 7$

Now try these 5.4

1. Write these numbers as a product of their prime factors.

   (a) 24   (b) 80   (c) 32   (d) 36   (e) 70   (f) 88

   (g) 90   (h) 68   (i) 140   (j) 300   (k) 453   (l) 525

2. This is Shannon's working for writing 324 as a product of its prime factors.

   Shannon has made a mistake.

   Explain her error and write the correct answer.

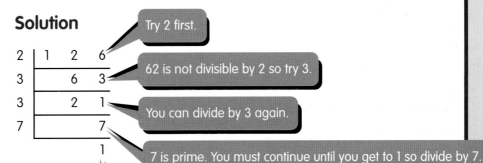

```
2 | 3  2  4
2 | 1  6  2
2 |    8  1
3 |    2  7
3 |       9
  |       3
```

So $324 = 2 \times 2 \times 2 \times 3 \times 3$
$= 2^3 \times 3^2$

3. Express 1001 as a product of primes.

4. 120 written as a product of its prime factors is $2^3 \times 3 \times 5$.

   (a) Express 360 as a product of its prime factors.

   (b) Express 1200 as a product of its prime factors.

5.5 Lowest common multiple

The **lowest common multiple** of a set of numbers is the smallest number that is a multiple of all the numbers in the set.

You can use the abbreviation LCM for lowest common multiple.

Here are some multiples of 4.

4, 8, 12, 16, 20, 24, 28, 32, 36, ...

Some multiples of 6 are

6, 12, 18, 24, 30, 36, ...

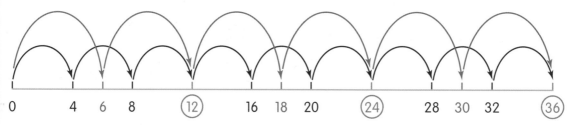

These are some **common multiples** of 4 and 6.

12, 24, 36, ...

They are in both lists.

12 is the smallest common multiple.

So 12 is the **lowest common multiple** of 4 and 6.

Example

Find the lowest common multiple of 10 and 14.

Solution

> List some multiples of 10 and of 14. Start with the smallest each time.

Multiples of **10**:   10,   20,   30,   40,   50,   60,   (70,)   80,   ...

Multiples of **14**:   14,   28,   42,   56,   (70,)   ...

> You can stop at 70 as this is the first multiple of 14 that is in the multiples of 10 list.

The lowest common multiple of 10 and 14 is 70.

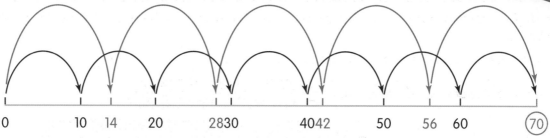

You can find the lowest common multiple of three or more numbers by an extension of this method.

The common multiples must be in all the lists.

Continued ..

Example

Find the lowest common multiple of 2, 3 and 6.

Solution

Multiples of **2:   2,   4,   6,   8,   10,   ...**

Multiples of **3:   3,   6,   9,   12,   ...**

Multiples of **6:   6,   12,   ...**

The lowest common multiple of 2, 3 and 6 is 6.

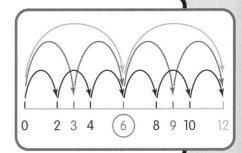

Now try these **5.5**

① Find the lowest common multiple of these pairs of numbers.

(a) 2 and 5   (b) 3 and 4   (c) 6 and 9
(d) 7 and 14   (e) 8 and 10   (f) 6 and 10
(g) 12 and 8   (h) 50 and 10

② Find the lowest common multiple of these sets of numbers.

(a) 2, 3 and 4   (b) 4, 5 and 10   (c) 2, 6 and 8
(d) 5, 8 and 10   (e) 2, 3, 4 and 5   (f) 150, 200 and 300

5 Puzzle

Julie's watch gains 1 minute every hour.
Kate's watch loses 1 minute every hour.
Adam's watch has stopped altogether.
Whose watch keeps the best time?

⚠ Don't forget there are 60 minutes in an hour.

③ The chairs in a school hall can be set out in rows of 8, 10 or 12.

The school caretaker uses a mixture of rows of 8, 10 and 12 chairs.

What is the smallest number of chairs he sets out that is a multiple of these three numbers?

④ A bus stop is used by three bus routes.

The number 64 leaves every 7 minutes.
The number 54 leaves every 10 minutes.
The number 92 leaves every 15 minutes.

Buses on all three routes leave together at 9 a.m.

(a) When do a number 64 and a number 54 next leave at the same time?

(b) When do a number 54 and a number 92 next leave at the same time?

(c) When do buses on all three routes next leave at the same time?

5.6 Highest common factor

The **highest common factor** of a set of numbers is the largest number that is a factor of all the numbers in the set.

You can use the abbreviation HCF for highest common factor.

The factors of 12 are   **1, 12,   2, 6,   3, 4**   ◀ Work out the factor pairs.

In order: 1,   2,   3,   4,   6,   12   ◀ Writing the factors in order makes it easier to compare the factors of different numbers.

The factors of 30 are   **1, 30,   2, 15,   3, 10,   5, 6**

Continued ...

In order: **1, 2, 3, 5, 6, 10, 15, 30**

①②③ 4 5 ⑥   10   12   15   30

These are the **common factors** of 12 and 30.

1, 2, 3 and 6

They are in both lists.

6 is the largest common factor.

So 6 is the **highest common factor** of 12 and 30.

You can find the highest common factor of three or more numbers by an extension of this method.

The common factors must be in all the lists.

Example

Find the highest common factor of 16, 20 and 36.

Don't mix up lowest common multiple and highest common factor. The lowest common multiple is always greater than (or equal to) the largest number; the highest common factor is always less than (or equal to) the smallest number.

Solution

Factors of 16: 1, 2, 4, 8, 16

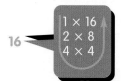

1 × 16
2 × 8
4 × 4

Factors of 20: 1, 2, 4, 5, 10, 20

1 × 20
2 × 10
4 × 5

Factors of 36: 1, 2, 3, 4, 6, 9, 12, 18, 36

1 × 36
2 × 18
3 × 12
4 × 9
6 × 6

The highest common factor of 16, 20 and 36 is 4.

①②3 ④5 6   8 9 10   12   16 18 20   36

Now try these 5.6

❶ Find the highest common factor of these pairs of numbers.

   (a) 6 and 8   **(b)** 9 and 12   **(c)** 10 and 15
   (d) 14 and 21   **(e)** 3 and 27   **(f)** 18 and 24
   (g) 30 and 50   **(h)** 25 and 45

❷ Find the highest common factor of these sets of numbers.

   (a) 4, 6 and 8   **(b)** 12, 16 and 20
   (c) 16, 32 and 40   **(d)** 9, 30 and 60
   (e) 24, 28, and 40 **(f)** 300, 400 and 500

Continued…

3 What is the largest number of children who can share equally 96 chocolates and 64 toffees?

4 Puzzle

When books are printed a certain number of pages are printed onto a large sheet of paper.

The large sheets are then folded and glued together to make the book. The number of large sheets used for each book depends on how many pages the finished book will have, as the number of pages printed on to each large sheet is always the same.

Jane looks at two of her books.
One has 96 pages.
The other has 160 pages.

How many pages do you think were printed on the large sheets used to make these books?

6 Decimals

Subject links
- science
- design and technology
- PHSE

Coming up ...

- comparing and ordering decimals
- multiplying whole numbers and decimals by 10, 100 and 1000
- dividing whole numbers and decimals by 10, 100 and 1000
- using division to convert a fraction to a decimal
- solving problems involving decimals

Chapter starter

When you go on holiday abroad, you exchange British Pounds for the currency of the country you are visiting. Currency can be bought at banks, at the Post Office and at travel agents. You buy the currency at an exchange rate that can change every day. The exchange rates are usually advertised on a board like this:

1 British Pound buys						
	USA	1.8629	Dollar		Kenya	122.2300	Shilling
	Eurozone	1.2664	Euro		Mexico	18.6900	Peso
	New Zealand	2.2863	Dollar		Pakistan	115.9700	Rupee
	Canada	1.8687	Dollar		South Africa	13.9100	Rand
	Egypt	9.4852	Pound		Switzerland	2.0348	Franc
	Hungary	312.7700	Forint		Taiwan	54.0700	Dollar
	India	68.2700	Rupee		Thailand	56.7400	Baht
	Israel	6.3044	Shekel				

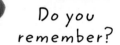
Continued ...

Do you remember?
- how to add and subtract whole numbers
- how to multiply and divide whole numbers by 10, 100 and 1000
- that lengths can be measured in metres, centimetres and millimetres

Key word

integer
fraction
digit
decimal
place value
tenth
hundredth
thousandth

Notice from the table that although usually we only use two decimal places when working with money, exchange rates use four.

Example

How many Swiss Francs will 30 British Pounds buy?

Solution

Firstly, look up the exchange rate.

From the table, 1 British Pound buys 2.0348 Swiss Francs.

So, 30 British Pounds can buy 30 × 2.0348 = 61.044 Swiss Francs. However, because exchange rates have four decimal places, the answer is 61.0440 Swiss Francs.

① How many Euros will 10 British Pounds buy?

② How many Canadian Dollars will 25 British Pounds buy?

③ How many Pakistani Rupees will 100 British Pounds buy?

When you return from holiday, you may have some foreign currency left and you may want to exchange it back into British Pounds. The exchange rate works in the opposite direction.

Example

How many British Pounds will 750 Thai Baht buy?

Solution

Firstly, look up the exchange rate.

From the table, 1 British Pound buys 56.7400 Thai Baht, so divide 750 Thai Baht by the exchange rate:

750 ÷ 56.7400 = 13.2182 British Pounds

④ How many British Pounds will 250 New Zealand Dollars buy?

⑤ How many British Pounds will 1000 South African Rand buy?

Investigation

Why do exchange rates use four decimal places?

6.1 Ordering decimals

Hint
Use a table.
Always start at the left-hand side when comparing numbers.

You can use place value to compare and order decimals.

Example

Which is bigger, 5.72 or 5.74?

Solution

U	.	t	h
5	.	7	2
5	.	7	4

Compare the units. They are the same.

Compare the tenths. They are the same.

Compare the hundredths. 4 is bigger than 2.

You can write this as 5.74 > 5.72. > means 'is bigger than'.

So 5.74 is bigger than 5.72.

Continued ...

You can check your answer on a number line.

5.72   5.74

5.70   5.80

Example

Write these decimals in order of size.

0.35   0.289   1.3

Start with the smallest.

Solution

Compare the whole number (units) parts.
They are the same.

Compare the whole number (units) parts.
1 is bigger than 0.
So 1.3 is the largest number.

Th	H	T	U	.	t	h	th
			0	.	3	5	
			0	.	2	8	9
			1	.	3		

Compare the tenths.
2 is smaller than 3.
So 0.289 is smaller than 0.35.

⚠ It is a common error to think that the largest number is the one with the most digits.
Use a table and fill in empty spaces after the decimal point with zeros to help you when comparing decimals.

The order is 0.289, 0.35, 1.3.

You can check your answer on a number line.

0.289 0.35   1.3

0   0.2 0.3   0.5   1.0   1.5

Now try these 6.1

1 Copy these numbers and write the symbol < or > in the boxes.

(a) 3.4 ☐ 3.6

(b) 1.93 ☐ 1.9

(c) 6.7 ☐ 6.65

(d) 3.01 ☐ 3.1

(e) 29.845 ☐ 29.485

2 Write each set of numbers in order of size. Start with the biggest.

(a) 2.3   2.7   2.1

(b) 0.256   0.3   0.27

(c) 0.014   0.14   0.2

3 Write each set of numbers in order of size. Start with the smallest.

(a) 5.6   5.59   5.68   (b) 0.81   0.8   0.9

(c) 3.5   3.48   3.53

4 Write this set of numbers in order of size. Start with the smallest.

6.03   6.1   6.04

5 Write these in order of size. Start with the biggest.

3.002   2.99   2.994   2.9

6 Write these in order of size. Start with the smallest.

1.1   1.11   1.011   1.01

7 Write these in order of size. Start with the biggest.

0.37   0.367   0.376   0.637

Continued ..

⑧ Jordan, Megan, Dan and Jess took part in a sponsored walk.

Write the amounts in order, smallest first.

I raised £2.

I raised 95p.

I raised £1.50.

I raised £1.25.

⑨ **Puzzle**

(a) Arrange the numbers in order, smallest first.
What word do the letters spell?

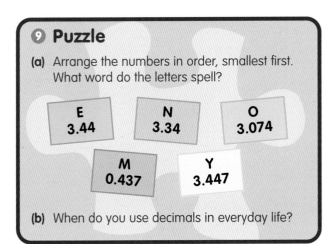

E 3.44

N 3.34

O 3.074

M 0.437

Y 3.447

(b) When do you use decimals in everyday life?

⑩ Write the numbers that are halfway between these numbers.

(a) 3.5 and 3.7
(b) 6.17 and 6.19
(c) 0.3 and 0.4
(d) 2.04 and 2.05
(e) 2.16 and 2.17
(f) 0.3 and 0.6
(g) 0.99 and 1

Hint
You can use a number line to help you with this question.

6.2 Multiplying by 10, 100 and 1000

You should already know how to multiply integers by 10, 100 and 1000.

You use the same method to multiply decimals by 10, 100 and 1000.

● When you multiply a number by **10** you move the digits **one** place to the left.
● When you multiply a number by **100** you move the digits **two** places to the left.
● When you multiply a number by **1000** you move the digits **three** places to the left.

Multiplying a positive number by 10, 100 or 1000 has the effect of increasing the number.

Example

Work out these.

(a) 3.84 × 10
(b) 2.657 × 100
(c) 1.86 × 1000

Solution

(a) 3.84 × 10 = 38.4

Th	H	T	U	.	t	h
			3	.	8	4
		3	8	.	4	

(b) 2.657 × 100 = 265.7

Th	H	T	U	.	t	h	th
			2	.	6	5	7
	2	6	5	.	7		

Continued ...

(c) $1.86 \times 1000 = 1860$

Th	H	T	U	.	t	h	th
			1	.	8	6	0
1	8	6	0	.			

You need to put a zero in the units column to show that there are no units.

If there are no digits after the decimal point you do not need to have a decimal point in your answer. You can write 1860.0 as 1860.

Now try these 6.2

1 Work out these.
- **(a)** 2.86×10
- **(b)** 14.85×10
- **(c)** 2.7×10
- **(d)** 234.9×10
- **(e)** 5.34×10
- **(f)** 0.86×10

2 Work out these.
- **(a)** 3.985×100
- **(b)** 4.7×100
- **(c)** 4.067×100
- **(d)** 3.9×100
- **(e)** 0.98×100
- **(f)** 0.002×100

3 Work out these.
- **(a)** 1.2347×1000
- **(b)** 8.743×1000
- **(c)** 3.5×1000
- **(d)** 93×1000
- **(e)** 0.57×1000
- **(f)** 20×1000

4 Work out these.
- **(a)** 6.007×10
- **(b)** 1.1×100
- **(c)** 0.586×1000
- **(d)** 19×10
- **(e)** 3.87×10
- **(f)** 47×100
- **(g)** 300×10
- **(h)** 6.34×100
- **(i)** 523×10

5 To convert centimetres to millimetres you multiply by 10.
How many millimetres are there in 3.6 cm?

6 To convert metres to centimetres you multiply by 100.
How many centimetres are there in 5.3 m?

7 To convert kilometres to metres you multiply by 1000.
How many metres are there in 8.6 km?

8 To convert kilograms to grams you multiply by 1000.
How many grams are there in 3.5 kg?

9 Work out these.
- **(a)** $1.395\,22 \times 10\,000$
- **(b)** $83.729\,63 \times 10\,000$
- **(c)** $6.9365 \times 10\,000$
- **(d)** $8.543 \times 10\,000$

6.3 Dividing by 10, 100 and 1000

You should already know how to divide integers by 10, 100 and 1000.

You use the same method to divide decimals by 10, 100 and 1000.

- When you divide a number by **10** you move the digits **one** place to the right.
- When you divide a number by **100** you move the digits **two** places to the right.
- When you divide a number by **1000** you move the digits **three** places to the right.

Dividing a positive number by 10, 100 or 1000 has the effect of decreasing that number.

Continued

Example

Work out these.

(a) 27.4 ÷ 10

(b) 4581.3 ÷ 100

(c) 27 ÷ 1000

Solution

(a) 27.4 ÷ 10 = 2.74

Th	H	T	U	.	t	h
		2	7	.	4	
			2	.	7	4

(b) 4581.3 ÷ 100 = 45.813

Th	H	T	U	.	t	h	th
4	5	8	1	.	3		
	4	5	.	8	1	3	

(c) 27 ÷ 1000 = 0.027

Th	H	T	U	.	t	h	th
		2	7	.			
			0	.	0	2	7

> It is usual to put a 0 in the units column to show that there are 0 units. Write 0.027 rather than .027.

> You need to put a 0 in the tenths column to show that there are 0 tenths.

Now try these 6.3

1 Work out these.
- **(a)** 45 ÷ 10
- **(b)** 6.5 ÷ 10
- **(c)** 358.1 ÷ 10
- **(d)** 84.2 ÷ 10

2 Work out these.
- **(a)** 158 ÷ 100
- **(b)** 34.4 ÷ 100
- **(c)** 990.4 ÷ 100
- **(d)** 589.6 ÷ 100

3 Work out these.
- **(a)** 137 ÷ 1000
- **(b)** 45 ÷ 1000
- **(c)** 50.612 ÷ 1000
- **(d)** 4678.2 ÷ 1000

4 Work out these.
- **(a)** 0.18 ÷ 10
- **(b)** 2.6 ÷ 1000
- **(c)** 0.065 ÷ 10
- **(d)** 5.803 ÷ 100

5 To convert centimetres to metres you divide by 100. Convert 165 cm to metres.

6 To convert metres to kilometres you divide by 1000. Convert 2500 m to kilometres.

7 To convert grams to kilograms you divide by 1000. Convert 256 g to kilograms.

8 To convert millimetres to centimetres you divide by 10. Convert 77 mm to centimetres.

9 Brain strain

Work out these.
- **(a)** 27 034.23 ÷ 10 000
- **(b)** 70 032.772 ÷ 10 000
- **(c)** 6775.903 ÷ 10 000
- **(d)** 23.2339 ÷ 10 000

6.4 Adding and subtracting decimals

Your knowledge of place value will help you when you add and subtract decimals.

Example

Work out 5.67 + 2.84.

Solution

You can use a place value table to help you.

The table helps you give each digit its correct place value.

> These are the carried digits.

U	.	t	h
5	.	6	7
2	.	8	4
8	.	5	1
	1		1

Continued ...

When you use the column method you line up the decimal points and digits in the same way but without drawing the table.

```
  5 . 6 7
+ 2 . 8 4
─────────
  8 . 5 1
  1   1
```

Example

Work out 19.5 + 0.743.

Hint
Fill the spaces in the columns with zeros to help you line up the digits correctly.

Solution

T	U	.	t	h	th
1	9	.	5	0	0
0	0	.	7	4	3
2	0	.	2	4	3
	1	1			

```
  1 9 . 5 0 0
+ 0 0 . 7 4 3
─────────────
  2 0 . 2 4 3
     1 1
```

Example

Work out 4.6 – 1.87.

Put a zero in the empty space to show that there are no hundredths in 4.6.

Solution

U	.	t	h
³4	.	¹⁵5̸	¹0
1	.	8	7
2	.	7	3

You can't subtract 7 from 0 so break down the 6 tenths into 5 tenths and 10 hundredths. It is the same method you use when subtracting integers.

```
  ³4 . ¹⁵5̸ ¹0
-  1 . 8 7
───────────
   2 . 7 3
```

Use a zero to show that there are no hundredths in 4.6. It helps you to line up the digits correctly.

You can check your calculation using a number line.

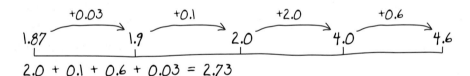

2.0 + 0.1 + 0.6 + 0.03 = 2.73

Now try these 6.4

❶ Puzzle

In these number pyramids, two numbers next to each other are added to find the number in the box above. Copy and complete the pyramids.

(a)

3.8

1.3 2.5 3.4

(b)

0.73 1.34

0.02

(c)

4.67

2.42

1.17

Continued …

Puzzle

In these puzzles, the number in the square is the sum of the numbers in the circles on either side.

Copy and complete the puzzles.

(a)

(b)

(c)

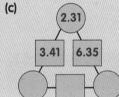

3 Work out these.

   (a) 2.06 + 1.72   (b) 8.57 – 3.25
   (c) 5.7 + 2.9   (d) 3.73 – 1.36

4 Work out these.

   (a) 20.7 + 3.42   (b) 2.94 – 1.6
   (c) 0.724 + 0.88   (d) 3.4 – 0.72

5 Work out these.

   (a) 26.8 + 153.4   (b) 234.1 – 38.5
   (c) 9.3 + 25.81   (d) 0.88 – 0.206

6 Work out these.

   (a) 16.1 – 2.208   (b) 6 – 3.7
   (c) 14 – 5.9   (d) 1 – 0.734

7 Work out these.

   (a) 34.05 – 9.78   (b) 2.004 – 1.348
   (c) 5.017 – 2.878   (d) 0.5 – 0.41

8 Jake visits a games shop to spend his birthday money.

This is what he buys.

Game: Spider Warrior Attacks	£37.99
Game: Virtual Ju-Jitsu	£29.69
Game controller handset	£11.49

How much does he spend?

9 Shefali is buying her lunch.

This is what she chooses.

sandwich	£1.99
small bag crisps	36p
small bag dried fruit	45p
chocolate bar	40p
small carton orange juice	24p

   (a) How much does she spend altogether?
   (b) She pays with a £10 note.
      How much change does she get?

10 Mark is doing up an old chair to sell on the internet.

He needs to replace the seat.

The picture shows the dimensions of the chair.

He has to cut four pieces of wood to make the seat.

Each piece must be 2 mm shorter than the dimension of the chair.

   (a) What lengths of wood must he cut?
   (b) What length of wood does he need altogether?
   (c) He has a 2-metre length of wood.
      How much does he have left over?
   (d) Do you think the leftover piece will really be the length you have calculated?

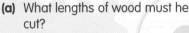

Hint
To convert from centimetres to metres, divide by 100.
To convert from millimetres to centimetres, divide by 10.

You probably think of the fraction $\frac{3}{4}$ as meaning '3 parts out of 4', which is certainly true.

$\frac{3}{4}$ can also be thought of as '3 divided by 4' and this gives you a handy way to convert fractions into their decimal equivalents.

Example

Convert $\frac{3}{4}$ into a decimal.

Solution

Carry out a long division, 3 divided by 4.

```
    0 . 7 5
4 ) 3 . 0
    2   8
      2 0
      2 0
        0
```

So $\frac{3}{4} = 0.75$

For some fractions it is convenient to write them with a denominator of 10 or 100 first.

This makes the division much easier.

Example

Convert $\frac{9}{20}$ into a decimal.

Solution

$\frac{9}{20} = \frac{45}{100}$ Multiply both the numerator and the denominator by 5.

$45 \div 100 = 0.45$

So $\frac{9}{20} = 0.45$.

For harder questions you may want to use a calculator.

Example

Convert $\frac{3}{7}$ into a decimal.

Round your answer to 3 decimal places.

Solution

Using a calculator, $3 \div 7 = 0.428\ 571\ 428\ 6\ldots$

This value is between 0.428 and 0.429, so to three decimal places we need to choose between 0.428 and 0.429.

Since it lies above 0.4285 it is closer to 0.429.

So $\frac{3}{7} = 0.429$ (to 3 decimal places).

① Convert these fractions to decimals.

(a) $\frac{4}{5}$ (b) $\frac{1}{4}$ (c) $\frac{7}{20}$ (d) $\frac{1}{5}$

(e) $\frac{3}{10}$ (f) $\frac{21}{50}$ (g) $\frac{11}{20}$ (h) $\frac{5}{8}$

(i) $\frac{13}{20}$ (j) $\frac{12}{25}$

② Convert these fractions to decimals.

Round your answers to 3 decimal places.

(a) $\frac{1}{3}$ (b) $\frac{2}{3}$ (c) $\frac{1}{6}$ (d) $\frac{5}{6}$

(e) $\frac{1}{9}$ (f) $\frac{4}{9}$ (g) $\frac{1}{11}$ (h) $\frac{7}{11}$

(i) $\frac{1}{7}$ (j) $\frac{4}{7}$

③ The fraction $\frac{1}{16}$ is exactly equal to 0.0625.

Use this information to convert these fractions into exact decimals.

(a) $\frac{3}{16}$ (b) $\frac{7}{16}$ (c) $\frac{15}{16}$ (d) $\frac{1}{8}$

(e) $\frac{11}{16}$ (f) $\frac{1}{32}$

④ Write these fractions in order of size, starting with the smallest.

$\frac{11}{15}$ $\frac{24}{29}$ $\frac{7}{9}$ $\frac{36}{41}$

⑤ Write these fractions in order of size, starting with the largest.

$\frac{14}{25}$ $\frac{18}{31}$ $\frac{27}{40}$ $\frac{67}{102}$

Accuracy and rounding

Subject links
● science
● geography
● design and technology

Coming up …

● rounding positive whole numbers to the nearest 10, 100 and 1000
● rounding decimals to the nearest whole number and to one decimal place
● estimating the answer to a calculation

Chapter starter

When repairing a window the measurements need to be exact.

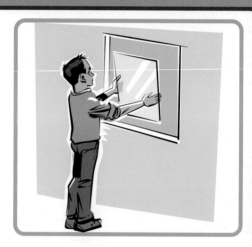

Do you remember?
● rules of arithmetic
● about place value
● decimal numbers
● units for measuring including their abbreviations

When using many recipes the measurements do not need to be exact.

You do not need to measure 40 grams of butter exactly.

It would not matter if you used 38 grams or 43 grams.

You do not need to measure 100 millilitres of milk exactly.

It would not matter if you used 105 millilitres or 97 millilitres.

SCRAMBLED EGGS
40 GRAMS OF BUTTER
3 EGGS
100 MILLILITRES OF MILK

Key words

estimate
estimation
approximate
approximation
round
rounding
convention
multiple
accuracy
decimal place

Continued …

Decide whether the following need to be exact or not. Give reasons for your answers.

1. A teacher wants to know the number of pupils she is taking on a school trip to London.

2. A reporter wants to know, for a magazine article, the number of mobile phones sold in Britain last year.

3. The school canteen wants to know how many pupils will have lunch in the school canteen tomorrow.

4. A scientist wants to know the distance from the Earth to the Moon in kilometres.

5. A builder wants to know the mass of bricks that can be carried on a lift.

6. A salesman wants to know the time taken to travel by car between Brighton and Bristol.

7. A bank manager wants to know how much money was taken out of a cashpoint machine.

7.1 Rounding to the nearest 10, 100 or 1000

Hint
Another word for an estimate is an approximation.

If you do not need to use the exact value of a number you can use an **estimate**.

One way of making an estimate is to round the number.

Dan did a survey of the number of music downloads the pupils in his class made last year.

He finds that the average number is 58 per pupil.

Dan says

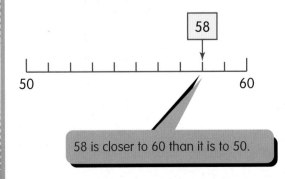

My class made approximately 60 music downloads each last year.

Dan has rounded 58 to the nearest 10.

58 is closer to 60 than it is to 50.

In Mia's class the average number was 55.

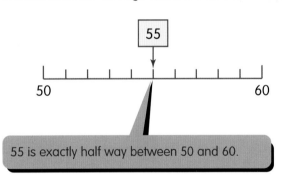

55 is exactly half way between 50 and 60.

By **convention**, you round up to the larger number.

55 rounded to the nearest 10 is 60.

You don't have to draw a number line.

Think of the multiple of 10 above and below the number you are rounding.

Then decide which it is closer to.

Continued ...

Su Ling organises a charity collection at her school.

She collects £429.

Hint
429 has 4 hundreds so the multiple of 100 below it is 400. The next multiple of 100 is 500.

We collected over £400.

Su Ling has rounded £429 to the nearest £100.

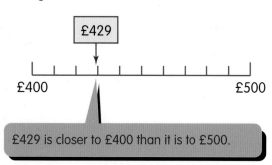

£429

£400   £500

£429 is closer to £400 than it is to £500.

Again, you don't have to draw a number line.

Think of the multiple of 100 above and below the number you are rounding.

Then decide which it is closer to.

Mr and Mrs Crawford are house hunting.

The price of the house they look at is £124 750.

This one costs £125 000.

Mrs Crawford has rounded £124 750 to the nearest £1000.

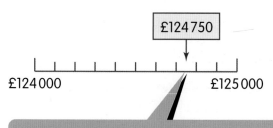

£124 750

£124 000   £125 000

£124 750 is closer to £125 000 than £124 000.

Without using a number line, the multiple of 1000 below 124 750 is 124 000.

The next multiple of 1000 is 125 000.

£124 750 is closer to £125 000 than £124 000.

Now try these 7.1

1. Remember Su Ling raised £429 for charity.
   What is this to the nearest £10?

2. Jamie is weighing flour to make a pizza base.
   Estimate the mass of the flour to the nearest 100 grams.

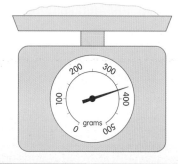

3. The table shows the heights of the four highest waterfalls in the world.

Waterfall	Height in metres
Angel Falls	979
Yosemite Falls	737
Mardalsfossen-South	655
Tugela Falls	614

   (a) Round each height to the nearest 10 metres.

   (b) Which two of the waterfalls have the same height when rounded to the nearest 100 metres?

Continued

4 The diameter of the Earth at the Equator is 12 756 kilometres.

Jenny says that this is 12 000 kilometres rounded to the nearest 1000 kilometres.

Is she correct?

Give a reason for your answer.

5 The diagram shows the end of a rope.

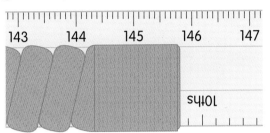

How long is the rope to the nearest

(a) 10 centimetres

(b) 100 centimetres?

6 Round these numbers to the stated accuracy.

(a) 79 to the nearest 10

(b) 4568 to the nearest 1000

(c) 433 to the nearest 10

(d) 560 to the nearest 100

(e) 7939 to the nearest 100

(f) 42 580 to the nearest 1000

(g) 65 555 to the nearest 100

(h) 85 to the nearest 10

(i) 536 399 to the nearest 1000

(j) 250 to the nearest 100

7 (a) Round 2975 to the nearest 1000.

(b) Round 2975 to the nearest 100.

(c) Round 2975 to the nearest 10.

8 (a) Find a number that gives the same answer when rounded to the nearest 10 and to the nearest 100.

(b) Find a number that gives the same answer when rounded to the nearest 100 and to the nearest 1000.

(c) Find a number that gives the same answer when rounded to the nearest 10, to the nearest 100 and to the nearest 1000.

9 This is part of a newspaper report on a rock concert.

> The concert was attended by a crowd of about 25 000 people

You are not told the level of accuracy the reporter has used.

What are the smallest and largest possible sizes of the crowd if the reporter rounded the size to

(a) the nearest 1000

(b) the nearest 100?

10 Brain strain

Jordan correctly rounds 2448 to the nearest 10.

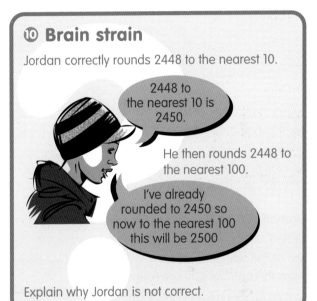

2448 to the nearest 10 is 2450.

He then rounds 2448 to the nearest 100.

I've already rounded to 2450 so now to the nearest 100 this will be 2500

Explain why Jordan is not correct.

In Chapter 6, section 6.1 you learnt about place value in decimals.

The decimal 257.8 has 1 decimal place

There is one digit to the right of the decimal point.

The digit 8 stands for 8 tenths, or 0.8, and is in the first decimal place.

The decimal 3.64 has 2 decimal places.

There are two digits to the right of the decimal point.

The digit 6 stands for 6 tenths, or 0.6, and is in the first decimal place.

The digit 4 stands for 4 hundredths, or 0.04, and is in the second decimal place.

Decimals can be rounded to the nearest whole number.

Look at the whole numbers immediately above and below the number you are rounding.

Then decide which it is closer to.

Example

A line is measured as 24.7 cm.

Round the length to the nearest centimetre.

Solution

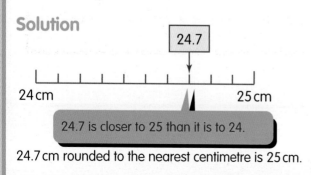

24.7 is closer to 25 than it is to 24.

24.7 cm rounded to the nearest centimetre is 25 cm.

You don't have to draw a number line.

Look at the digit in the first decimal place.

If it is less than 5, just write the integer part of the number.

If it is 5 or more, add one to the units digit.

Don't write the decimal point or any digits after it.

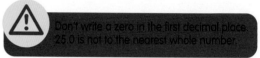

24.7 — You have 7 tenths. 7 tenths is closer to 1 than it is to 0. You add 1 to the units.

24.7 cm rounded to the nearest centimetre is 25 cm.

⚠ Don't write a zero in the first decimal place. 25.0 is not to the nearest whole number.

Example

Round 3.298 kg to the nearest kilogram.

Solution

Using a number line

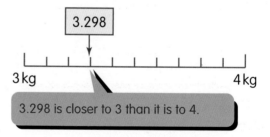

3.298 is closer to 3 than it is to 4.

3.298 kg rounded to the nearest kilogram is 3 kg.

Without drawing a number line

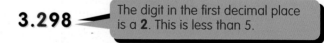

3.298 — The digit in the first decimal place is a **2**. This is less than 5.

You leave the units digit unchanged.

Don't write the decimal point or any digits after it.

Hint
You do not need to look at the digits in the second or third decimal place.

3.298 kg rounded to the nearest kilogram is 3 kg.

Continued ...

Decimals can also be rounded to 1 decimal place.

The digit in the first decimal place represents tenths. You are rounding to the nearest tenth.

Example

Round 46.18 to 1 decimal place.

Solution

Using a number line

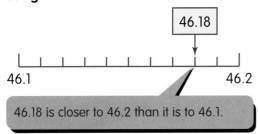

46.18 is closer to 46.2 than it is to 46.1.

46.18 rounded to 1 decimal place is 46.2.

Without drawing a number line

You don't have to draw a number line.

Look at the digit in the second decimal place.

If it is less than 5, do not change the digit in the first decimal place.

If it is 5 or more, add one to the digit in the first decimal place.

46.18 — The digit in the second decimal place is an 8. This is more than 5.

You add one to the digit in the first decimal place.

Don't write any digits to the right of the first decimal place.

46.18 rounded to 1 decimal place is 46.2.

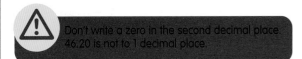

⚠ Don't write a zero in the second decimal place. 46.20 is not to 1 decimal place.

Example

Round 7.95 to 1 decimal place.

Solution

Using a number line

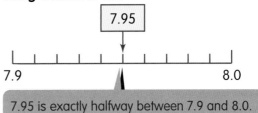

7.95 is exactly halfway between 7.9 and 8.0.

By convention, you round up to 8.0.

7.95 rounded to 1 decimal place is 8.0.

You need the zero in the first decimal place to show that you have rounded to 1 decimal place.

Without drawing a number line

7.95 — The digit in the second decimal place is a 5.

Look at the digit in the second decimal place.

This is a 5.

You add 1 to the digit in the first decimal place.

The digit in the first decimal place is 9.

Adding 1 makes 10 so you put a zero in the first decimal place and you make the units digit one bigger.

7.95 rounded to 1 decimal place is 8.0.

You need the zero in the first decimal place to show that you have rounded to 1 decimal place.

Now try these 7.2

1. Here are some calculator displays. Round each number to the nearest whole number.

   (a) 6.37   (b) 13.49

   (c) 3.6   (d) 20.45

   (e) 19.8   (f) 1.71

   (g) 26.79   (h) 3.5

   (i) 100.5

2. Here are some more calculator displays. Round each number to 1 decimal place.

   (a) 2.16   (b) 10.68

   (c) 5.94   (d) 4.07

   (e) 38.24   (f) 12.39

   (g) 1.97   (h) 0.93

   (i) 154.06   (j) 6.65

   (k) 15.99   (l) 1.858

   (m) 0.9099   (n) 27.555

   (o) 9.96

3. **Puzzle**

   A number has 2 decimal places.
   When it is rounded to 1 decimal place the answer is 5.8.
   Write down all the possible numbers that the number could be.

4. Round these weights to the nearest tenth of a kilogram.

   (a) 35.44 kg

   (b) 7.98 kg

   (c) 290.85 kg

   (d) 0.4545 kg

   (e) 49.99 kg

   Hint
   The digit in the first decimal place represents tenths so the question is asking you to round to 1 decimal place.

7.3 Making estimates and approximations

Rounding is not the only way of making an estimate.

It is important to look at the context when you are estimating.

Steve works out that he needs 2.3 litres of paint.

The paint comes in 1-litre tins.

2.3 litres to the nearest litre is 2 litres.

Steve has to buy 3 litres of paint, however, otherwise he would run out of paint before he had finished the room.

People often make an estimate of how much a number of items are going to cost.

One reason is to make sure they are not overcharged.

Another reason is because they only have a certain amount of money to spend.

Alisha has a £20 note in her purse.

She wants to buy these items.

Book	£3.49
CD	£8.72
Birthday card	£1.69
Printer cartridge	£6.40

She rounds each of the prices to the nearest pound.

£3 + £9 + £2 + £6 = £20
I will have enough money.

Continued

When Alisha goes to pay she finds that she does not have enough money.

Alisha's estimate of £20 is close to the actual total of £20.30 but to be sure she has enough money she needs to use a different method.

She needs to make each price up to the next pound.

£4 + £9 + £2 + £7 = £22

There are times when you need to make an approximation to a problem.

For example, you can work out an approximation to check an answer is approximately correct.

 An approximation is done without a calculator.

An approximation should use numbers that make the calculation easy to work out.

Six friends sell their old toys on the internet and make a profit of £171.

They share the money equally.

Emily decides to do an approximation to work out roughly how much they will each receive.

How much will we each receive?

Here are some approximations she can use.

Calculation	Good choice?	Bad choice?
170 ÷ 10	Easy to work out. 170 is very close to 171.	10 is not very close to 6.
170 ÷ 6	170 is very close to 171 and 6 is exact	Not easy to work out.
180 ÷ 6	Easy to work out. 180 is quite close to 171 and 6 is exact.	
200 ÷ 5	Easy to work out. 5 is close to 6.	200 is not very close to 171

180 ÷ 6 = 30 and is easy to work out.

Can you think of any other calculations that could have been used?

Hint
You need to be able to work out the estimate quickly without a calculator so choose one that is easy to work out.

Use your calculator to work out 171 ÷ 6 and the four choices.

Does 180 ÷ 6 give an answer close to the exact answer?

Example

Estimate the answer to 419 × 27.

Solution

You need a calculation that is easy to work out.

419 × 27 ≈ 400 × 30 = 12 000

The symbol ≈ means 'is approximately equal to'.

Can you think of any other calculations that could have been used?

Use your calculator to work out 419 × 27.

Was 400 × 30 a good choice?

With a friend

Discuss which are good approximations and which are bad approximations for each of these calculations.

Give reasons for your answers.

Are there any other approximations you could use?

Use your calculator to find the exact answers and the approximate answers.

Was the approximation you chose close to the actual answer?

❶ Which is the best approximation for 51.7 − 38.9?

(a) 517 − 389   (b) 52 − 39   (c) 51 − 38

❷ Which is the best approximation for 9.3 × 4.8?

(a) 9 × 4   (b) 9 × 5   (c) 10 × 5

❸ Which is the best approximation for 3.5 × 2.5?

(a) 3 × 5   (b) 4 × 3   (c) 3 × 3

(d) 3 × 2

Now try these 7.3

1. Estimate the answers to these calculations.

   Show the numbers that you use.

   (a) 498 + 207 + 98   (b) 1520 − 585

   (c) 98 + 99 + 104   (d) 8029 − 2892

   (e) 360 × 12   (f) 480 × 19

   (g) 73 ÷ 6.95   (h) 249 ÷ 51

   (i) 48 × 2.9   (j) 32 196 ÷ 14.8

2. 1 kilogram is about 2.2 pounds.

   A suitcase weighs 18 kilograms.

   Estimate its weight in pounds.

3. A set of walking guide books is published.

   There are seven books altogether in the series and each one costs £7.99.

   Estimate the total cost of the whole set of books.

4. A coach company has 11 coaches.

   Each coach can hold 58 passengers.

   Estimate the total number of passengers that all 11 coaches can hold.

5. The bank will exchange £1 for 1.42 Euros.

   (a) How many Euros will you get for £10?

   (b) How many Euros will you get for £5?

   Juan has £489.50. He takes this to the bank and changes it for Euros.

   (c) Estimate the number of Euros that Juan should receive.

6. Estimate the answer to 21.4^2.

7. Six friends attend a concert.

   The tickets cost £21.50 each and they share a taxi that costs £40 altogether. Estimate the total cost for all six friends.

8. Here are four suggested answers to the calculation 38.3×1.9.

   (a) 7.277   (b) 72.77

   (c) 727.7   (d) 7277

   One of them is correct.

   Use estimation to decide which one is the correct answer.

9. Nine workmates win a lottery prize of £14 892.

   They share the prize equally between them all.

   Work out an estimate of the amount that each one receives.

10. Rachel works out $\dfrac{218}{11.7 \times 9.1}$ on her calculator.

    She writes down the answer as 20.475 251 24.

    Use estimation to show that Rachel's answer is wrong.

    What mistake do you think she has made?

Multiplying and dividing

Subject links
- design and technology
- science

Coming up …

- multiplying a three-digit integer by a two-digit integer
- multiplying a decimal with 1 or 2 decimal places by a single-digit integer
- dividing a decimal with 1 or 2 decimal places by a single-digit integer
- solving word problems involving multiplication and division
- using procedures to check whether your answers are correct

Do you remember?
- the multiplication facts to 10 × 10
- how to add and subtract positive integers and decimals
- how to multiply by 10 and 100
- how to estimate the answer to a calculation

Chapter starter

Six children and two leaders from the 1st Pitlochry Scouts are going to cycle from Dundee to Pitlochry.

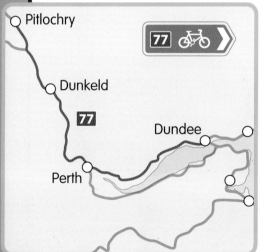

1 Transport to Dundee for the group and their bikes costs £56.

The cost is shared equally between the eight people in the group.

(a) How much do they each pay?

(b) Why do you think they are starting at Dundee rather than Pitlochry?

2 The distance is 54 miles.

They estimate they can cycle 6 miles in an hour.

How long will the ride take altogether?

3 Overnight accommodation costs £12 each.

How much does it cost for the whole group?

4 The leaders say each person's luggage should weigh 6 kg at the most.

(a) What is the most the group's luggage should weigh?

Actually, each of the children's bags only weighs about 4 kg.

The leaders have to carry first aid kits, bicycle repair kits and other emergency supplies.

Their bags weigh 7 kg each.

(b) How much does the group's luggage weigh?

Key words

integer

decimal

multiply

divide

estimate

approximation

remainder

There are different ways to multiply one number by another number.

The examples show two of these methods: the grid method and long multiplication.

Example

Find the product of 247 and 26.

Solution

Grid method

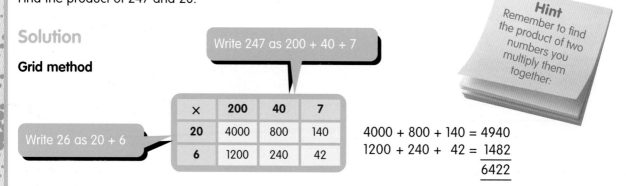

Write 247 as 200 + 40 + 7

Write 26 as 20 + 6

×	200	40	7
20	4000	800	140
6	1200	240	42

$$4000 + 800 + 140 = 4940$$
$$1200 + 240 + 42 = 1482$$
$$6422$$

Hint
Remember to find the product of two numbers you multiply them together.

A good approximation for 247×26 is $200 \times 30 = 6000$

The answer of 6422 is about right.

Long multiplication

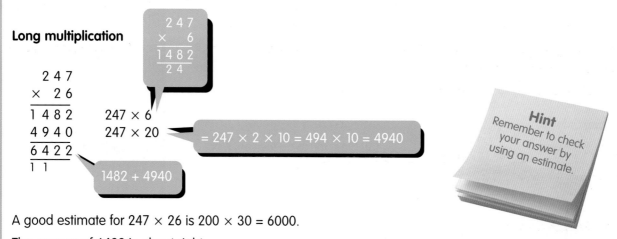

$$
\begin{array}{r}
2\,4\,7 \\
\times \quad 6 \\
\hline
1\,4\,8\,2 \\
2\,4 \\
\end{array}
$$

$$
\begin{array}{r}
2\,4\,7 \\
\times \quad 2\,6 \\
\hline
1\,4\,8\,2 \\
4\,9\,4\,0 \\
\hline
6\,4\,2\,2 \\
1\,1 \\
\end{array}
$$

247×6

247×20

$= 247 \times 2 \times 10 = 494 \times 10 = 4940$

$1482 + 4940$

Hint
Remember to check your answer by using an estimate.

A good estimate for 247×26 is $200 \times 30 = 6000$.

The answer of 6422 is about right.

Investigation

Work out each pair of calculations and say what you notice.

(a) 132×14 and 2×4 **(b)** 257×36 and 7×6 **(c)** 129×24 and 9×4

(d) 517×37 and 7×7 **(e)** 651×98 and 1×8

① Find the product of each pair of numbers.

(a) 54 and 8   (b) 43 and 12

(c) 7 and 126   (d) 147 and 15

(e) 52 and 314   (f) 521 and 63

② An ounce is approximately 28 grams.
A muffin weighs 4 ounces.
How many grams do six muffins weigh?

③ Mrs Knight's school is 34 miles away from her home.
She works 195 days a year.
How many miles does she drive to and from school in total in a year?

④ **Brain strain**

Jon buys 35 multipacks of crisps to sell at his youth club.

Each multipack contains 12 bags of crisps.

Jon sells each bag of crisps for 20p.

How much money does he make?

⑤ Tom and Megan have worked out 236 × 48.

The answer is 1328.

No, the answer is 11 328.

Who is correct?

8.2 Multiplying decimals

In the same way as for multiplying integers, there are different methods you can use.

When multiplying decimals, one technique is to ignore the decimal point while you do the calculation and replace it in the final answer.

You will need to find an estimate for the final answer.

Example
A portion of fish and chips cost £4.28.
Mr Corelli buys six portions of fish and chips for his family.
How much does he pay?

Solution
The cost is £4.28 × 6.
A good approximation for £4.28 × 6 is £4 × 6 = £24.
The answer is approximately £24.

Grid method ignoring the decimal point

Ignoring the decimal point the calculation is 428 × 6.

Write 428 as 400 + 20 + 8.

Notice that there are two places after the decimal point in the question and two places after the decimal point in the answer.

×	400	20	8
6	2400	120	48

2400 + 120 + 48 = 2568

The answer is approximately £24 so £4.28 × 6 = £25.68.

Continued...

Grid method using decimals

You may feel confident enough to work with the decimal number using the grid method.

Write 4.28 as 4.0 + 0.2 + 0.08.

×	4.0	0.2	0.08
6	24.0	1.2	0.48

24.0 + 1.2 + 0.48 = 25.68

Notice that there are two places after the decimal point in the question and two places after the decimal point in the answer.

```
  2 4 . 0
    1 . 2
+ 0 . 4 8
_____
  2 5 . 6 8
```

If you don't do the addition mentally, make sure you line up the decimal points.

Check: The answer is approximately £24 so this answer is about right.

Short multiplication

Ignoring the decimal point the calculation is 428 × 6.

```
    4 2 8
  ×     6
  _____
  2 5 6 8
    1 4
```

The answer is approximately £24 so £4.28 × 6 = £25.68.

Example

Work out 327.8 × 9.

Solution

A good approximation for 327.8 × 9 is 300 × 10 = 3000.
The answer is approximately 3000.

Grid method ignoring the decimal point

Ignoring the decimal point the calculation is 3278 × 9.

Write 3278 as 3000 + 200 + 70 + 8.

×	3000	200	70	8
9	27 000	1800	630	72

27 000 + 1800 + 630 + 72 = 29 502

Notice that there is one place after the decimal point in the question and one place after the decimal point in the answer.

The answer is approximately 3000 so 327.8 × 9 = 2950.2.

Continued...

Grid method using decimals

You may feel confident enough to work with the decimal number using the grid method.

> Write 327.8 as 300 + 20 + 7 + 0.8.

×	300	20	7	0.8
9	2700	180	63	7.2

2700 + 180 + 63 + 7.2 = 2950.2

Short multiplication

Ignoring the decimal point the calculation is 3278 × 9.

```
  3 2 7 8
×       9
─────────
2 9 5 0 2
  2 7 7
```

> Notice that there is one place after the decimal point in the question and one place after the decimal point in the answer.

The answer is approximately 3000 so 327.8 × 9 = 2950.2.

Now try these 8.2

① Work out these.

(a) 0.7 × 8

(b) 0.06 × 4

(c) 0.02 × 0.6

(d) 0.4 × 0.03

(e) 2.41 × 7

(f) 4.8 × 6.4

(g) 6.35 × 12

(h) 0.3 × 0.8

(i) 0.5 × 0.04

(j) 0.09 × 0.3

(k) 38.4 × 0.8

(l) 5.6 × 3.8

(m) 0.3 × 0.12

(n) 7.2 × 0.36

(o) 12 × 0.02

(p) 1.8 × 0.02

(q) 3.5 × 6.2

(r) 16 × 0.09

(s) 0.006 × 6

(t) 2.16 × 1.2

(u) 0.1 × 0.2

Use your answers in order to decode the message.

A	D	E	G	I
0.036	16.87	0.24	60.3	25.781
L	**N**	**O**	**R**	**S**
0.012	76.2	30.72	2.592	21.7
T	**U**	**W**	**Y**	**!**
1.44	21.28	5.6	0.027	0.02

② Brain strain

Use the fact that 136 × 17 = 2312 to write down the answers to these.

(a) 13.6 × 17

(b) 1.36 × 1.7

(c) 0.136 × 1.7

As for multiplication, there are different ways you can do division.

The examples show some of the different methods.

Example
Work out $216 \div 18$.

Solution
$216 \div 18 \approx 200 \div 20 = 10$

> Whichever method you use, it is a good idea to make an estimate of the answer first.

Using a number line

You could count on in steps of 18.

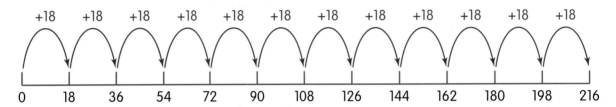

There are 12 steps of 18 to get to 216.

So $216 \div 18 = 12$.

You can be more efficient than this.

You know $18 \times 10 = 180$.

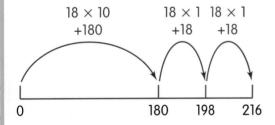

$10 + 1 + 1 = 12$.

So $216 \div 18 = 12$.

Repeated subtraction

You can subtract 18 repeatedly until you cannot take any more away.

$216 - 18 = 198$	$108 - 18 = 90$
$198 - 18 = 180$	$90 - 18 = 72$
$180 - 18 = 162$	$72 - 18 = 54$
$162 - 18 = 144$	$54 - 18 = 36$
$144 - 18 = 126$	$36 - 18 = 18$
$126 - 18 = 108$	$18 - 18 = 0$

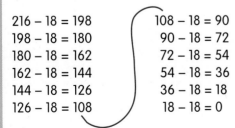

You have taken away 12 lots of 18.

So $216 \div 18 = 12$.

You can be more efficient than this.

You know $18 \times 10 = 180$.

$216 - 180 = 36$ — You have taken away 10 lots of 18.

$36 - 18 = 18$ — You have taken away 11 lots of 18.

$18 - 18 = 0$ — You have taken away 12 lots of 18.

So $216 \div 18 = 12$.

You can write your calculation like this.

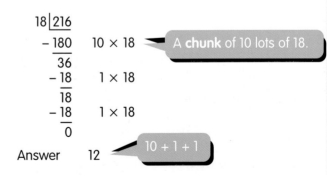

A **chunk** of 10 lots of 18.

Answer   12 $10 + 1 + 1$

If you know $2 \times 18 = 36$ you can be even more efficient.

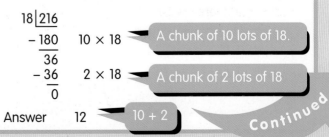

A chunk of 10 lots of 18.

A chunk of 2 lots of 18

Answer   12 $10 + 2$

Continued ...

Short division

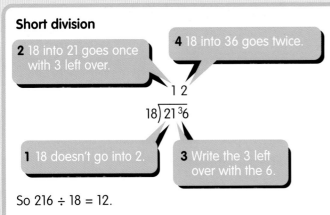

2 18 into 21 goes once with 3 left over.

4 18 into 36 goes twice.

1 18 doesn't go into 2.

3 Write the 3 left over with the 6.

$$18\overline{)21\,^36}$$
$$1\quad2$$

So $216 \div 18 = 12$.

Example

A school trip has 254 pupils and teachers in total. How many 35-seater coaches do they need?

Solution

The answer is found by calculating $254 \div 35$.

$254 \div 35 \approx 300 \div 40 = 7.5$.

Using a number line

$35 \times 10 = 350$ is too much. You can halve it to find 35×5.

$35 \times 5 = 175$

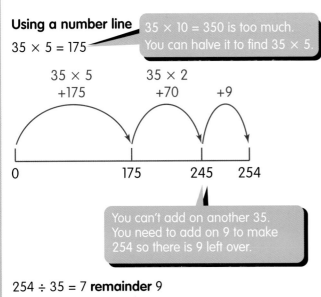

35×5 35×2
$+175$ $+70$ $+9$

0 175 245 254

You can't add on another 35. You need to add on 9 to make 254 so there is 9 left over.

$254 \div 35 = 7$ **remainder** 9

The **remainder** is the number left over.

The people on the school trip will completely fill 7 coaches and there will be 9 people left over.

Therefore 8 coaches are needed.

Hint
Remember to look at your answer in the context of the question. This is especially important when there is a remainder.

Repeated subtraction

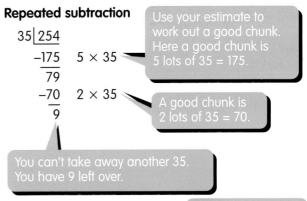

$$35\overline{)254}$$
$$-175 \quad 5 \times 35$$
$$\overline{79}$$
$$-70 \quad 2 \times 35$$
$$\overline{9}$$

Use your estimate to work out a good chunk. Here a good chunk is 5 lots of $35 = 175$.

A good chunk is 2 lots of $35 = 70$.

You can't take away another 35. You have 9 left over.

Answer   7 **remainder** 9

The **remainder** is the number left over.

The people on the school trip will completely fill 7 coaches and there will be 9 people left over.

Therefore 8 coaches are needed.

Short division

$$35\overline{)254}$$

35 into 2 doesn't go. 35 into 25 doesn't go either!

This method doesn't work very well for this example.

You have to know or be able to work out that $35 \times 7 = 245$.

$$35\overline{)254}$$
$$245$$
$$\overline{9}$$
$$7$$

$35 \times 7 = 245$

This is the remainder. The remainder is the number left over.

The people on the school trip will completely fill 7 coaches and there will be 9 people left over.

Therefore 8 coaches are needed.

1 Work out these.

(a) 152 ÷ 8   (b) 384 ÷ 12

(c) 378 ÷ 14   (d) 682 ÷ 22

(e) 513 ÷ 27   (f) 923 ÷ 13

2 Work out these.

Make sure you write down the remainder.

(a) 745 ÷ 7   (b) 736 ÷ 19

(c) 436 ÷ 21   (d) 896 ÷ 42

(e) 621 ÷ 11   (f) 947 ÷ 37

3 658 football fans are going by coach to see an away match.

Each coach can seat 54 people.

How many coaches do they need to hire?

4 Brain strain

Freya works out that 415 ÷ 18 = 23 remainder 1.

Write down the answer to 18 × 23.

Explain how you know.

5 Isobel has £12.40 worth of credit on her mobile phone.

A phone call costs her 15p per minute.

How many whole minutes of phone calls can she make?

8.4 Dividing decimals

You can use the same methods you used to divide integers to divide a decimal by an integer.

Example

Work out 25.2 ÷ 4.

Solution

25.2 ÷ 4 ≈ 24 ÷ 4 = 6.

> Make an estimate of the answer first.

Using a number line

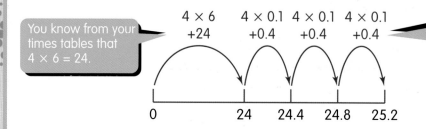

You know from your times tables that 4 × 6 = 24.

4 × 6 +24   4 × 0.1 +0.4   4 × 0.1 +0.4   4 × 0.1 +0.4

You need a decimal number. 4 × 0.1 = 0.4.

0   24   24.4   24.8   25.2

6 + 0.1 + 0.1 + 0.1 = 6.3. So 25.2 ÷ 4 = 6.3.

Continued ..

Repeated subtraction

```
4|25.2
 -24      6 × 4
 ───
   1.2
 -0.4     0.1 × 4
 ────
   0.8
 -0.4     0.1 × 4
 ────
   0.4
 -0.4     0.1 × 4
 ────
     0
```

A good chunk is 6 lots of 4 = 24

Now you need a decimal number.
A good chunk is 0.1 lots of 4 = 0.4

Answer   6.3 ◄ 6 + 0.1 + 0.1 + 0.1

Short division

4 4 into 12 goes 3 times.

2 4 into 25 goes six times with 1 left over.

```
    6. 3
 4)25.¹2
```

1 Make sure you line up the decimal points.

3 Write the 1 left over with the 2.

So 25.2 ÷ 4 = 6.3.

Hint
You can check your answer by working backwards.
6.3 × 4 = 25.2

Example

Ben pays £22.68 for 9 packs of trading cards.
How much is one pack?

Solution

One pack will cost £22.68 ÷ 9.
Estimate: 22.68 ÷ 9 ≈ 20 ÷ 10 = 2.

Using a number line

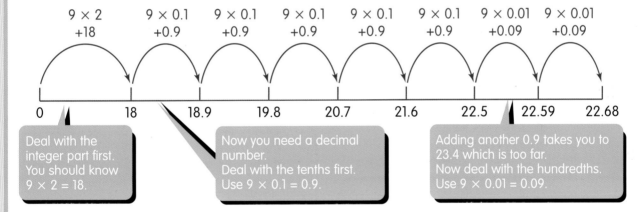

Deal with the integer part first.
You should know 9 × 2 = 18.

Now you need a decimal number.
Deal with the tenths first.
Use 9 × 0.1 = 0.9.

Adding another 0.9 takes you to 23.4 which is too far.
Now deal with the hundredths.
Use 9 × 0.01 = 0.09.

2 + 0.1 + 0.1 + 0.1 + 0.1 + 0.1 + 0.01 + 0.01 = 2.52

So 22.68 ÷ 9 = 2.52

One pack of trading cards costs £2.52. ◄ Remember to answer the question.

You can be more efficient.

Half of 9 is 4.5.

So 9 × 0.5 = 4.5.

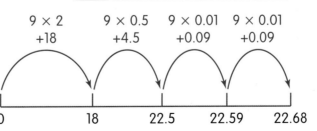

2 + 0.5 + 0.01 + 0.01 = 2.52

So 22.68 ÷ 9 = 2.52.

One pack of trading cards costs £2.52.

Continued ...

Repeated subtraction

Next you need to deal with the tenths.
Work out
0.1 lots of 9 = 0.9
0.2 lots of 9 = 1.8
0.3 lots of 9 = 2.7
0.4 lots of 9 = 3.6
0.5 lots of 9 = 4.5
0.6 lots of 9 = 5.4
which is too many

Then deal with the hundredths.
0.01 lots of 9 = 0.09

Use your tables to work out how many lots of 9 to take away.

```
 9│22.68
  − 18      2 × 9
  ─────
    4.68
  − 4.5     0.5 × 9
  ─────
    0.18
  − 0.09    0.01 × 9
  ─────
    0.09
  − 0.09    0.01 × 9
  ─────
    0
```

Answer   2.52

2 + 0.5 + 0.01 + 0.01 = 2.52

So 22.68 ÷ 9 = 2.52.

One pack of trading cards costs £2.52.

Short division

4 9 into 46 goes 5 times with 1 left over.

2 9 into 22 goes 2 times with 4 left over.

6 9 into 18 goes 2 times.

```
   2.5 2
 9)22.⁴6¹8
```

1 Make sure you line up the decimal points.

5 Write the 1 left over with the 8.

3 Write the 4 left over with the 6.

So 22.68 ÷ 9 = 2.52.

One pack of trading cards costs £2.52.

Hint
You can check your answer by working backwards.
2.52 × 9 = 22.68

Now try these 8.4

① Work out these.

(a) 6.4 ÷ 4
(b) 8 ÷ 0.1
(c) 12 ÷ 0.4
(d) 12.1 ÷ 11
(e) 0.05 ÷ 0.2
(f) 0.049 ÷ 7

② (a) Sally has saved £8.45 in 5p coins.
How many coins does she have?

(b) Ben has saved £12.42 in 2p coins.

③ Puzzle

Toby has saved some 5p and 2p coins.
He has 100 coins altogether.
He has saved £3.08.
How many coins of each value does he have?

④ Brain strain

Rob buys a one-year travel pass for his journey to work.

The travel pass costs £874.16.

Rob works 49 weeks a year.

How much does Rob pay to travel to work each week?

⑤ Brain strain

A group of eight friends go out for a meal.

The meal costs £155.

How much should each person pay?

Is it possible for each person to pay the same amount?

9 Symmetry

Subject links
- geography
- art
- design and technology

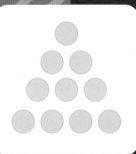

Coming up ...
- reflection symmetry
- rotation symmetry

Chapter starter

1. Place ten counters in a triangle like this.

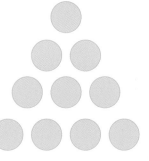

2. Move some counters so that the pattern is turned upside down.

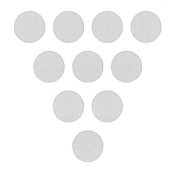

3. What is the smallest number of counters you need to move?

Do you remember?
- how to measure angles
- how to label angles and lines
- how to recognise acute, obtuse, reflex and right angles
- that angles in a triangle add up to 180°
- that there are 360° in a full turn

Key words

horizontal

vertical

origin

symmetry

symmetrical

reflection symmetry

reflect

line of symmetry

axis of symmetry

mirror line

vertex (plural: vertices)

rotation symmetry

order of rotation symmetry

> **With a friend**
>
> What do you notice about these words?   What about this one?
>
> CODE   BOX   HOOD
>
> HIDE   BEE   DIE
>
> ⊢OℲⱯ⊢O

Note
A **line of symmetry** is sometimes called an **axis of symmetry** or a **mirror line**.

A **line of symmetry** is the line about which a word or an object is reflected.

Some shapes don't have any lines of symmetry.

Some shapes have more than one line of symmetry.

Lines of symmetry can be horizontal, vertical or sloping.

Hint
You can use a mirror to help you find lines of symmetry.

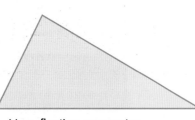

No reflection symmetry

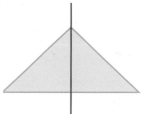

One line of symmetry

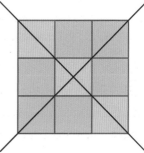

Two lines of symmetry

Now try these 9.1

Hint
Turning a shape round will help you find all the lines of symmetry, especially if any are sloping.

❶ Copy these shapes and draw in any lines of symmetry.

❷ Which of these road signs have one line of symmetry?
Which have no lines of symmetry?
Write down the number of lines of symmetry for each sign.

Continued …

3 (a) Turn this sign round so the aeroplane is pointing vertically upwards.

Now copy it and draw in its line of symmetry.

(b) Copy these shapes and find all their lines of symmetry.

4 Copy these signs.

Draw in all the lines of symmetry.

5 Copy these diagrams.

On each diagram colour in two more squares so that each pattern has one line of symmetry.

(a)   (b)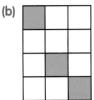

(c)   (d)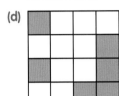

6 Puzzle

Kevin writes his name, and puts a mirror next to it.

He writes his name in different ways, as shown.

He notices that some letters always look the same. Which ones?

Do the same with your own name.

What names or words can you find which are unchanged when reflected?

9.2 Rotation symmetry

This shape does not have reflection symmetry.

However it does have rotation symmetry.

The shape could fit into a hole of the same shape and size in three different positions. This is because it can turn round (or rotate) and still look exactly the same.

You can see this if you colour in one of the small triangles.

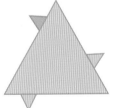

First position

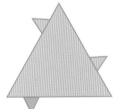

Second position

Third position

The shape has **rotation symmetry of order 3**.

Continued ...

Look at these shapes.

This shape has rotation symmetry of order 2.

This shape has rotation symmetry of order 4.

Now try these 9.2

1. What is the order of rotation symmetry of these shapes?

2. Copy the shapes below.

For *each* shape, shade in two more cells to make a pattern with rotation symmetry.
For each shape, write down the order of rotation symmetry.

(a)

(b)

(c)

3 Puzzle

Put these shapes together to make a shape with rotation symmetry of order 2.

4 Puzzle

Mr Simmons is a baker.
He makes a white loaf which he called 'SNOWWIS'.
Can you explain why he chose that name?
What other names or words behave in a similar way?

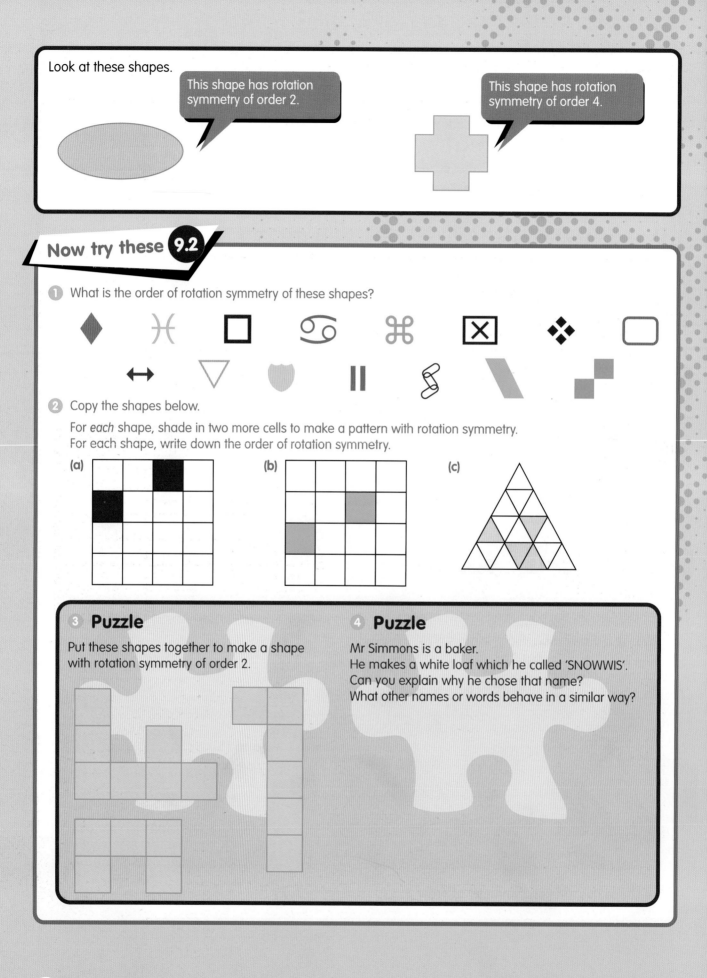

9.3 Combining reflection and rotation symmetry

Some shapes have both reflection symmetry and rotation symmetry.
The shape on the right is an example.

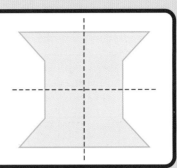

It has two lines of symmetry.
It has rotation symmetry of order 2.

Now try these 9.3

① Puzzle

Draw a shape with reflection symmetry but no rotation symmetry.

② Puzzle

Draw a shape with rotation symmetry but no reflection symmetry.

Note
A shape without rotation symmetry is said to have rotation symmetry of order 1.

③ Puzzle

Copy this shape.

Colour one square to make a shape with one line of reflection symmetry and rotation symmetry of order 1.

④

Make five more copies of the shape in question 3.

Colour the grid to make a shape for each line of the table below.

Number of squares to colour	Number of lines of reflection symmetry	Order of rotation symmetry
2	1	1
2	0	2
3	1	1
4	2	2
4	1	1

⑤ Brain strain

A magic square is one where the numbers in each row and each column add up to the same total.

Here are two very special magic squares.
Can you see what is so special about them?

96	11	89	68
88	69	91	16
61	86	18	99
19	98	66	81

8818	1111	8188	1881
8181	1888	8811	1118
1811	8118	1181	8888
1188	8881	1818	8111

Continued...

Investigation

On a 3 by 3 grid, there are three different ways to shade in one square.

(i) 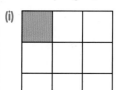   (ii) 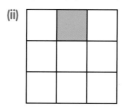   (iii)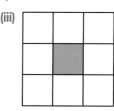

All other arrangements are reflections or rotations of these patterns.

1 Copy each one, and write down
   (a) the order of rotation symmetry
   (b) the number of lines of reflection symmetry.

2 Investigate further.

O Triangles and quadrilaterals

Subject links
- design and technology
- art
- geography

Coming up …

- properties of triangles
- properties of quadrilaterals
- solving problems involving triangles and quadrilaterals
- finding the coordinates of points determined by geometric information

Chapter starter

① A square is cut up into three pieces like this.

The blue shape is a trapezium.

It has four sides.

Two of its sides are parallel to each other.

(a) What are the other two shapes called?

(b) Rearrange the three pieces to make a different trapezium.

There are two possible answers.

Can you find them both?

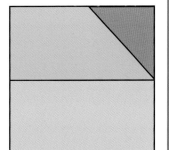

② What shapes can you make with these pieces?

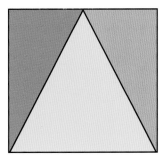

Draw the shapes you can make.

Name as many as you can.

Do you remember?

- how to draw and measure angles
- how to classify angles
- that angles in a triangle add up to 180°
- how to recognise reflection and rotation symmetry

Key words

two-dimensional (2-D)
triangle
equilateral triangle
isosceles triangle
scalene triangle
right-angled triangle
angle
quadrilateral
square
rectangle

parallelogram
rhombus
kite
isosceles trapezium
trapezium
parallel
opposite
adjacent
coordinates
rotation symmetry
reflection symmetry

A **triangle** is a two-dimensional shape consisting of three straight sides.

Triangles can be divided into different types.

Name	Length of sides	Size of angles
Equilateral triangle	all sides equal	all three angles equal
Isosceles triangle	two sides equal	two angles equal
Scalene triangle	all sides different	all angles different
Right-angled triangle	sides can be different lengths or two sides can be equal	one right angle

Did you know?
Equilateral comes from Latin. It means 'equal sides'.
Isosceles comes from Greek. It means 'equal sides' too.
In mathematics **equilateral** means 3 equal sides and **isosceles** means 2 equal sides.

Now try these 10.1

1 Match these labels with the triangles on the right.

Equilateral triangle

Isosceles triangle

Scalene triangle

Right-angled triangle

Some triangles will have more than one label.

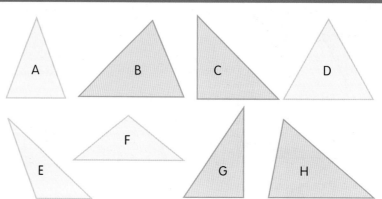

2 Toni wants to draw an obtuse-angled triangle.

Which types of triangle can she draw?

A **quadrilateral** is a two-dimensional shape consisting of four straight sides.

Quadrilaterals can have sides that are all different lengths with no parallel pairs and angles that are all different sizes.

The table shows some special quadrilaterals.

Hint
Adjacent means 'next to each other'.

Research
There is one more special quadrilateral.
What is its name?
What is special about it?

Name	Sides	Angles
Square	All sides equal; two pairs of parallel sides	All four angles are 90°
Rectangle	Opposite sides equal; two pairs of parallel sides	All four angles are 90°
Parallelogram	Two pairs of sides which are equal and parallel	Two pairs of equal angles
Rhombus	All sides equal; two pairs of parallel sides	Two pairs of equal angles
Kite	Two pairs of adjacent sides which are equal	One pair of equal angles
Isosceles trapezium	One pair of opposite sides which are parallel; the other pair are equal length	Two pair of equal angles
Trapezium	One pair of opposite sides parallel; opposite sides different lengths	All angles different

Now try these 10.2

1. What different quadrilaterals can you think of which have opposite sides with the same length?

2. Draw a kite with no right angles.

3. Draw a kite with one right angle.

4. Draw a kite with two right angles.

5. Explain why you cannot draw a kite with four right angles.

6. What three differences can you think of between a rhombus and a rectangle?

7. (a) I have four sides.
The sides next to each other are the same length.
What am I?

   (b) I have four sides.
All my sides are the same length but my angles aren't all equal.
What am I?

   (c) I have four sides.
Two of them are parallel.
What am I?

   (d) I have four sides.
Both pairs of opposite sides are parallel.
What am I?

Continued ...

8 Cut a square into two identical pieces with one straight cut.

Here are three different ways.

 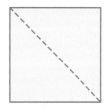 

Arrange the two pieces in a different way.

You must only put equal sides together, and the shapes cannot overlap.

So you can do this …

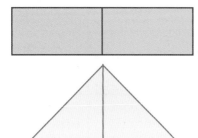

… but you cannot do this.

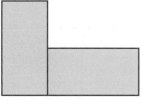

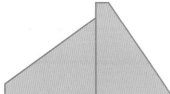

What different shapes can you make?

9 You have two identical isosceles triangles.

Join the triangles by putting equal sides together.

What different shapes can you make?

Draw and name each one.

10 Puzzle

For each group of four shapes, think of a fact which makes the **red** one the odd one out.
Give as many different reasons as you can.

For example: **Rectangle**, Rhombus, Square, Kite
Possible answers:
The rectangle is the only one whose diagonals do not cross at right angles.
The rectangle is the only one without two equal sides next to each other.

(a) Rectangle, Parallelogram, **Square,** Trapezium
(b) Rectangle, **Triangle,** Square, Trapezium
(c) Rectangle, Parallelogram, Kite, **Trapezium**
(d) **Rectangle**, Parallelogram, Trapezium, Rhombus
(e) Equilateral triangle, Square, **Rectangle,** Rhombus.

11 How many different quadrilaterals can you make on a 3 by 3 pinboard?

Draw them all.

Label each one square, rectangle, parallelogram, trapezium, kite, arrowhead or scalene.

Hint
The answer is a prime number.

You use the properties of special triangles and quadrilaterals to solve problems.

Example

Plot the points A(5, 7), B(8, 4) and C(5, 1).

Join them in order.

Plot a fourth point, D, to make a square.

This is one method.
All the angles of a square are 90°.
Draw lines at right angles to the sides AB and BC.
They meet at the point D.
This method is easier to use when a pair of sides is vertical or horizontal.

This is another method.
Opposite sides are parallel and equal in length.
To get from B to A you go left three squares and up three squares.
So to get from C to D you go left three squares and up three squares.
You can use this method to find a point when the sides are equal and parallel even if angles are not right angles.

Solution

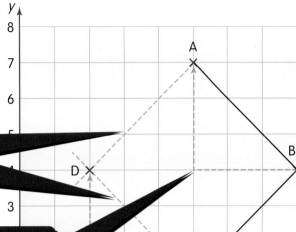

Now try these 10.3

For each of questions **1** to **5** you will need a coordinate grid from 0 to 10.

1. Plot the points A(7, 7), B(7, 2) and C(2, 2). Join them in order.
   Mark a fourth point, D, to make a square.

2. Plot the points A(4, 7), B(10, 7) and C(8, 3). Join them in order.
   Mark a fourth point, D, to make a parallelogram.

3. Plot the points A(5, 9), B(7, 5) and C(5, 1). Join them in order.
   Mark a fourth point, D, to make a kite.

4. Plot the points A(4, 6), B(5, 6) and C(8, 2). Join them in order.
   Mark a fourth point, D, to make an isosceles trapezium.

5 Puzzle

Plot the points (3, 7) and (6, 4). These are two vertices of a square.
Plot two more points to make a square.
There are three possible answers. Try to find them all.

Continued...

With a friend

1 Follow the flow chart for each of these shapes.

square   rhombus   kite   **trapezium**   parallelogram   rectangle

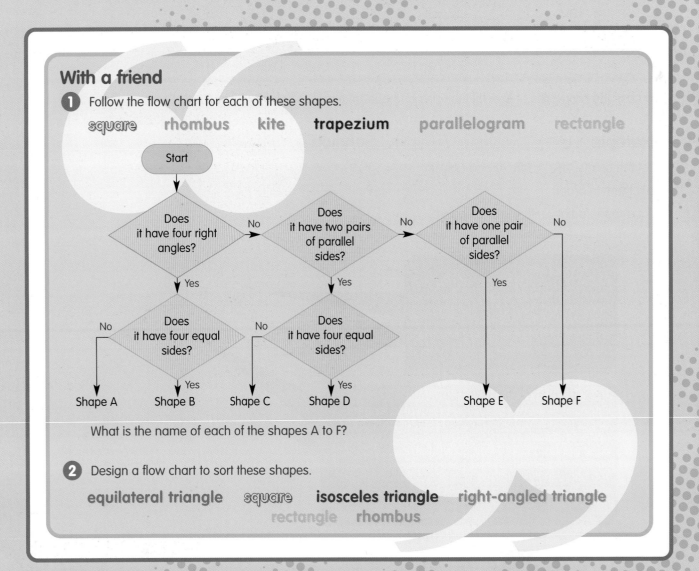

What is the name of each of the shapes A to F?

2 Design a flow chart to sort these shapes.

equilateral triangle   square   **isosceles triangle**   **right-angled triangle**
rectangle   rhombus

1

Perimeter and area

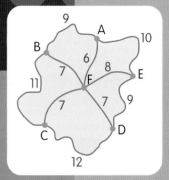

Coming up ...

- finding the perimeter of a rectangle
- finding the area of a rectangle
- finding the perimeter and area of a shape made from rectangles
- solving word problems involving length, perimeter and area

Do you remember?
- how to measure with a ruler
- how to work with centimetres and millimetres

Chapter starter

The map shows the distances in miles between 6 towns A, B, C, D, E and F.

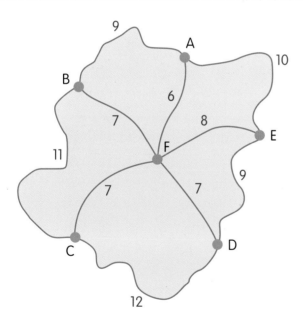

Bill lives at town A.

He needs to visit towns B, C, D E and F before returning to town A.

He can visit the towns in any order he likes.

What is the shortest journey he can make if he starts from A and visits B, C, D, E and F before returning home to town A?

Key words

length
width
perimeter
centimetre (cm)
millimetre (mm)
area
square centimetre (cm²)
square millimetre (mm²)

The **length** of a rectangle is how long one side is, usually one of the longer sides.

The **width** of a rectangle is how long one of the shorter sides is.

The **dimensions** of a rectangle are the length and width.

The **perimeter** of a rectangle is the distance around the outside.

Perimeter is measured in units such as centimetres (cm), millimetres (mm) and metres (m).

The perimeter of the rectangle below is 16 cm.

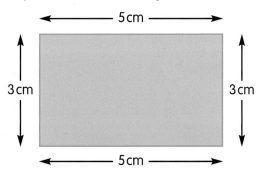

5 cm + 3 cm + 5 cm + 3 cm = 16 cm

Now try these 11.1

1 Find the perimeters of the rectangles A, B, C, D, E and F.

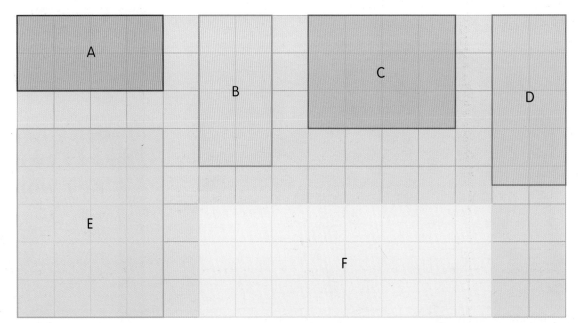

2 Find the perimeter of these rectangles.

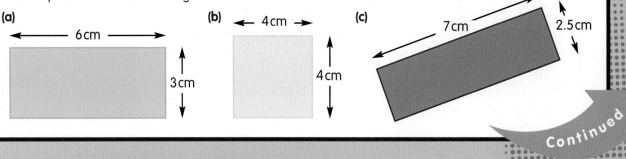

(a) 6 cm, 3 cm

(b) 4 cm, 4 cm

(c) 7 cm, 2.5 cm

Continued ...

3 This table shows the length, width and perimeter of different rectangles.
Copy and complete the table. The first one is done for you.

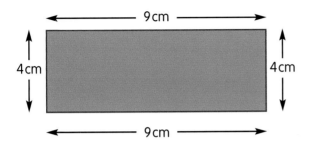

Length	Width	Perimeter
9 cm	4 cm	26 cm
8 cm	2 cm	
11 mm	7 mm	
3 m	2 m	
6 cm		`20 cm
	4 cm	32 cm
	2.5 cm	13 cm
6.5 cm		15 cm
4.3 cm	2.4 cm	
7.1 cm		20 cm

4 Which of these rules are correct for finding the perimeter of a rectangle?

(a) length + width = perimeter
(b) 2 × length + 2 × width = perimeter
(c) 2 × length + width = perimeter

(d) (length + width) × 2 = perimeter
(e) length × width = perimeter
(f) 2 × (length + width) = perimeter

5 The shapes in this question have been made of two rectangles.
Each rectangle is 5 cm long and 3 cm wide, like the one on the right.
Find the perimeter of each shape.

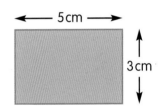

(a)

(b)

(c)

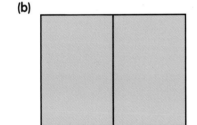

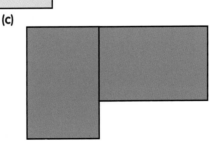

Hint
Don't forget where you started!
Why not start at the top left-hand corner every time, so you know when you have been all the way round?

6 Puzzle

How many different shapes can you draw with a perimeter of 12 cm?
Rules: All angles must be right angles.
All sides must be a whole number of centimetres long.

The area of a shape is how much flat space there is inside it.

Area is measured in square units, for example square centimetres (written cm²), or square millimetres (mm²).

A square centimetre is a square with all sides 1 cm long.

1 cm

1 cm

With a friend

You can find the area of the shapes below by counting the squares.
Write down the area of each of these rectangles.

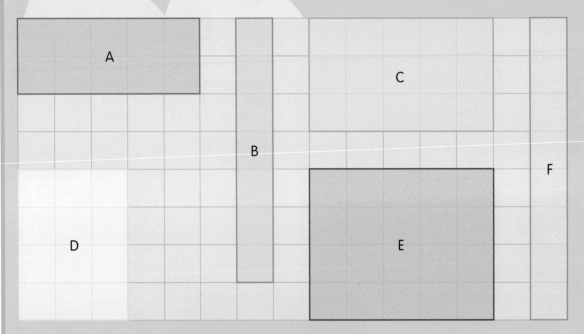

The length of shape E is 5 cm, so 5 squares fit along the length.
The width of shape E is 4 cm, so there are 4 rows of squares.
Altogether there are 4 lots of 5 squares, so the area is 4 × 5 = 20 cm².
So the area of a rectangle = the length × the width.
You can write that like this.

Area = *l* × *w*

length   width

Check this works for all the rectangles above.

Now try these 11.2

Do not use a calculator for questions **1** to **5**.

1 Find the area of these rectangles.

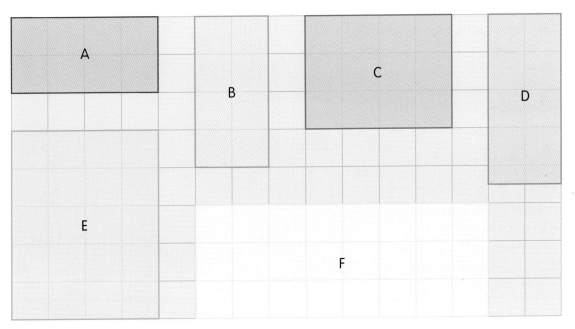

2 Find the area of these rectangles.

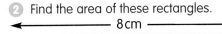

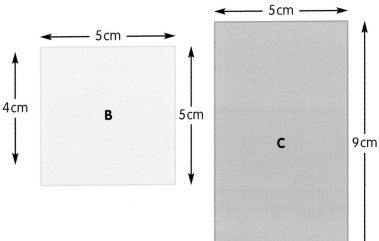

---

3 Puzzle

Draw 4 different rectangles with an area of 30 cm².
Write down the perimeter of each one.

What do you notice about the shape of your rectangles and the perimeter?

4 Puzzle

Draw these rectangles, all with a perimeter of 18 cm.
(a) Area = 18 cm², perimeter = 18 cm.
(b) Area = 20 cm², perimeter = 18 cm.
(c) Area = 8 cm², perimeter = 18 cm.

What other rectangles can you find with a perimeter of 18 cm?

Continued ...

5 A farmer has 20 fence panels. Each panel is 1 m long.

He designs a pen for his sheep, using a wall as one side.
The diagram shows one example.

He checks he can make this pen, by adding up the fence panels.

4 m + 1 m + 2 m + 3 m + 1 m + 2 m + 7 m = 20 m

Count the squares to find the area of the pen.

What other areas of pen can he make using 20 metres of fencing?

Draw some and work out the area of each one.

What is the largest area he can make?

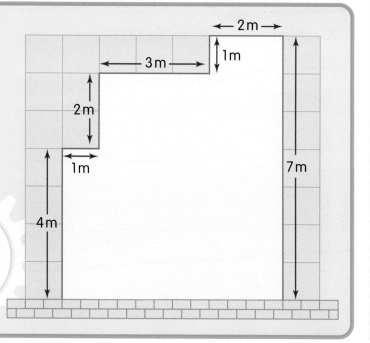

6 Brain strain

Can you find a rectangle with an area of 120 cm² and a perimeter of 68 cm?

Can you find a rectangle with an area of 162 cm² and a perimeter of 66 cm?

7 Brain strain

How many rectangles can you find where the number of centimetres in the perimeter is equal to the number of square centimetres in the area?

11.3 Shapes made of rectangles

These two rectangles both have a perimeter of 14 cm.

The one on the left has an area of 12 cm². The one on the right has an area of 10 cm².

Area of A = $l \times w$ = 4 × 3 = 12 cm².

Area of B = $l \times w$ = 5 × 2 = 10 cm².

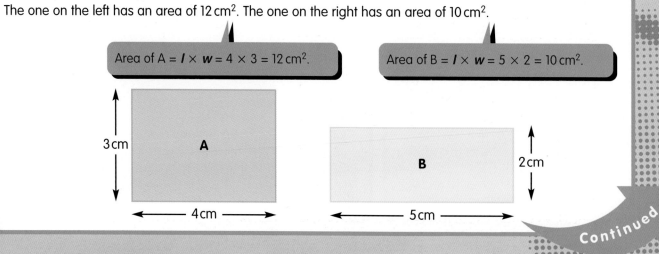

Continued ...

If they are put together, the area of the new shape is 12 cm² + 10 cm² = 22 cm².

The two areas are simply added together.

The perimeters cannot be added.

Look at the diagram.

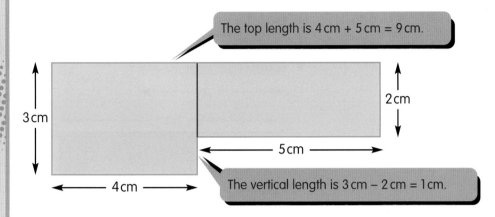

The top length is 4 cm + 5 cm = 9 cm.

3 cm

2 cm

5 cm

4 cm

The vertical length is 3 cm − 2 cm = 1 cm.

The red line is not part of the outside of the new shape.

The new perimeter = 9 cm + 2 cm + 5 cm + 1 cm + 4 cm + 3 cm = 24 cm.

Now try these 11.3

1. Find the area and perimeter of each of these shapes.

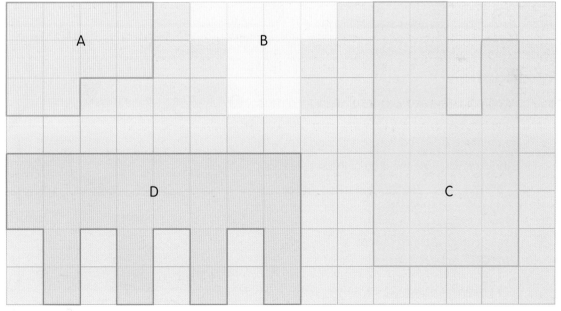

A

B

D

C

Continued ...

② Find the area and perimeter of each of these shapes.

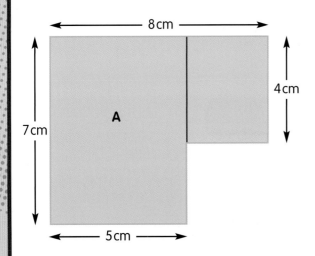

Hint
You will find it easier to find the area if you draw the shapes first, and split them into rectangles. The first one has been done for you.

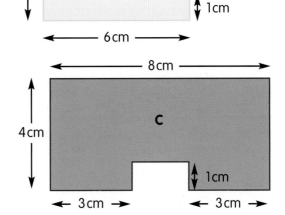

③ Puzzle

If possible, draw a shape which follows the rules for each question part.
(a) An area of $12\,cm^2$ and a perimeter of $16\,cm$.
(b) An area of $16\,cm^2$ and a perimeter of $12\,cm$.
(c) An area of $12\,cm^2$ and a perimeter of $20\,cm$.
(d) An area of $20\,cm^2$ and a perimeter of $20\,cm$.
(e) An area of $13\,cm^2$ and a perimeter of $15\,cm$.

④ Brain strain

(a) Draw some shapes with a perimeter of $10\,cm$. What different areas can you make?

(b) Draw some shapes with an area of $10\,cm^2$. What different perimeters can you make?

Investigation

❶ The diagram below shows a set of stairs for a doll's house.

There are three stairs, each $1\,cm$ high and $1\,cm$ wide.

Find the perimeter and the area of the set of stairs.

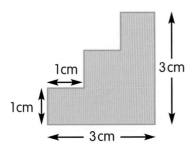

❷ Now find the perimeter and area of a set of four stairs.

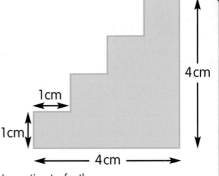

❸ Investigate further.

You know that the area of a rectangle can be calculated by multiplying the length by the width, as this works out how many squares it takes to fill it.

This rectangle is 6 cm long and 4 cm wide.

Its area is length × width = 6 cm × 4 cm = 24 cm^2.

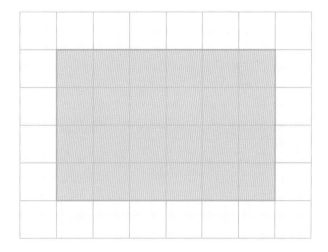

You can cut a triangle from one end of the rectangle and move it to the other.

It makes a parallelogram but the area is unchanged.

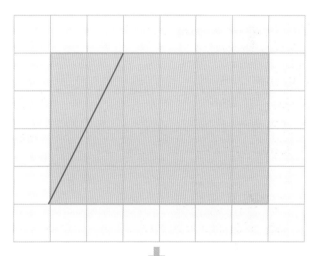

So the parallelogram has a base of 6 cm and a height of 4 cm.

It has an area of 24 cm^2.

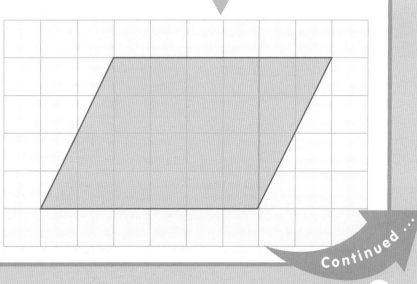

Continued ···

This parallelogram is made from the same rectangle.

So it also has an area of 6 cm × 4 cm = 24 cm².

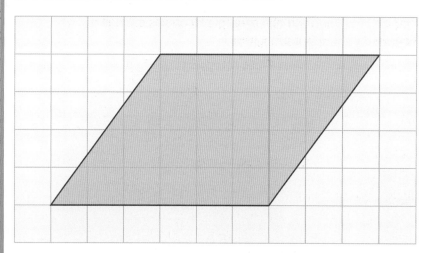

The area of a parallelogram = base x perpendicular height or A = b x h.

Now try these 11.4

① Calculate the area of these parallelograms.

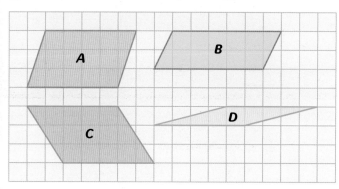

② Calculate the area of these parallelograms.

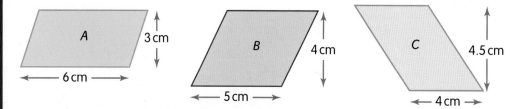

③ Calculate the area of these parallelograms.

(a) Base = 8 cm, height = 6 cm

(b) Base = 4.5 cm, height = 4 cm

(c) Base = 5.4 cm, height = 4.7 cm

When a parallelogram is cut in half along a diagonal, it produces two congruent triangles.

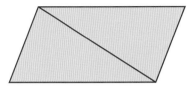

You know that the formula for the area of the parallelogram is Area = $b \times h$.

The triangle is exactly half the parallelogram, so the formula for the area of a triangle is

Area = $b \times h \div 2$.

This can be written as

$$A = \tfrac{1}{2}bh.$$

Even obtuse-angled triangles are half a parallelogram.

Two of these triangles

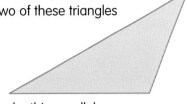

make this parallelogram.

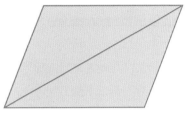

Note that the perpendicular height of an obtuse-angled triangle does not meet the base.

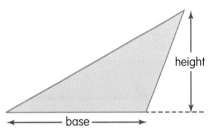

Now try these 11.5

1 Calculate the area of these triangles.

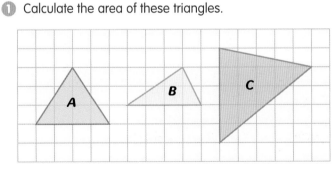

2 Calculate the area of these triangles.

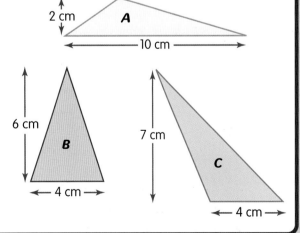

In the same way that a parallelogram can be split into two congruent triangles, it can also be cut into two congruent trapeziums.

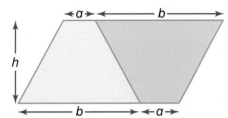

The length of the base of the parallelogram, $a + b$, is equal to the sum of the parallel sides of one of the trapeziums.

The area of the parallelogram is base × height or $(a + b) \times h$.

The area of one of the trapeziums is half of that or $\frac{1}{2}(a + b)h$.

$\frac{1}{2}(a + b)$ is the average of the parallel sides of one of the trapeziums, so you can write

Area of a trapezium = the average of the parallel sides x height or $\frac{1}{2}(a + b)h$.

Now try these 11.6

1 Find the area of these trapeziums.

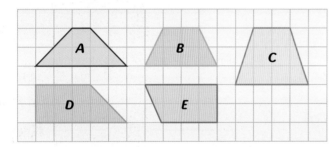

2 Find the area of these trapeziums.

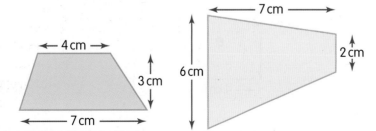

Constructions

Subject links
● design and technology

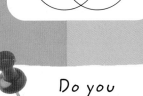

Coming up …

● constructing triangles given the length of two sides and the size of the angle between them
● constructing triangles given the length of a side and the size of two angles

Do you remember?
● how to draw lines to the nearest millimetre
● how to draw angles to the nearest degree
● that angles on a straight line add up to 180°
● the properties of special triangles and quadrilaterals

Chapter starter

1 Use a pair of compasses to draw a circle.

2 Put the point of your compasses on the circle and draw another circle, exactly the same size.

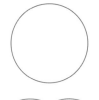

3 Use a point where the two circles cross as the centre of the next circle.

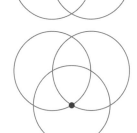

4 Continue in the same way around the original circle to make this pattern.

5 The blue section is inside three circles, which are coloured blue here to show you.

Colour your pattern using these rules.

● Sections inside just one circle: colour green.
● Sections inside two circles: colour red.
● Sections inside three circles: colour blue.
● Sections inside four circles: colour yellow.

Key words

construct
triangle
side
base
vertex (plural: vertices)
intersect

You use different methods to draw triangles depending on what information you are given.

In this section you learn how to construct a triangle given the length of two sides and the size of the angle between them, the **side-angle-side** case or **SAS** for short.

Example

Draw the triangle with these measurements.

AB = 4 cm
AC = 5 cm
Angle BAC = 72°

You will need
ruler
protractor

Solution

First draw a rough sketch without measuring so that you can see what the triangle looks like.

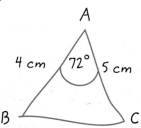

You can see that you have been given the lengths of two sides, and the angle in between them. This is the side-angle-side case or SAS for short.

It will be easier to draw the triangle if you know the length of the base and the size of a base angle.

Rotate your sketch.

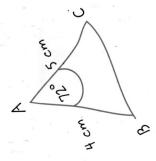

Now you are ready to make an accurate drawing.

Draw the side AB 4 cm long, and label it.

A ——————————— B

Then measure the angle of 72°.

Now draw AC, 5 cm long, and label the point C.

Make a small mark at 72°. Then use a ruler to draw a line from A through the mark. Draw the line 5 cm long.

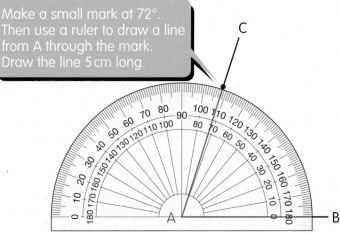

Finally, join points B and C to make the triangle.

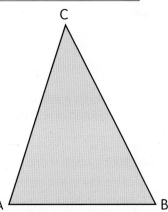

1 Make accurate drawings of these triangles.

(a)
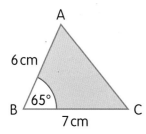
6 cm
65°
B
7 cm
C
A

(b)
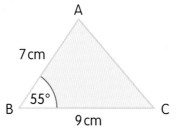
7 cm
55°
B
9 cm
C
A

(c) Measure the length of AC and the size of angles BAC and ACB on both your diagrams.

Write these measurements on your diagrams.

2 Make accurate drawings of these triangles.

(a)
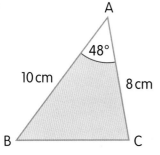
A
48°
10 cm
8 cm
B
C

(b)
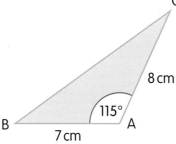
C
8 cm
115°
B
7 cm
A

(c) Measure the length of BC and the size of angles ABC and ACB on both your diagrams.

Write these measurements on your diagrams.

3 **Puzzle**

Draw this triangle accurately.
You haven't been given angle ABC, the angle between the two sides you know.

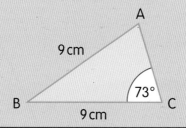
A
9 cm
73°
B
9 cm
C

4 Draw the triangle ABC, with AB = 11 cm, AC = 9 cm and angle BAC = 74°.

Measure the length of BC and the size of angles ABC and ACB.

5 Draw this diagram accurately.

Measure and label all the missing sides and angles.

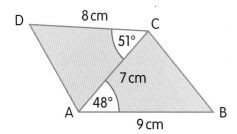
D
8 cm
C
51°
7 cm
48°
A
9 cm
B

6 **Brain strain**

Draw a rhombus ABCD with all sides 11 cm long and angle DAB = 48°.

In this section you learn how to construct a triangle given two angles and the length of the side between them, the **angle-side-angle** case or **ASA** for short.

Example

Draw the triangle with these measurements.

Angle ABC = 64°
BC = 5 cm
Angle ACB = 48°

You will need
ruler
protractor

Solution

Draw a rough sketch first.

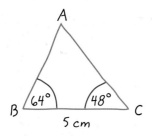

Then measure an angle of 48° at C.

Make a small mark at 48°.
Then use a ruler to draw a line
from C through the mark.
Draw the line.

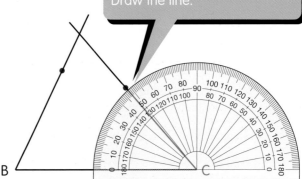

Turn the sketch round if necessary to make the side with the given length the base.

Draw the base BC, 5 cm long, and measure an angle of 64° at B.

You don't know how long AB is, so draw it longer than you think it should be.

The construction is complete!

You should not rub out your construction lines.

Make a small mark at 64°.
Then use a ruler to draw a line
from B through the mark.
Draw the line.

The third vertex of the
triangle is where the
lines cross.

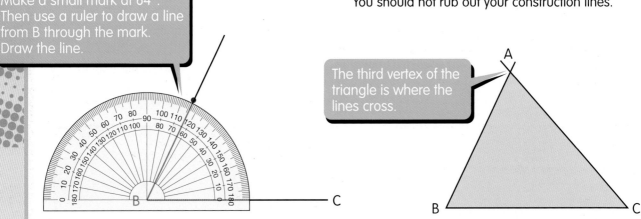

① Make accurate drawings of these triangles.

(a)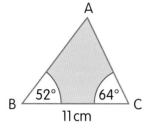

(b)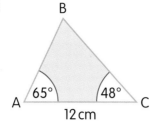

(c) Measure the length of AB on both your triangles.

Measure the length of AC and the size of angle BAC for your triangle for part **(a)**.

Measure the length of BC and the size of angle ABC for your triangle for part **(b)**.

Write these measurements on your diagrams.

Hint
Remember to draw a sketch first.

② Make accurate drawings of these triangles.

(a) AB = 9 cm
Angle CAB = 42°
Angle ABC = 53°

(b) AC = 11 cm
Angle BAC = 115°
Angle ACB = 32°

(c) Measure and label the sizes of all sides and angles on the triangles.

③ **Puzzle**

(a) Make a sketch of this triangle.
AB = 12 cm
Angle CAB = 52°
Angle ACB = 85°

(b) This isn't an ASA triangle. Why not?

(c) Use your knowledge of triangles to work out the size of angle ABC.

(d) Now make an accurate drawing of triangle ABC.

④ Adam is building a bike shelter.
He needs the shelter to be 1 metre wide.
He wants the roof to have a slope of 40°.

(a) Make an accurate drawing of the roof of the bike shelter.
Make the width of the shelter 10 cm.

(b) Use your drawing to find the height of the roof.

(c) Use your drawing to find the sloping length of the roof.

(d) The roof is to be made of a panel of wood.
Adam knows he can only cut the panel to the nearest 10 cm.
He wants to make the slope of the wood at least 40°.
What size should he cut the panel?

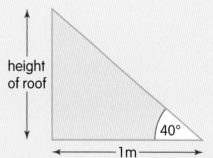

⑤ **Brain strain**

Make an accurate drawing of the trapezium.

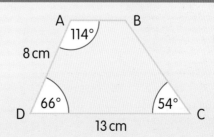

The **perpendicular bisector** of a line is a line that divides the first line into two equal lengths and is at right angles to it.

In this section you will learn how to construct the perpendicular bisector of a line using just a straight edge and a pair of compasses.

You will need
→ straight edge
→ compasses

Draw a line.

Open your compasses to more than half the length of the line.

Put the point of your compasses on one end of the line and draw two arcs, one on either side of the line.

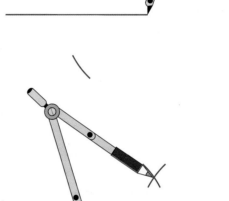

Keep your compasses open to the same distance.

Put the point of your compasses on the other end of the line.

Draw two more arcs to cut the first two.

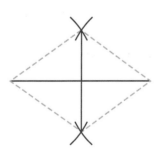

To draw the perpendicular bisector, join the points where the arcs cross.

As you keep your compasses open to the same distance, the blue shape is a rhombus.

The diagonals of a rhombus bisect at right angles.

> ### With a friend
> Draw a line 12 cm long.
>
> Use a straight edge and a pair of compasses to construct the perpendicular bisector. Ask your friend to check your drawing by measuring.
>
> The bisector should cut the line exactly at 6 cm and the lines should meet at right angles.

You will need
→ straight edge
→ compasses
→ ruler

1 Draw a large right-angled triangle.

Construct the perpendicular bisector of the shortest side.

Now construct the perpendicular bisector of the next shortest side.

Where do the perpendicular bisectors cross each other?

2 Draw a large acute-angled triangle.

Construct the perpendicular bisector of each side.

If your constructions are accurate, all three perpendicular bisectors should cross at a point.

Use this point as the centre of a circle.

Draw the circle so that it just touches all three vertices of the triangle.

3 Puzzle

What happens if you repeat question **2** with an obtuse-angled triangle?

4 Brain strain

Draw a large circle.

Now draw a quadrilateral so that each vertex is on the circle.

Construct the perpendicular bisector of one of the sides.

What happens?

Repeat for the other sides.

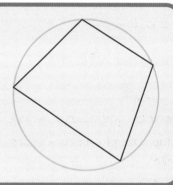

5 Follow these instructions to construct an isosceles triangle with a base of 8 cm and a height of 10 cm.

(a) Draw a horizontal line 8 cm long.

Label it AB.

(b) Draw the perpendicular bisector of AB and extend it to a point 10 cm above the line.

(c) Join the end of the perpendicular bisector to A and B.

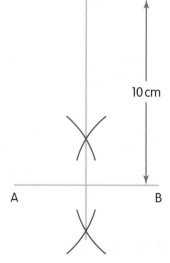

10 cm

A   B

Coming up …

- how to use letter symbols to represent unknown numbers or variables
- the meaning of the words term and expression
- how to substitute numbers into an expression

Chapter starter

Roman numerals are still used today for dates. You have probably seen them at the end of TV programmes and films.

I = 1	V = 5	X = 10	L = 50
C = 100	D = 500	M = 1000	

So III = 3   XV = 10 + 5 = 15

and DCL = 500 + 100 + 50 = 650

When a smaller numeral is written in front of a larger numeral it means 'subtract'.

So   IX = 10 – 1 = 9   and   CD = 500 – 100 = 400.

Look at how the Romans added and subtracted.

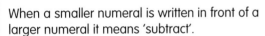

LXVI + XXVII = LXXXVVIII

> VV = X

= LXXXXIII

> It is easier to write IV as IIII.

> LXXXX = XC

= XCIII

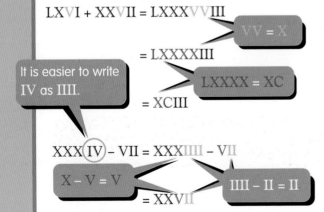

XXX(IV) – VII = XXXIIII – VII

> X – V = V

> IIII – II = II

= XXVII

Continued …

Continued …

Do you remember?
● about the order of operations

Key word

symbol
expression
term
substitution
substitute

1 Work out these.

   (a) XXII + XV   **(b)** LXV + XVII   **(c)** CLXXVII – LXVI

   (d) XCIX – XVI   **(e)** DCCLXXIX – CLXXV   **(f)** LXXIV + DCCXLII

   Check your answers by converting the Roman numerals into our number system.

2 Make up some questions of your own and share them with a friend.

3 The year 2000 uses only two Roman numerals (MM).

   Which year so far uses the most Roman numerals?

13.1   Letter symbols

You can use **symbols** to represent numbers.

For example 'a number plus 4' can be written using **letter symbols** like this.

n + 4   It doesn't matter which letter you use.

The letter *n* represents any number.

So *n* could be 2 or ‑0.68 or 3478 or $\frac{1}{2}$ or any number you can think of!

'*n* + 4' is called an **expression**.

An expression is a way of writing a statement using symbols and numbers.

There is no equals sign.

n + 4 has two **terms**: '*n*' and '4'.

Example

A shop sells CDs and DVDs.

(a) Write down an expression for the cost of two CDs.

   Use *c* for the cost in pounds of a CD.

(b) Write down an expression for the cost of two CDs and a DVD.

   Use *d* for the cost in pounds of a DVD.

You don't need to write the '×' signs.
So 2*c* means 2 × *c* or 2 lots of *c*.

Solution

(a) The cost of two CDs is *c* + *c* or 2 × *c* or 2*c*.

You should write numbers first then letters.
So 2*c* not *c*2.

(b) The cost of two CDs and a DVD is *c* + *c* + *d* or 2*c* + *d*.

2 lots of *c* plus 1 lot of *d*.

Note
You write *d* for the cost of one DVD rather than 1*d*.

① Rewrite the following using the correct notation.

(a) $5 \times a$ (b) $b \times 4$ (c) $c7$

② Write down how many terms there are in each of these expressions.

(a) $5a$ (b) $3b + 2c - 6d$ (c) $8 - 4c + 3d + 10e$

③ Here are four different expressions.

$n + 3$ $3 - n$ $n - 3$ $3n$

n represents any number.

Match together the following statements and the expressions above.

(a) 3 lots of a number   (b) a number add 3   (c) a number subtract 3
(d) subtract 3 from a number   (e) a number multiplied by 3   (f) 3 more than a number
(g) 3 less than a number   (h) subtract a number from 3

④ In this question n represents any number.

Explain in words each of the following expressions.

The first one has been done for you.

(a) $n + 10$ means 10 more than a number.

(b) $10 - n$ (c) $n - 10$ (d) $2n$ (e) $n \div 10$ (f) $10n - 10$ (g) $2 \times (10 + n)$

⑤ Use c for the cost in pounds of a CD.

Use d for the cost in pounds of a DVD.

Match the following statements with their correct expression.

Statements

The cost of three CDs

The cost of two CDs and three DVDs

The change from £50 when you buy a DVD

How much more a DVD costs than a CD

The change from £50 when you buy one CD and one DVD

Expressions

$c - d$ $2c + 3$ $50 - c + d$ $50 - d$

$3 + c$ $50 - c - d$ $3c$ $d - c$

$50 + d$ $d - 50$

⑥ A group of friends are playing a computer game.

Use p for the number of points that Tim scores.

(a) Mia scores **twice** as many points as **Tim**.

Write down an expression for the number points that Mia scores.

(b) Jamie scores **10 more** points than **Tim**.

Write down an expression for the number of points that Jamie scores.

(c) Peter scores **5 fewer** points than **Mia**.

Write down an expression for the number of points that Peter scores.

13.2 Substitution

Algebra follows the same rules as numbers.

Look at the expression $5a + 6$.

When, say, $a = 3$ you can find a value of the expression.

You do this by **substituting** $a = 3$ into the expression $5a + 6$.

So when $a = 3$ then $5a + 6$

Remember $5a$ means $5 \times a$ or 5 lots of a.

$= 5 \times a + 6$

Write 3 in place of a.

$= 5 \times 3 + 6$

Remember the order of operations: multiplication before addition.

$= 15 + 6$

$= 21.$

First	Brackets	( )
then	Division and Multiplication	$\div \times$
then	Addition and Subtraction	$+ -$

Example

Work out the value of $20 - 2a + bc$ when $a = 4$, $b = 3$ and $c = 5$.

Solution

Substitute $a = 4$, $b = 3$ and $c = 5$ into the expression $20 - 2a + bc$.

So when $a = 4$, $b = 3$ and $c = 5$

$20 - 2 \times a + b \times c$

Write the value in place of each letter.

$= 20 - 2 \times 4 + 3 \times 5$

$= 20 - 8 + 15$

Multiplication first.

$= 27.$

With a friend

Here is Anna's maths homework.

Which questions does she get right?

What mistakes does she make?

When $a = 5$ and $b = 2$ find the values of these expressions.
1. $b + 8 = 2 + 8 = 10$
2. $ab = 52$
3. $4 + 3b = 7 \times 2 = 14$
4. $7 - a + b = 7 - 5 + 2 = 4$

Now try these 13.2

1. Work out the value of $2x + 4$ when x has the following values.
   (a) $x = 2$ (b) $x = 3$ (c) $x = 5$

2. When $n = 4$ work out the value of these expressions.
   (a) $n + 5$ (b) $n - 1$ (c) $2n$ (d) $n \div 2$ (e) $3n + 1$ (f) $12 - n$

Continued ...

③ Work out the value of $2a + 4b - 5c$ using the following values for a, b and c.

(a) $a = 2$, $b = 3$ and $c = 1$
(b) $a = 9$, $b = 7$ and $c = 2$
(c) $a = 1$, $b = 0$ and $c = 0$
(d) $a = 4$, $b = 3$ and $c = 4$

④ When $r = 2$, $s = 3$ and $t = 1$, work out the value of these expressions.

(a) $2r$ (b) $3s + 1$ (c) $5t - 4$
(d) rs (e) $2rs$ (f) $rs + t$
(g) $r + s + t$ (h) $3r + 2s - 6t$ (i) $5r - 4s + 3t$

⑤ Use j for the cost in pounds of a pair of jeans.
Use t for the cost in pounds of a T-shirt.

(a) Write down an expression for the following statements.
  (i)   The cost of three T-shirts.
  (ii) The cost of one pair of jeans and three T-shirts.
  (iii) How much more jeans cost than T-shirts.

(b) Work out the value of each expression found in part (a) when $j = 35$ and $t = 12$.

---

⑥ Puzzle

When $a = 1$, $b = 2$ and $c = 3$, work out the value of these expressions.

(a) $a + b$ (b) $2a + b + c$
(c) $4b$ (d) $a + 3c$
(e) $2c - b$ (f) $c - b$
(g) bc (h) $c - b - a$
(i) $c - a$ (j) $c + 2$
(k) $4b + c$ (l) $8 - 7a$
(m) $3a + 3$ (n) $6a - bc$
(o) $12 - 5b$ (p) $4c - 2b - 3$

Key	
A	13
B	3
C	2
E	12
I	0
K	5
N	4
O	8
R	7
S	1
T	6
W	10
Y	11

Now use the key. Write the letter that matches your answer to part (a) in the first box below, and so on to crack the code.

Question:

What is ☐☐☐☐☐ and ☐☐☐☐☐☐?

Answer: A ☐☐☐☐☐!

---

⑦ Substitute $x = 5$, $y = 2$ and $z = 1$ into these expressions.

(a) $10 - (x + 4)$ (b) $8 - (x + z)$
(c) $x - (y + z)$ (d) $2 \times (y + 1)$
(e) $3 \times (y - z)$ (f) $(x - y + z) \div 2$
(g) $5(x + y)$ (h) $3(2x - z)$
(i) $4(x - 2y)$

⑧ Evaluate $5x^2$ when

(a) $x = 1$
(b) $x = 2$
(c) $x = 3$.

⑨ Evaluate these expressions when $y = 5$.

(a) $2y + 5$ (b) $7(2y + 5)$ (c) y^2
(d) $3y^2$ (e) $y^2 + 4$ (f) $40 - y^2$
(g) y^3 (h) $2y^3$ (i) $5 + 4y^3$

⑩ (a) Evaluate these expressions when $n = 2$, $n = 3$ and $n = 4$.

  (i) $\dfrac{n}{n}$ (ii) $\dfrac{2n}{n}$ (iii) $\dfrac{3n}{n}$

(b) What do you notice?

(c) What does $\dfrac{4n}{n}$ equal?

⑪ Evaluate $\dfrac{a + b}{2a}$ when

(a) $a = 3$ and $b = 9$
(b) $a = 2$ and $b = 10$
(c) $a = 1$ and $b = 7$
(d) $a = 5$ and $b = 0$.

Hint
Work out the brackets first.

Remember
Work out the value of the numerator and the denominator separately first. Then divide.

Expressions

$3 \times n$

Coming up ...

● simplifying expressions by collecting like terms
● multiplying a single term over a bracket

Chapter starter

Match together algebra cards which contain equivalent expressions.

Which expressions don't have a matching pair?

$3 \times n$	$2n + 6$	$4n - n$
$2n + n$	$2n + 3$	$n + n + n$
$6n$	$n - 3$	$2 \times (n + 3)$
$3 - n$	$2 + 1 + n$	$3n$
$2 \times 3 \times n$	$6n \div 2$	$n + 1 + 2$
$6 \times n$	$3 + n$	$n + 3$
$6n - 3n$	$n + 3 + n + 3$	$3 \times 2 \times n$
$n - 1 - 2$	$n + 3 - 2n$	$n + 2n + 3n$

Do you remember?

● how to use the grid method to multiply two numbers together
● the meaning of the words expression and term

Key words

expression
simplify
like terms
brackets
multiply out
expand

14.1 Simplifying expressions

$3 + 3 + 3 + 3 + 3$ can be written more simply as 5 lots of 3 or 5×3.

In the same way the expression $b + b + b + b + b$ can be written more simply as $5 \times b$ or $5b$.

> Remember b means 1 lot of b or $1 \times b$.

> Remember $5b$ means $5 \times b$ or 5 lots of b.

The expression has been **simplified** as it now has fewer terms.

You **simplify** an expression by collecting **like terms**.

Like terms are terms which contain the same letter symbols.

Look at these examples.

Example

Simplify $4b + 3b$.

Solution

$4b + 3b$

$= b + b + b + b + b + b + b$

> 4 lots of b add 3 lots of b is 7 lots of b.

$= 7b$

Example

Simplify $7x + 3x - 4x$.

Solution

$7x + 3x - 4x$

> 7 lots of x add 3 lots of x is 10 lots of x.
> 10 lots of x subtract 4 lots of x is 6 lots of x.

$= 6x$

Example

Simplify $9k + 3 - 2k + 7$

Solution

$9k + 3 \;(- 2k)\; + 7$

> First group together *like terms*. (You must keep a term together with the sign in front of it.)

$= 9k \;(- 2k)\; + 3 + 7$

> Like terms are terms which contain the same letters ($9k$ and $- 2k$) …

$= 7k + 10$

> … or numbers on their own ($+ 3$ and $+ 7$).

Example

Simplify $4 - 2y - 3 + 2y$.

Solution

$④ \;(- 2y)\; \;(- 3)\; (+ 2y)$

$= ④ \;(- 3)\; (- 2y) (+ 2y)$

> $0y$ means no lots of y so its value is zero.

$= 1 + 0y$

$= 1$

> $1 + 0 = 1$

With a friend

Ben writes down these answers on a worksheet.

Simplify: $10 - 3a$	Simplify: $4 + 6a$
Answer: $7a$	Answer: $10a$

How could you show Ben that he is wrong?

1 Simplify these.

(a) $a + a + a + a + a + a$
(b) $b + b$
(c) $c + c + c + c + c + c + c$
(d) $d + d + d$
(e) $e + e + e + e$
(f) $f + f + f + f + f$

2 Simplify these.

(a) $5a + 3a$
(b) $2b + 4b$
(c) $3c + 2c + 4c$
(d) $3d + 5d + 7d$
(e) $e + 2e + 3e + 4e$
(f) $9f + 7f + 5f + 3f + f$

3 Simplify these.

(a) $7r - 2r$
(b) $12s - 3s + 5s$
(c) $12t + 5t - 4t$
(d) $19u - 5u + 7u - 11u$
(e) $5v - 3v - v + 2v$
(f) $8w - 5w - 4w + 3w$

4 (a) Work out the value of these expressions when $a = 3$, $b = 4$ and $c = 5$.

(i) $5a - 4a$
(ii) $6b - 5b$
(iii) $10c - 4c - 5c$

Hint
Remember you should write 1x as x.

(b) Simplify the expressions given in part **(a)**.

5 Simplify these.

(a) $5p + 2p + 3 + 1$
(b) $7q - 2q + 5 - 2$
(c) $4r - 3r - 2 + 7$
(d) $4s + 5 - 3s - 4 - s$
(e) $4 + 4t + 5 - 3t$
(f) $2 + 9u + 1 - 7u - 3$
(g) $8v - 4v + 3 - 2v + 1$
(h) $5w - 2 + 3w - 2$
(i) $3 - 5x - 2 + 6x$
(j) $10 + 7y - 3y + 4y$

6 Write down an expression for the perimeter of these shapes then simplify each of your expressions.

(a)

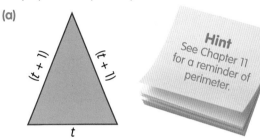

Hint
See Chapter 11 for a reminder of perimeter.

(b)

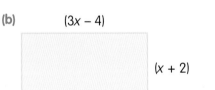

$(3x - 4)$

$(x + 2)$

7 (a) Emily draws the rectangle shown here.

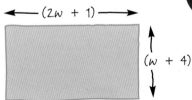

$(2w + 1)$

$(w + 4)$

The perimeter of this rectangle is $6w + 10$.

Is Emily right?

(b) Emily wants to find some other rectangles with a perimeter of $6w + 10$. She draws this rectangle as well.

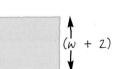

$(w + 2)$

Find an expression for the length of the rectangle.

(c) Using integers only, find as many rectangles with a perimeter of $6w + 10$ as you can.

Continued ...

⑧ Puzzle

Find an expression for the missing lengths in this shape.
Simplify your answers as far as possible.

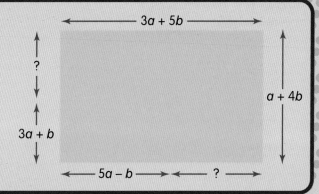

⑨ Brain strain

In these algebra walls the expression in each brick is found by adding the expressions in the two bricks underneath it.
Copy and complete these algebra walls.

(a)

	3x	
x	3x	5x

(b)

	y +4	
y		y

(c)

2x	3y	4x

(d)

	13x	
6x + 1		
	5x	

(e)

	4x + 5y	
2x		
		9y

(f)

	9f − 4e	
	6f − 3e	
3f − 2e		
	3f	

Algebraic expressions may sometimes include one or more brackets. To multiply out a bracket, you multiply *each* term in the bracket by the term outside the bracket.

Example

Expand the bracket in this algebraic expression.

$3(x + 2y)$ — **Expand** is another way of saying 'multiply out'.

Solution

$$3(x + 2y) = 3 \times x + 3 \times 2y$$
$$= 3x + 6y$$

There is a 3 in front of the bra
so you need 3 lots of x, which
3x, and 3 lots of 2y, which is

When you are asked to simplify an expression including a bracket, first multiply out the bracket and then collect like terms where possible.

Example

Simplify $\quad 3x + 4(x + 2y)$

Solution

$$3x + 4(x + 2y) = 3x + 4x + 8y$$
$$= 7x + 8y$$

Continued ...

You need to take care when there is a negative sign inside the bracket. Remember that you must keep the sign together with the term that follows it.

Example

Simplify $2(x + 8) + 4(x - 3)$

Solution

$2(x + 8) + 4(x - 3) = 2x + 16 + 4x - 12$ $4 \times -3 = -12$
$\qquad\qquad\qquad\quad = 2x + 4x + 16 - 12$
$\qquad\qquad\qquad\quad = 6x + 4$

Now try these 14.2

Simplify the expressions in questions **1** to **15**.

1. $4(x + 3y)$

2. $2(x + 5y)$

3. $3(2x + 7y)$

4. $5x + 3(2x + y)$

5. $12y + 2(3x + 2y)$

6. $4(x - 2y)$

7. $x + 2(x + 3) + 5$

8. $10 + 2(5x - 4)$

9. $3(2x + 10) + 2(5x - 3)$

10. $4(3x + 2) + 2(3x - 4)$

11. $5(2x - 2y) + 2(7x + 5y)$

12. $x + 3(3x - 5y) + 22y$

13. $2(3x + 4) + 6(x - 5) + 3$

14. $5(3x - 2) + 7(2x - 1)$

15. $3(3x + 4y + 5z) + 2(3x - 2y - z)$

16. **(a)** Arthur is n years old. Richard is 5 years older than Arthur.

    Write an expression for Richard's age.

    (b) David is twice as old as Richard.

    Write an expression for David's age.

    (c) Alan is as old as Arthur, Richard and David added together.

    Write an expression for Alan's age.

    Simplify your answer as far as possible.

17. Emily and Tom are simplifying $4(x + 3) - 2(x + 1)$.

The answer is $2x + 14$.

No – it's $2x + 10$.

Emily   Tom

(a) Substitute $x = 2$ into each of the three expressions.

(b) Who has definitely got the wrong answer?

Give a reason for your answer.

(c) Simplify $4(x + 3) - 2(x + 1)$.

Are either of them right?

Functions

Think of a number.

Coming up …

● using function machines
● drawing mapping diagrams
● finding the input of function machines
● finding the rule for function machines

Do you remember?
● how to write expressions using algebraic conventions
● that the inverse of multiplying by 2 is dividing by 2
● how to find the rule for a sequence from the pattern number

Chapter starter

1 Follow the instructions in the boxes.

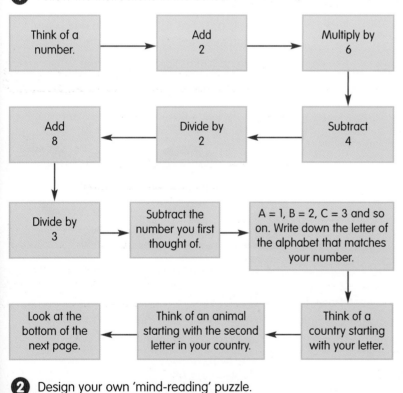

| Think of a number. | → | Add 2 | → | Multiply by 6 |

| Add 8 | ← | Divide by 2 | ← | Subtract 4 |

| Divide by 3 | → | Subtract the number you first thought of. | → | A = 1, B = 2, C = 3 and so on. Write down the letter of the alphabet that matches your number. |

| Look at the bottom of the next page. | ← | Think of an animal starting with the second letter in your country. | ← | Think of a country starting with your letter. |

2 Design your own 'mind-reading' puzzle.

Key words
function machine
rule
input
output
function
mapping
mapping diagram
inverse

A **function machine** uses a **rule** to turn one number (the input) into another number (the output).

This **function machine** uses the **rule** 'multiply by 2'.

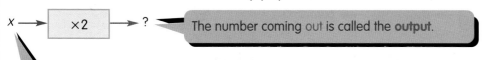

$x \longrightarrow \boxed{\times 2} \longrightarrow ?$

The number coming out is called the **output**.

The number going in is called the **input**.

So when the input is 5 the output is 10.

$5 \longrightarrow \boxed{\times 2} \longrightarrow 10$

output = input × 2

You can write down the rule for the function machine like this.

$$x \longrightarrow 2x$$

$x \times 2 = 2x$
Remember you don't write the × sign in algebra and you always write numbers first then letters.

This is called a **mapping**.

You say 'x maps on to $2x$'.

The inputs and outputs for a function machine can be shown in a table.

input	x	0	1	2	3	4	5
output	$x \longrightarrow 2x$	0	2	4	6	8	10

To find the output multiply the input by 2.

The inputs and outputs for a function machine can also be shown in a mapping diagram.

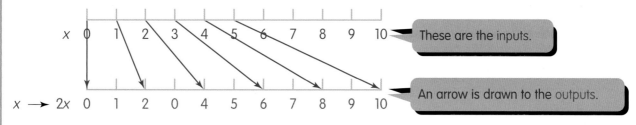

x 0 1 2 3 4 5 6 7 8 9 10

These are the inputs.

$x \longrightarrow 2x$ 0 1 2 0 4 5 6 7 8 9 10

An arrow is drawn to the outputs.

Now try these 15.1

1 For each function machine find the output when the input has these values.

(i) 4   (ii) 8   (iii) 12

(a) input $\longrightarrow \boxed{\times 5} \longrightarrow$ output   (b) input $\longrightarrow \boxed{+7} \longrightarrow$ output

(c) input $\longrightarrow \boxed{-3} \longrightarrow$ output   (d) input $\longrightarrow \boxed{\div 4} \longrightarrow$ output

Continued ...

Were you thinking of a Danish elephant?

2 For each function machine find the output when the input has these values.

    (i) 2   **(ii)** 5   **(iii)** 10

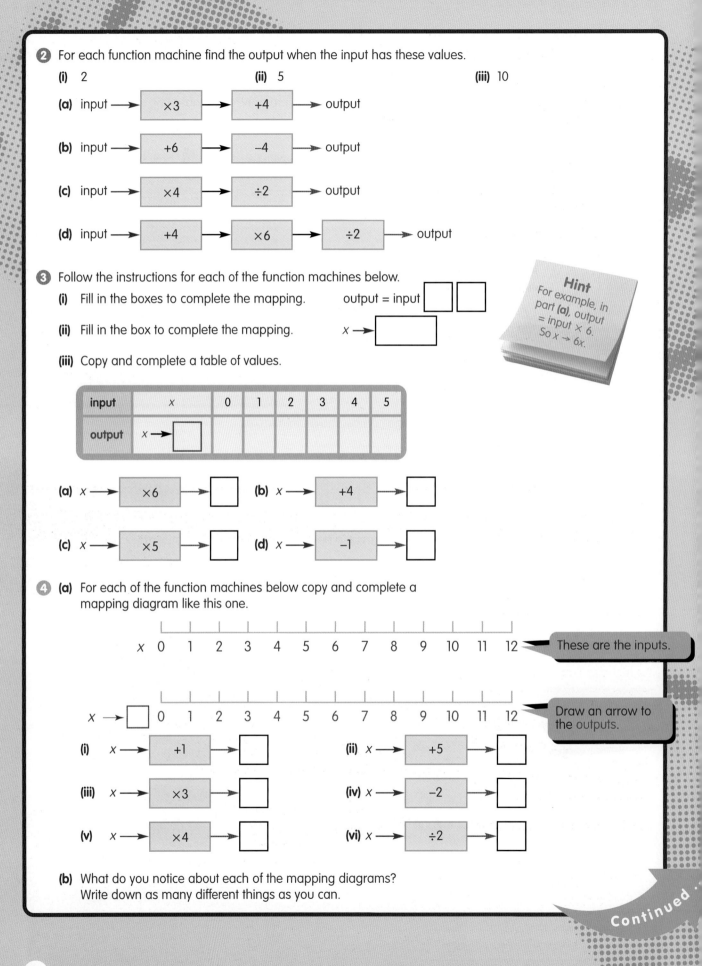

    (a) input ⟶ ×3 ⟶ +4 ⟶ output

    (b) input ⟶ +6 ⟶ −4 ⟶ output

    (c) input ⟶ ×4 ⟶ ÷2 ⟶ output

    (d) input ⟶ +4 ⟶ ×6 ⟶ ÷2 ⟶ output

3 Follow the instructions for each of the function machines below.

    (i) Fill in the boxes to complete the mapping.   output = input ☐ ☐

    (ii) Fill in the box to complete the mapping. x ⟶ ☐

> **Hint**
> For example, in part **(a)**, output = input × 6.
> So $x \to 6x$.

    (iii) Copy and complete a table of values.

input	x	0	1	2	3	4	5
output	$x \to$ ☐						

    (a) x ⟶ ×6 ⟶ ☐   **(b)** x ⟶ +4 ⟶ ☐

    (c) x ⟶ ×5 ⟶ ☐   **(d)** x ⟶ −1 ⟶ ☐

4 **(a)** For each of the function machines below copy and complete a mapping diagram like this one.

x 0   1   2   3   4   5   6   7   8   9   10   11   12 ← These are the inputs.

x ⟶ ☐   0   1   2   3   4   5   6   7   8   9   10   11   12 ← Draw an arrow to the outputs.

    (i) x ⟶ +1 ⟶ ☐   **(ii)** x ⟶ +5 ⟶ ☐

    (iii) x ⟶ ×3 ⟶ ☐   **(iv)** x ⟶ −2 ⟶ ☐

    (v) x ⟶ ×4 ⟶ ☐   **(vi)** x ⟶ ÷2 ⟶ ☐

    (b) What do you notice about each of the mapping diagrams?
    Write down as many different things as you can.

Continued

Investigation

1

These two function machines are the same.

Is Su Ling right?
Give a reason for your answer.

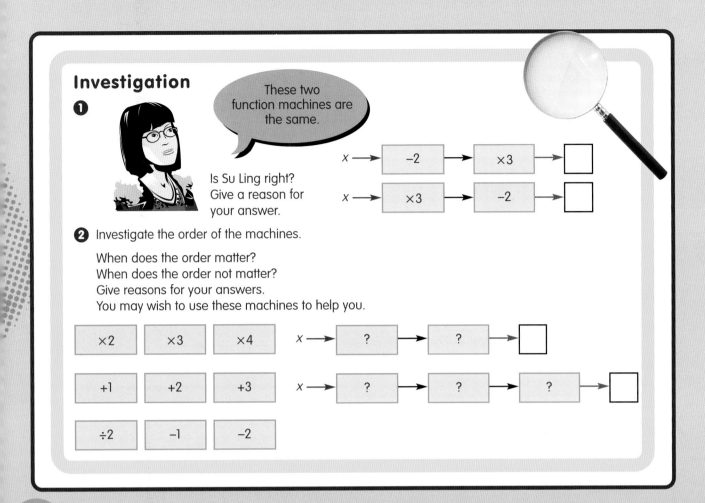

2 Investigate the order of the machines.

When does the order matter?
When does the order not matter?
Give reasons for your answers.
You may wish to use these machines to help you.

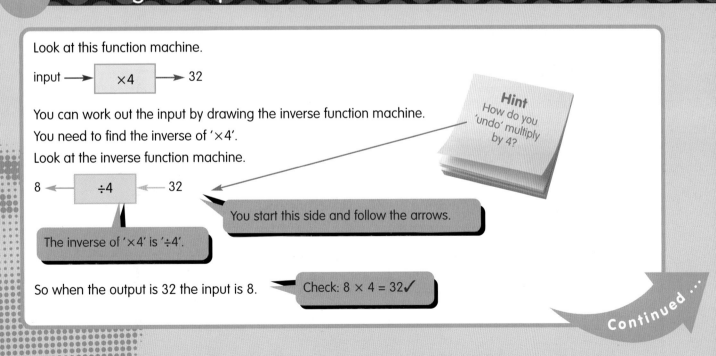

Look at this function machine.

input ⟶ ×4 ⟶ 32

You can work out the input by drawing the inverse function machine.
You need to find the inverse of '×4'.
Look at the inverse function machine.

Hint
How do you 'undo' multiply by 4?

8 ⟵ ÷4 ⟵ 32

You start this side and follow the arrows.

The inverse of '×4' is '÷4'.

So when the output is 32 the input is 8.

Check: 8 × 4 = 32 ✓

Continued ...

Example

Find the input for this function machine.

input ——→ | ÷5 | ——→ | +10 | ——→ 30

Solution

Draw the inverse function machine.

100 ←—— | ×5 | ←—— | −10 | ←—— 30

The inverse of '÷5' is '×5'.   The inverse of '+10' is '−10'.

So when the output is 30 the input is 100.   Check: 100 ——→ | ÷5 | ——→ | +10 | ——→ 30 ✓

Now try these 15.2

1. Fill in the boxes to complete these statements.

   (a) The inverse of '×2' is ☐☐   (b) The inverse of '÷5' is ☐☐

   (c) The inverse of '+7' is ☐☐   (d) The inverse of '−6' is ☐☐

2. Follow the instructions for each of these function machines.

   (i) Draw the inverse function machine.   (ii) Find the input.

   (a) ☐ ——→ | +3 | ——→ 7 (b) ☐ ——→ | −2 | ——→ 12 (c) ☐ ——→ | ×7 | ——→ 63

   (d) ☐ ——→ | +9 | ——→ 10 (e) ☐ ——→ | ÷5 | ——→ 21 (f) ☐ ——→ | −11 | ——→ 11

3. Follow the instructions for each of these function machines.

   (i) Draw the inverse function machine.   (ii) Find the input.

   (a) ☐ ——→ | +5 | ——→ | ÷3 | ——→ 5 (b) ☐ ——→ | −6 | ——→ | ×3 | ——→ 3

   (c) ☐ ——→ | +8 | ——→ | −5 | ——→ 11 (d) ☐ ——→ | ×2 | ——→ | ×5 | ——→ 30

   (e) ☐ ——→ | ÷9 | ——→ | +9 | ——→ 10 (f) ☐ ——→ | ×7 | ——→ | −3 | ——→ 60

4. Find the input when the *output* has these values.   (a) 20   (b) 30   (c) 0

   input ——→ | −4 | ——→ | ×5 | ——→ output

Hint
Remember there were two types of rules.
One type was for finding the next term of a sequence from the previous term.
The other type was for finding any term of a sequence from the pattern number.
It is the second type of rule that is useful when working with function machines.

In Chapter 3 you learnt about finding the rule of a sequence from the pattern number.

This will help you with finding the rule of a function machine.

When you use the sequence 1, 2, 3, …, as inputs, it is like inputting the pattern number.

The outputs you get are like the terms of the sequence.

Look at this function machine:

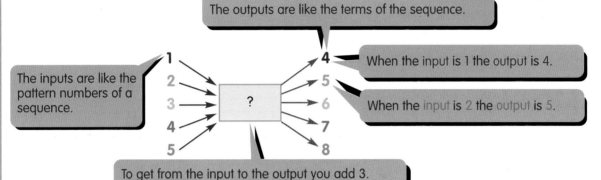

The outputs are like the terms of the sequence.

The inputs are like the pattern numbers of a sequence.

When the input is 1 the output is 4.

When the input is 2 the output is 5.

To get from the input to the output you add 3.

The rule for the function machine is

  output = input + 3

  or $x \longrightarrow x + 3$.

You saw earlier in the chapter that some function machines have two parts.

In Chapter 3 some of the sequences you met had two parts to their rules.

Function machines with two parts are like sequences with two parts to their rule.

Example

Complete this function machine:

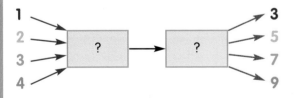

Solution

The outputs are increasing by 2 each time.

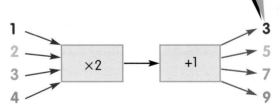

To get from the input to the output you have to multiply by 2 then add 1.

Check: $1 \longrightarrow 1 \times 2 + 1 = 3$ ✓

$2 \longrightarrow 2 \times 2 + 1 = 5$ ✓

$3 \longrightarrow 3 \times 2 + 1 = 7$ ✓

$4 \longrightarrow 4 \times 2 + 1 = 9$ ✓

① Copy and complete these function machines.

(a) 2 → [?] → 7   (b) 8 → [?] → 5

(c) 12 → [?] → 19   (d) 6 → [?] → 0

② Copy and complete these function machines.

(a) 8 → [?] → 2   (b) 5 → [?] → 50

(c) 7 → [?] → 1   (d) 9 → [?] → 36

③ Follow the instructions for each of the following function machines.

(i) Copy and complete the function machine.

(ii) Write down its rule.

(a)
1		5
2		6
3	[?]	7
4		8
5		9

(b)
6		4
7		5
8	[?]	6
9		7
10		8

(c)
1		8
2		16
3	[?]	24
4		32
5		40

④ Copy and complete these function machines.

(a)
1			1
2	[×4]	[?]	5
3			9
4			13

(b)
1			6.5
2	[÷2]	[?]	7
3			7.5
4			8

(c)
1			4
2	[?]	[+1]	7
3			10
4			13

(d)
1			5
2	[?]	[+3]	7
3			9
4			11

⑤ **Puzzle**

(a) Copy and complete this function machine. You should use integers (whole numbers).

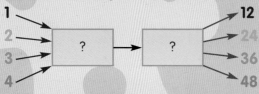

1			12
2	[?]	[?]	24
3			36
4			48

(b) How many different answers can you find?

(c) This two-part machine can be simplified into a single-part machine:

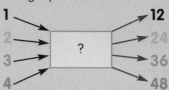

1		12
2	[?]	24
3		36
4		48

What is its rule?

6 Interpreting data

Subject links
- geography
- science

Coming up ...

- finding and using information from diagrams and graphs

Chapter starter

These are the racing and mountain bikes sold by a shop one day in December.

1 How many racing and mountain bikes were sold altogether?

2 How many of the bikes were yellow?

3 How many of the bikes were neither yellow nor green?

4 How many of the bikes were

 (a) green (b) mountain bikes (c) green mountain bikes?

5 Racing and mountain bikes made up half of the total number of bikes sold that day.

 How many bikes were sold altogether?

6 How can you arrange the data to make it easier to find the answers to questions like these?

Do you remember?

- the meaning of the word frequency
- how to read the scales of a graph
- how to calculate simple fractions of an amount
- the percentage equivalents of simple fractions

Key words

table
bar chart
bar-line graph
frequency
horizontal axis
vertical axis
pie chart
sector

16.1 Interpreting tables

Information is sometimes written in tables.

A table has column and row headings which help you to find information.

Example

This table gives information about three fuels that can be used in cars.

It shows some of the things that are produced when fuel burns.

✓ shows a substance is produced when the fuel burns.

✗ shows a substance is not produced when the fuel burns.

Fuel	Physical state	Energy provided (kJ/kg)	Carbon monoxide	Sulphur dioxide	Water
Petrol	liquid	48 000	✓	✓	✓
Hydrogen	gas	121 000	✗	✗	✓
Ethanol (alcohol)	liquid	30 000	✓	✗	✓

(a) Which fuel is a gas?

(b) Which fuel provides

(i) the most energy (ii) the least energy?

(c) Which fuel produces carbon monoxide and sulphur dioxide?

(d) Scientists say that if hydrogen is used as a fuel there will be less pollution.

Do you agree?

Give a reason for your answer making use of the table.

Solution

This column tells you how much energy the fuels provide.

These headings tell you what is produced when the fuel burns.

Fuel	Physical state	Energy provided (kJ/kg)	Carbon monoxide	Sulphur dioxide	Water
Petrol	liquid	48 000	✓	✓	✓
Hydrogen	gas	121 000	✗	✗	✓
Ethanol (alcohol)	liquid	30 000	✓	✗	✓

This is the biggest number in this column.

This is the smallest number in this column.

Find gas in the table.

(a) Hydrogen is a gas.

(b) (i) Hydrogen provides the most energy – 121 000 kJ/kg.

(ii) Ethanol provides the least energy – 30 000 kJ/kg.

(c) Petrol produces both carbon monoxide and sulphur dioxide.

(d) Yes, as burning hydrogen only produces water.

It does not produce carbon monoxide or sulphur dioxide, which are both pollutants.

1 The table shows the distances in miles between the capital cities of England, Northern Ireland, Scotland and Wales.

(a) What is the distance between Belfast and Edinburgh?

(b) Which two cities are
  (i) closest together
  (ii) furthest apart?

Distances (miles)

Belfast			
241	Cardiff		
143	307	Edinburgh	
322	133	332	London

This is the distance between Belfast and London.

2 The table shows the mass of water, fat, fibre and vitamin C in 100 g of potatoes cooked in different ways.

	Water (g)	Fat (g)	Fibre (g)	Vitamin C (mg)
Chips	57	7	2	9
Boiled, peeled potato	80	hardly any	1	6
Potato baked in its skin	63	hardly any	3	14

(a) Which way of cooking potatoes contains
  (i) the most fibre (ii) the least fibre?

(b) Which part of a potato contains the most vitamin C? How do you know?

16.2 Interpreting bar charts

A bar chart is made up of vertical or horizontal bars.

All the bars are the same width.

The bar or bars for each category are separated by spaces.

The height or length of the bar is used to represent the frequency.

The best bar charts use rectangles to represent the data.

They all use the height or length of the bar to represent the frequency.

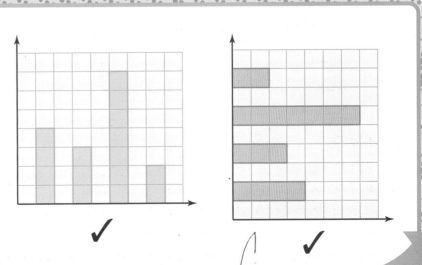

✓   ✓

Continued ...

In this chart, there are two bars for each year.

They are touching because together they make up the whole population for the year.

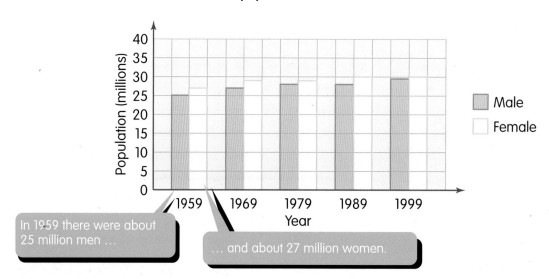

UK population 1959 to 1999

In 1959 there were about 25 million men ...

... and about 27 million women.

This type of bar chart is useful for comparing two or more subgroups.

It is easy to compare the number of men and women in the population in each of the years.

You can see quickly that, in the years shown, there were more women than men in the population.

It is more difficult to find the total population.

In this chart, each bar is divided into two.

The two parts are touching and together they show the total population for the year.

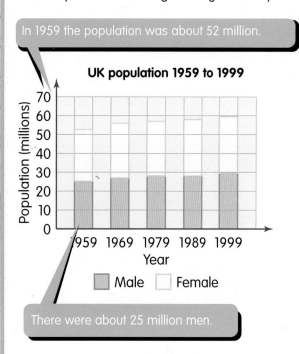

In 1959 the population was about 52 million.

UK population 1959 to 1999

There were about 25 million men.

This type of bar chart is useful when you are interested in the total.

You can also find out information about different subgroups.

You can see quickly that the population grew each year.

It is also easy to see that the number of men grew each year.

It is more difficult to tell if the number of women grew each year.

There are three things that can help you to find information from a bar chart.

● A title
● Labels on the horizontal axis
● Labels and scales on the vertical axis

There may also be a key, like in the charts showing the UK population.

It tells you what the different colours or shading represent.

① Ellis carried out a test to find out how well things dissolved in water.

The bar chart shows his results.

(a) Which of the things Ellis tested was easiest to dissolve?

(b) Which of the things Ellis tested was most difficult to dissolve?

(c) Write the four items Ellis tested in order of solubility. Put the item that dissolved best first.

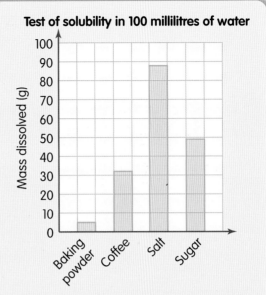

Test of solubility in 100 millilitres of water

② This bar-line graph shows the number of pupils in class 7A who had a school meal on each day of one week.

(a) How many more pupils had a school meal on Wednesday than on Monday?

(b) Chips are served on only two days. On which days do you think chips are served? Give a reason for your answer.

(c) How many school meals did Class 7A eat altogether during the week?

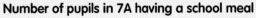

Number of pupils in 7A having a school meal

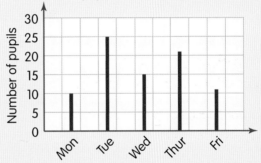

③ This bar chart shows the results of a study into changes in the whale population.

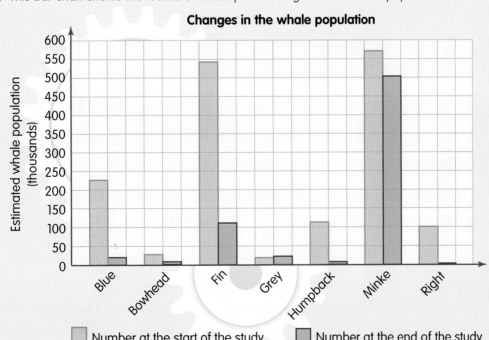

Changes in the whale population

☐ Number at the start of the study   ☐ Number at the end of the study

Continued ...

(a) Estimate the number of minke whales at the start of the study.

(b) Which of the whales shown now has the smallest population?

(c) Which type of whale has increased in number?

(d) Estimate the reduction in the number of blue whales.

4 The members of a youth club were asked what they would like to do most on an activity evening.
This chart shows the results.

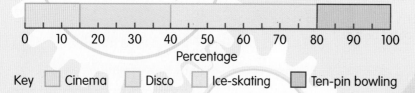

Key ▢ Cinema ▢ Disco ▢ Ice-skating ▢ Ten-pin bowling

(a) Which was the least popular activity?

(b) Which was the most popular activity?

(c) What percentage chose ice-skating?

(d) One activity was chosen by twice as many people as another activity.
What were the two activities?

Note

This type of chart shows how the whole group is divided. The width of each section tells you the percentage. You can't say how many people chose an activity because you don't know how many people are in the youth club.

With a friend

1 Write down at least ten things that you know from looking at the bar chart below.

2 Compare your answer to question **1** with a friend's answer.

3 Why do you think there is a difference between the two sets of data?

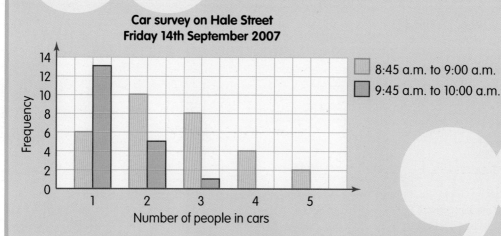

Line graphs are made by joining up points plotted on a graph.

There are three things that can help you to find information from a line graph.

● A title
● Labels and scales on the horizontal axis
● Labels and scales on the vertical axis

Example

A baby is weighed at birth and each week after that.

The mass is recorded on a line graph.

(a) What was the mass of the baby at birth?

(b) What was the mass of the baby at 6 weeks?

(c) When did the baby lose weight?

(d) How much mass did the baby gain in the first 9 weeks of his life?

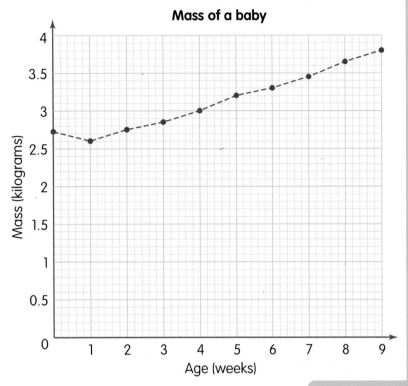

Solution

(a) At birth the baby weighed 2.7 kilograms.

(b) After 6 weeks the baby weighed 3.3 kilograms.

(c) The baby lost weight between birth and being weighed after a week.

This is where the graph goes down.

(d) At birth, the baby's mass was 2.7 kilograms.

After 9 weeks, his mass was 3.8 kilograms.

The baby gained 1.1 kilograms.

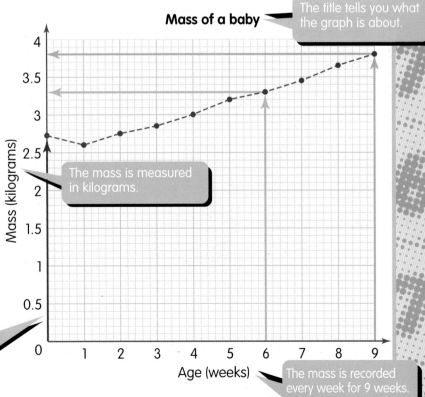

The title tells you what the graph is about.

The mass is measured in kilograms.

There are five squares between 0 and 0.5, so each square represents 0.1 kg.

The mass is recorded every week for 9 weeks.

① The graph shows the average monthly temperature in the Sahara desert.

Average monthly temperature in the Sahara desert

(Graph: Temperature (degrees Celsius) on vertical axis from 0 to 40, Month on horizontal axis from Jan to Dec)

(a) How many degrees Celsius does each small square on the vertical axis represent?

(b) What is the average temperature in October?

(c) Which two months have the same average temperature?

(d) Which is the coldest month? What is the temperature in that month?

(e) Which is the hottest month? What is the temperature in that month?

(f) What is the difference in average temperature between the hottest and the coldest months?

Investigation

Sometimes you will find two sets of information displayed on the same diagram.
A common example is temperature and rainfall for different places.

These two graphs show the average rainfall and average temperature for Christchurch in New Zealand and London in England.

□ Average temperature in degrees Celsius
◆ Average rainfall in millimetres

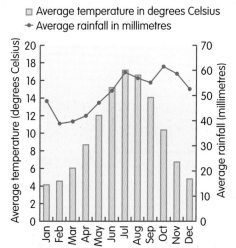

□ Average temperature in degrees Celsius
◆ Average rainfall in millimetres

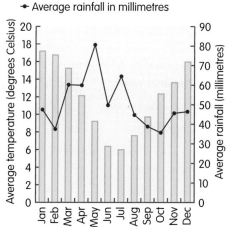

① Discuss with a friend which graph belongs to which city.
How do you know?

② Rose and her family live in London.
They are planning to move to Christchurch.
In what ways will they find the weather different from London?

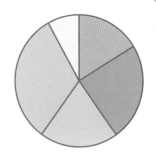

Pie charts are used to show how something is divided up.

In a pie chart a circle is divided into sectors.

A key is often given to show what the different sectors represent.

The clearest pie charts use a circle divided into sectors.

Example

This pie chart shows how water is used in an average household in the United Kingdom.

(a) Which item uses about one third of the water?
How do you know?

(b) About what percentage of the water is used for flushing the toilet?
How do you know?

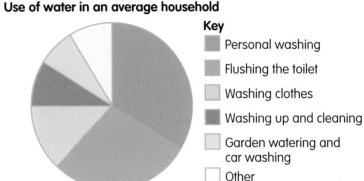

Use of water in an average household

Key
- Personal washing
- Flushing the toilet
- Washing clothes
- Washing up and cleaning
- Garden watering and car washing
- Other

Solution

(a) Personal washing uses about one third of the water.
The pink sector is about one third of the circle.

(b) So about 25% of the water is used for flushing the toilet (a quarter is 25%).
The blue sector is about a quarter of the circle.

In the example, you can't say how many litres of water were used.

However, if you are given the total number of litres used, then you can work out how much is used for each sector.

Example

An average person uses 150 litres of water per day.

Use this fact and the information in the pie chart in the previous example to answer this question.

How many litres of water does an average person use in a day for personal washing?

Solution

Personal washing uses about $\frac{1}{3}$ of the water. $\frac{1}{3}$ of 150 litres = 50 litres.

To find $\frac{1}{3}$, divide by 3. 150 ÷ 3 = 50

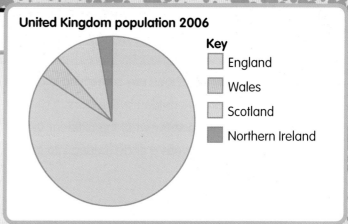

Now try these 16.4

① This pie chart compares the populations of the countries of the United Kingdom in 2006.

Write the countries in order of population starting with the smallest.

United Kingdom population 2006

Key
- England
- Wales
- Scotland
- Northern Ireland

② The pie chart shows the results of 20 netball matches played by one team.

(a) How many matches were won?
How do you know?

(b) How many matches were lost?
How do you know?

Results of netball matches

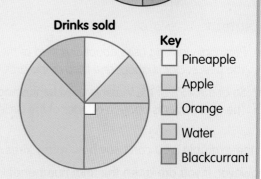

③ During one break time 40 drinks were sold from a drinks machine.

The pie chart shows the drinks that were sold.

(a) Which three drinks sold the same amount?

(b) How many orange drinks were sold?

(c) Five apple drinks were sold.

How many bottles of water were sold?
How do you know?

Drinks sold

Key
- Pineapple
- Apple
- Orange
- Water
- Blackcurrant

④ The pie charts here show the ages of pedestrians and cyclists under the age of 16 injured on Shropshire roads in 2005.

(a) In which age group were there the fewest injuries?

(b) In which age group were there the most injuries?

(c) Why is there no 5–7 category on the cyclists' pie chart?

(d) 20 cyclists were injured altogether.

Estimate the number of cyclists injured who were aged 12–15.

(e) 63 pedestrians were injured altogether.

Estimate the number of pedestrians injured who were aged 12–15.

Age of pedestrians under 16 injured in Shropshire in 2005

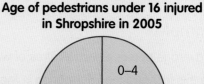

Age of cyclists under 16 injured in Shropshire in 2005

17 Averages and range

Subject links
- science
- geography
- physical education

Coming up …

- the mode and the modal class
- the mean and median
- the range
- comparing sets of data

Do you remember?
- how to do mental and written calculations
- how to interpret tables, diagrams and graphs

Chapter starter

According to a survey, an average Year 7 girl

- has a height of 153 centimetres
- wears size 3 shoes
- eats meat on 4 days each week
- eats 2.7 portions of fruit each day
- eats 2.8 portions of vegetables each day
- lives in a semi-detached house
- walks to school
- exercises on 3.5 days every week
- cleans her teeth twice a day.

According to a survey, an average Year 7 boy

- has a height of 153 centimetres
- wears size 4 shoes
- eats meat on 3.9 days each week
- eats 2.7 portions of fruit each day
- eats 2.8 portions of vegetables each day
- lives in a semi-detached house
- walks to school
- exercises on 4.7 days every week
- cleans his teeth twice a day.

1. Are you an average Year 7 boy or girl?
2. What does average mean?
3. How can you find the average height of a Year 7 boy or girl?
4. How can you find the most common way a Year 7 boy or girl travels to school?

Key words

average
mode
modal class
mean
median
range

The **mode** is the item in a set of data that occurs the most often. It is the **most common** item.

There can be more than one mode in a set of data.
The mode is the only average that does not have to be a number.

Example

Class 7F recorded the weather for ten days.

Monday	Tuesday	Wednesday	Thursday	Friday

Monday	Tuesday	Wednesday	Thursday	Friday

What type of weather is the mode?

Solution

It was rainy three times.
It was cloudy three times.
It was sunny four times.
It was sunny more times than any other type of weather.
So the mode is sunny.

Example

Find the mode of these numbers.

12, 10, 10, 14, 13, 14

Solution

10 and 14 both occur twice.

The other numbers occur once.

So there are two modes, 10 and 14.

Hint
If there are a lot of values, it is helpful to write them in order.

Example

Which letter is the mode?

M, O, D, A, L

Solution

Each of the letters occurs once.

So there is no mode.

Continued...

Example

The table shows the results of rolling a dice 60 times.

What is the **modal score**?

'What is the modal score?' is another way of asking 'What score is the mode?'

Score	Frequency
1	11
2	9
3	13
4	10
5	8
6	9

Solution

The modal score is 3 because 3 appears 13 times, which is more than any other number.

⚠️ Remember that the mode is 3 not 13!

Now try these 17.1

1. Find the mode or modes for each set. If there is no mode explain why.
   (a) 4, 7, 2, 7
   (b) ➕, ✳, ◗, ▪, ◗, ➕, ◗
   (c) dog, cat, dog, rabbit, cat, cat, rabbit, mouse
   (d) 43, 45, 43, 40, 45, 46
   (e) A, V, E, R, A, G, E
   (f) 12, 17, 13, 16, 11, 17, 18, 15, 11
   (g) scissors, stone, stone, paper, scissors, scissors, stone, paper, scissors, stone, paper, stone, stone, paper
   (h) 6.1, 6.9, 6.8, 6.4, 6.3, 6.8
   (i) 10p, 20p, 5p, £1, 50p, 10p, 10p, 5p, 20p, £1, 5p
   (j) 6, 8, 11, 3, 5, 9, 10, 2, 7
   (k) P.E., maths, science, maths, Spanish, science, P.E., maths

2. The pupils in Year 7 chose which theme park they would like to go to for a day out.

   The results are shown in the pie chart. Which theme park was the mode? How do you know?

3. Find the modal item or items in each frequency table.

(a)

Animal	Frequency
Cow	52
Sheep	81
Horse	2

(b)

Type of house	Frequency
Detached	23
Semi-detached	32
Flat	16
Bungalow	4
Terrace	21

(c)

Sport	Frequency
Cricket	29
Football	33
Rugby	42
Athletics	17
Hockey	35

When data is put into groups the **modal group** or **modal class** is the group or class that has the highest frequency or occurs the most often.

Age in years	Frequency
Under 14	10
14–17	4
18–24	5
25–34	3
35–50	4
Over 50	4

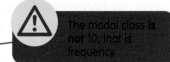

The modal class **is not 10**, that is frequency.

The modal group or class is **Under 14** because there are more people in this group than in any other.

Now try these 17.2

① Find the modal class or modal classes for each grouped frequency table.

(a)

Number of letters per word	Frequency
1–3	56
4–6	76
7–9	23
10–13	7

(b)

Length of film to the nearest minute	Frequency
60–89	1
90–119	28
120–149	14
150–179	2

(c)

Height of pupil to the nearest centimetre	Frequency
130–139	35
140–149	34
150–159	19
160–169	6

(d)

Time to run 100 m to the nearest second	Frequency
11–12	1
13–14	23
15–16	23
17–18	5

② The list below shows the lengths, to the nearest second, of 20 television advertisements shown on one evening.

57 52 37 16 14
28 31 42 35 18
36 31 33 27 54
39 26 33 11 35

(a) Copy and complete the frequency table.

(b) What is the modal class for the length of television advertisements?

Length of advertisement to the nearest second	Tally	Frequency
1–10		
11–20		
21–30		
31–40		
41–50		
51–60		

When people use the word *average* they are often talking about the **mean**.

To find the mean you *add* up all the values and *divide* by the number of values.

You can write this as $\text{mean} = \dfrac{\text{the sum of all the values}}{\text{the number of values}}$

Example

Find the mean of these numbers.

9, 5, 10, 4, 14

Solution

$\text{Mean} = \dfrac{\text{the sum of all the values}}{\text{the number of values}}$

$= \dfrac{9 + 5 + 10 + 4 + 14}{5}$

$= \dfrac{42}{5}$

$= 8.4$

> Add up all the values.
> $9 + 5 + 10 + 4 + 14 = 42$

> Divide by the number of values. There are five values altogether.

> The mean does not have to be a whole number. Do not round the value to the nearest whole number.

If you know the mean and the number of values you can work out the sum of the values.

Example

These three cards have numbers on the other side.

The mean of the numbers is 5.

(a) What do the three numbers add up to?

(b) Another card is added and the mean is now 7.

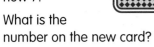

What is the number on the new card?

Solution

(a) The mean of the three numbers is 5.

$\text{Mean} = \dfrac{\text{the total of the three numbers}}{\text{the number of cards}}$

$5 = \dfrac{\text{the total of the three numbers}}{3}$

So the total of the three numbers is 15.

> Ask yourself what number divided by 3 equals 5.

(b) The mean of the four numbers is 7.

$\text{Mean} = \dfrac{\text{the total of the four numbers}}{\text{the number of cards}}$

$7 = \dfrac{\text{the total of the four numbers}}{4}$

> Another card has been added so there are now four numbers.

> total of four cards

> total of three cards

Number on fourth card = 28 − 15 = 13.

Continued...

You can work out the mean from a frequency table.

Example

The table shows the number of goals England scored in the Euro 2008 qualifying rounds.

Number of goals	Number of matches
0	3
1	2
2	1
3	5
4	0
5	1
Total	12

What was the mean number of goals scored in each match?

Solution

Mean number of goals per match = $\dfrac{\text{total number of goals}}{\text{number of matches}}$.

Add a column to your table to find the total number of goals.

Number of goals	Number of matches	Total number of goals
0	3	$0 \times 3 = 0$
1	2	$1 \times 2 = 2$
2	1	$2 \times 1 = 2$
3	5	$3 \times 5 = 15$
4	0	$4 \times 0 = 0$
5	1	$5 \times 1 = 5$
Total	12	24

They scored no goals in three matches.

They scored one goal in two matches.
So in those two matches they scored a total of two goals.

They scored three goals in five matches.
So in those five matches they scored a total of 15 goals.

This is the total number of matches played.

Add the numbers in this column to find the total number of goals scored in all the matches.

Mean number of goals per match = $\dfrac{\text{the total number of goals}}{\text{number of matches}}$

$$= \frac{24}{12}$$

$$= 2$$

1 Find the mean of each set of numbers.

  (a) 32,   36
  (b) 50,   20,   20
  (c) 7,   12,   11,   10
  (d) 15,   10,   5,   10,   20
  (e) 1.1,   1.3,   1.9,   2.2,   3.5
  (f) $1\frac{1}{2}$, $2\frac{3}{4}$, $2\frac{1}{2}$, $1\frac{1}{4}$

2 Write down these numbers.

  (a) Two different numbers with a mean of 6
  (b) Three different numbers with a mean of 6
  (c) Five different numbers with a mean of 6

3 Jane played four rounds of golf.
These are her scores.

72   75   67   66

Work out Jane's mean score.

4 In cricket, a player's batting average is the total number of runs he has scored divided by the number of times he was out.

These are the runs Asif scored in six games.

30 (out),   25 (not out),   35 (out),   42 (out),
27 (not out),   21 (out)

  (a) How many times was Asif out?
  (b) What is Asif's batting average for these games?

5 Puzzle

These four cards have numbers on the other side.
The mean of the numbers is 3.

  (a) What do the four numbers add up to?
  (b) Another card is added and the mean is now 6. What is the number on the new card?

6 These are the number of guests staying at Paula's hotel each day for one week.

Day	Number of guests
Mon	23
Tues	19
Weds	15
Thurs	21
Fri	40
Sat	40
Sun	10

Work out the mean number of guests each day.

7 Brain strain

Look back at the example about the mean number of goals England scored per match in the qualifying rounds of Euro 2008.

Do you think the mean number of goals scored gives you a good idea of England's scores in the matches?

Continued...

8 The table shows the number of raffle tickets bought by the pupils in a class.

Number of tickets	Number of pupils
0	3
1	12
2	15
3	2
4	1
5	2
Total	35

What was the mean number of tickets bought by each pupil?

17.4 The median

The **median** is the *middle* number when all the numbers have been put *in order.*

Example

Find the median of these numbers.

3, 7, 2, 5, 9

Solution

Put the numbers in order.

2, 3, (5,) 7, 9

The middle number is 5.

The median is 5.

When there are two middle numbers, the median is halfway between the two numbers.

Example

Find the median of these numbers.

5, 9, 7, 3, 3, 13

Solution

Put the numbers in order.

3, 3, (5, 7,) 9, 13

The middle numbers are 5 and 7.

The number halfway between 5 and 7 is 6. So 6 is the median.

The mean of 5 and 7 is $\dfrac{5+7}{2} = \dfrac{12}{2} = 6$
So the median is 6.

When the middle numbers are the same the median will be that number.

For example if the two middle numbers are 32 and 32 the median will be 32.

1. Find the median of each set of numbers.

   (a) 6, 4, 9

   (b) 9, 12, 0, 8, 5

   (c) 32, 24, 64, 27, 12, 90, 43

   (d) 10, 6, 8, 4

   (e) 13, 10, 4, 3, 16, 9

   (f) 20, 17, 33, 29, 23, 43, 8, 23

   (g) 1.3, 2.5, 1.7, 4.9, 3.6

   (h) $4\frac{3}{4}$, $6\frac{1}{2}$, $5\frac{1}{4}$, $1\frac{1}{2}$, $3\frac{1}{4}$, $2\frac{3}{4}$

   (i) 2.5, $5\frac{1}{4}$, 6.9, $4\frac{1}{2}$, 3.5, 1.0

2. Write down these.

   (a) Five different numbers with a median of 8.

   (b) Six different numbers with a median of 8.

③ **Puzzle**

These five cards have a number on one side.
When the cards are put in order the median is 1.
Write down three different possibilities for the numbers on the five cards.

17.5 The range

The **range** is the difference between the largest and smallest numbers in a set.

The range is not an average.

range = the largest number – the smallest number

Example

Find the range of these numbers.

7, 3, 8, 2, 5, 1

Hint
If there are a lot of values, it is helpful to write them in order.

Solution

The largest number is 8.

The smallest number is 1.

The range = the largest number – the smallest number
$$= 8 - 1 = 7.$$

The range is not 1 to 8 or 1–8.
The range is a single number.

1. Find the range of the following sets.

   (a) 8, 3, 7, 1, 3, 5

   (b) 72, 13, 54, 49, 90

   (c) 6.2, 4.9, 1.6, 8.5, 0.9

   (d) $8\frac{3}{4}$, $13\frac{1}{2}$, $7\frac{1}{4}$, $2\frac{1}{2}$, $11\frac{1}{4}$, $15\frac{3}{4}$

   (e) 6.3, $8\frac{1}{4}$, 12.9, $15\frac{1}{2}$, 3.5, 11.0

   (f) 6, ⁻5, 11, ⁻8, 9, ⁻15

Continued...

3 The list shows the birth weight in grams of each of the puppies in a litter.

415,   451,   408,   444,   373,
392,   435,   402,   428

What is the range of the birth weights of the puppies?

3 The table shows the length of some films.

Film	Length
Harry Potter and the Order of the Phoenix	2 hours 18 minutes
Mr Bean's Holiday	1 hour 30 minutes
Shrek the Third	1 hour 32 minutes
Snow White and the Seven Dwarfs	1 hour 23 minutes
Star Wars Episode III: Revenge of the Sith	2 hours 26 minutes
The Lord of the Rings: The Return of the King	3 hours 30 minutes

What is the range of the lengths of the films in minutes?

4 Puzzle

The range of the numbers on these three cards is 4.
What are the two numbers that could be on the third card?

5 Brain strain

The table shows the midday temperature in degrees Celsius of four cities on the 1st January.

City	Temperature (°C)
London	3.9
Paris	3.5
Rome	13.5
Moscow	⁻10.2

What is the range of the temperatures?

6 Puzzle

(a) Write down five numbers with a mode of 5 and a range of 7.
(b) Write down three numbers with a mean of 6 and a range of 6.
(c) Write down five different numbers with a mean of 3 and a median of 3. What is the range of your numbers?

7 The bar chart shows the number of newspapers Helen delivered each day.
For the number of newspapers delivered, find

(a) the mean
(b) the median
(c) the mode
(d) the range.

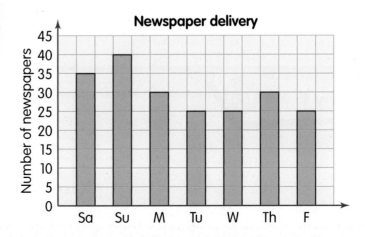

17.6 Comparing data

You can use the range and one or more of the averages to compare two sets of data.

Now try these 17.6

1. Look at the numbers on these five cards.

   (a) Explain why
      (i) the mean is 5
      (ii) the median is 6
      (iii) the mode is 2
      (iv) the range is 6.

6	**2**	**7**	**2**	**8**

   (b) Write a set of five numbers with a median of 6 and a mode of 2 but with a higher mean than the numbers for part (a).

2. The bar charts show the points scored by boys and girls in a fantasy football league.

   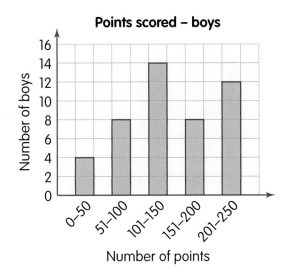

   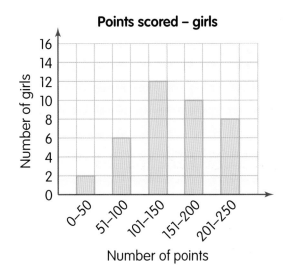

   For each statement below decide whether it is true, false or you cannot tell.

   Explain your answers and show any working out that you do.

   (a) There are more boys than girls in the fantasy football league.

   (b) The mean number of points is 143 for the boys and 147 for the girls.

   (c) The modal class is the same for the boys and the girls.

   (d) The range is the same for the boys and the girls.

3. These are the scores Jane and Guy got the last three times they went ten-pin bowling together.

Jane	110	108	115
Guy	117	96	123

   (a) Work out the mean and range of the scores for each person.

   (b) Who would you choose for your team?

      Give a reason for your answer.

18 Negative numbers

Subject links
- geography
- food technology
- PHSE

Coming up ...

- positioning positive and negative numbers on a number line
- adding and subtracting using positive and negative numbers
- using the sign change key on a calculator

Chapter starter

Every golf course has a number of strokes (or shots) in which the course should be completed.

This is known as par for that course.

The 2007 Open Golf Championship was played at Carnoustie.

The par for that course is 71.

Tiger Woods took 69 strokes.

This is 2 less than 71. His score was ⁻2.

Ian Poulter took 73 strokes.

This is 2 more than 71. His score was ⁺2.

Do you remember?
- what an integer is
- what the symbols < and > mean
- adding and subtracting positive integers
- how to use a number line
- how to work out the range of a set of numbers

Here are some golf courses and their pars.

Course	Carnoustie	Birkdale	Troon	Muirfield	Hoylake
Par	71	70	71	71	72

1. Write these scores using a ⁺ or a ⁻.
   (a) Vijay Singh plays Hoylake in 70 strokes.
   (b) Paul Casey plays Muirfield in 74 strokes.

2. Ernie Els has a score of ⁻3 after playing Troon. How many strokes did he take?

3. Mike Weir has a score of ⁻1 after playing Birkdale. How many strokes did he take?

Key word

integer

positive

negative

plus

sum

minus

difference

inverse operation

Temperatures are usually measured in degrees Celsius (°C).

In the United Kingdom (UK) the temperature is usually greater than 0 °C.

But in the winter months the temperature can fall below 0 °C.

> 0°C is sometimes called freezing point.

This means that the temperature will be a negative number.

The lowest recorded temperature in London was ⁻10 °C.
This is 10 °C less than 0 °C.

In other countries the temperature will often be below 0 °C for long periods.

In the town of Vladivostock in Russia temperatures below ⁻20 °C have been recorded from November to March.

A thermometer is like a vertical number line.

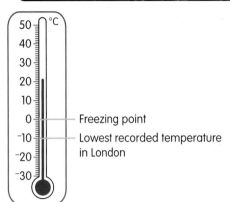

Freezing point

Lowest recorded temperature in London

Example

The temperature is ⁻1°C.

The temperature falls by 3 °C.

What is the new temperature?

Solution

The number that is three less than ⁻1 is needed.

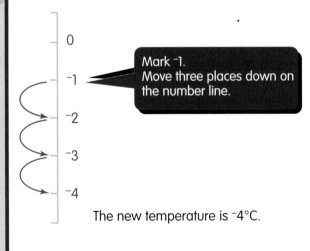

> Mark ⁻1.
> Move three places down on the number line.

The new temperature is ⁻4°C.

Example

The temperature is ⁻7°C.

The temperature rises by 4 °C

What is the new temperature?

Solution

The number that is 4 more than ⁻7 is needed.

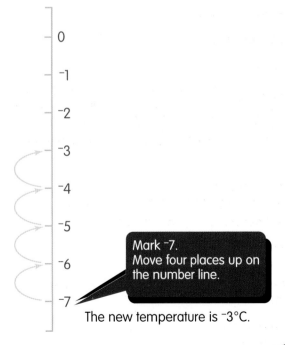

> Mark ⁻7.
> Move four places up on the number line.

The new temperature is ⁻3°C.

Continued ...

Research

1 What is the lowest recorded temperature in the UK?

2 Find the ten places in the world that have the lowest average temperatures.

3 Draw a number line showing the ten places and their average temperatures.

Now try these 18.1

1 Copy and complete this table.

	Temperature now	Change	Temperature later
(a)	3 °C	decreases by 5 °C	
(b)	⁻2 °C	increases by 3 °C	
(c)	⁻3 °C	decreases by 1 °C	
(d)	0 °C	increases by 6 °C	
(e)	⁻4 °C	decreases by 2 °C	
(f)	⁻2 °C	rises by 2 °C	
(g)	⁻1 °C		⁻5 °C
(h)	⁻6 °C		⁻14 °C
(i)	0 °C		⁻7 °C
(j)	⁻10 °C		⁻5 °C

2 Mathematical Mansion has eight floors above ground level and three floors below ground level.

The owner, Miss Calculation, calls ground level Floor 0.

The fifth floor above ground level is called Floor ⁺5.

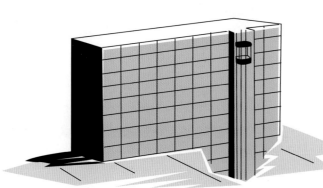

(a) What is the top floor called?

(b) What is the bottom floor called?

(c) Mr Point is on Floor ⁺6 and needs to go to Floor ⁻2.

How many floors does he need to go down?

(d) Ms Take starts on the bottom floor and travels to the top floor.

Then she goes to ground level before going to Floor ⁻2 and finally back to the top floor.

How many floors did she travel through?

18.2 Negative numbers on a calculator

To enter a negative number you use the [–] key on your calculator.

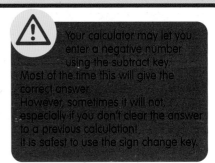

Your calculator may let you enter a negative number using the subtract key.
Most of the time this will give the correct answer.
However, sometimes it will not, especially if you don't clear the answer to a previous calculation!
It is safest to use the sign change key.

Example

(a) Add ⁻36 and ⁻88.

(b) Work out the difference between 274 and negative 356.

Solution

(a) These are the keys to press to add ⁻36 and ⁻88.

[–] 3 6 + [–] 8 8

This is what your calculator should show.

–124

(b) These are the keys to press to work out the difference between 274 and negative 356.

2 7 4 – [–] 3 5 6

This is what your calculator should show.

630

Now try these 18.2

1 Use your calculator to work out these.

(a) 35 + ⁻57	**(b)** ⁻39 + 68	**(c)** 567 – ⁻76	**(d)** ⁻62 – ⁻44
(e) ⁻573 + 345	**(f)** 438 + ⁻235	**(g)** ⁻721 – ⁻848	**(h)** 6.5 – ⁻4.2
(i) ⁻2.7 + 15.4	**(j)** ⁻8.9 – 14.1	**(k)** 23.7 + ⁻77	**(l)** ⁻9.3 – ⁻10.8
(m) 6427 + ⁻5796	**(n)** 14 – ⁻52 + 13	**(o)** ⁻37 – ⁻63 – ⁻19	

(p) Add negative 37 to negative 459.

(q) What is negative 506 subtract 235?

(r) Find the sum of 413, negative 562 and negative 99.

---

2 Puzzle

In this number pyramid, two numbers are added to find the number in the box above.
Copy and complete the pyramid.

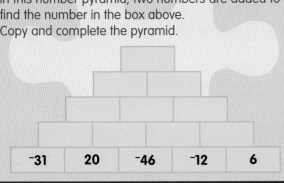

3 Puzzle

In this number pyramid, the number in the box above is found by *subtracting* the number on the left from the number on the right in the two boxes below.

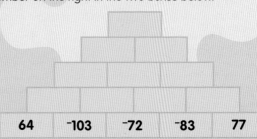

Continued ...

The number pyramid in Puzzle 2 has bottom row: ⁻31, 20, ⁻46, ⁻12, 6

The number pyramid in Puzzle 3 has bottom row: 64, ⁻103, ⁻72, ⁻83, 77

4 This is part of Jake's bank statement.

A bank statement tells you what amounts have been taken out of and put into an account.

The balance is the amount of money in the account.

SO means standing order. It is a payment made automatically. It is the same amount each time. Standing orders are often monthly.

CHQ means cheque.

BP means bank payment. It is a one-off payment which you instruct your bank to make.

Date	Payment type and details		Paid out	Paid in	Balance	
09 Jul	Balance brought forward				47.93	
10 Jul	SO	Savings account	100.00		52.07	D
12 Jul	CHQ	100003	23.56		75.63	D
12 Jul	BP	Holiday	1320.00		1395.63	D
12 Jul	DD	TV licence	11.37		1407.00	D
15 Jul	ATM	Cash @ 18:40	40.00		1447.00	D
17 Jul	CR	Salary		1000.00	447.00	D
20 Jul	SO	Rent	350.00		797.00	D

DD means direct debit. It is similar to a standing order except the amount can change. Jake pays for his TV licence by direct debit. If the cost of the TV licence goes up, the amount of the direct debit is increased automatically.

ATM stands for automated teller machine, in other words a cashpoint.

CR stands for credit. It indicates that money has been received into the bank account.

Banks put a D after the balance if it is negative. It means the account is overdrawn. More money has been spent than was in the account.

This is part of Jake's next statement.

Date	Payment type and details	Paid out	Paid in	Balance	
09 Aug	Balance brought forward			812.16	D

(a) Does Jake have more or less in his account than he did on 20th July? By how much?

(b) These are the next few payments and credits. Write them as they would appear on his bank statement.

On 10th August, Jake's standing order is paid into his savings account.

On 12th August, the direct debit for Jake's TV licence is paid. The amount is £11.41.

On 14th August, Jake's friend pays him his half of the holiday cost.

Jake puts the money straight into his bank account.

At 7:30 p.m. on 15th August, Jake takes out £40 from his local cashpoint.

On 17th August, Jake's salary is paid into his account.

On 20th August, the standing order for Jake's rent comes out of his account.

Also on 20th August, Jake pays for his shopping with his debit card.

He spends £36.92.

The code for his debit card is MAE.

9 Fractions

Subject links
- PHSE
- design and technology

Coming up ...

- finding equivalent fractions
- writing a fraction in its lowest terms
- converting a simple decimal to a fraction
- adding and subtracting simple fractions
- multiplying a fraction by an integer
- finding a fraction of an amount

Do you remember?
- how to read and write fractions
- multiplication tables up to 10×10
- inverse operations

Chapter starter

$\frac{1}{4}$ of this rectangle is blue.

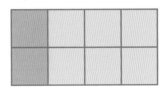

1 Copy the rectangle.

Colour squares to show a fraction with the same numerator but a different denominator.

How many different fractions can you show?

Use a new diagram to show each fraction.

2 How many fractions with a numerator of 1 and different denominators can you show using these rectangles?

(a)  (b)

Key words
fraction
numerator
denominator
equivalent fractions
cancel
lowest terms
decimal

In this rectangle 4 squares out of 12 are blue so $\frac{4}{12}$ is blue.

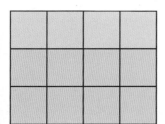

In this rectangle 1 row out of 3 is blue so $\frac{1}{3}$ is blue.

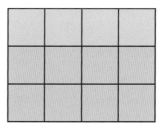

But in both rectangles, the same amount is blue so $\frac{4}{12}$ is the same as $\frac{1}{3}$ or $\frac{4}{12} = \frac{1}{3}$.

You say that $\frac{4}{12}$ and $\frac{1}{3}$ are **equivalent fractions**.

Equivalent fractions can be found by multiplying or dividing the numerator and the denominator by the same number.

Here are some fractions equivalent to $\frac{12}{16}$.

$$\overset{\div 2}{\frac{12}{16} = \frac{6}{8}}\underset{\div 2}{} \qquad \overset{\div 4}{\frac{12}{16} = \frac{3}{4}}\underset{\div 4}{} \qquad \overset{\times 2}{\frac{12}{16} = \frac{24}{32}}\underset{\times 2}{} \qquad \overset{\times 100}{\frac{12}{16} = \frac{1200}{1600}}\underset{\times 100}{}$$

Example

Copy and complete this to show equivalent fractions.

$$\frac{2}{9} = \frac{\square}{27}$$

You are given both the denominators. How do you get from 9 to 27?

Solution

$$\overset{\times 3}{\frac{2}{9} = \frac{6}{27}}\underset{\times 3}{}$$

To make equivalent fractions you must multiply (or divide) the numerator and the denominator by the same number.

9 has been multiplied by 3 to give 27.

When you write a fraction as an equivalent fraction using smaller numbers you are **simplifying** the fraction.

To simplify a fraction you divide the numerator and the denominator by the same number.

This is called **cancelling**.

$$\overset{\div 2}{\frac{4}{12} = \frac{2}{6}}\underset{\div 2}{}$$

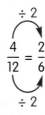
Continued ...

You can divide the numerator and the denominator by 2 again.

When you write a fraction as an equivalent fraction using the smallest possible numbers, you are writing the fraction in its **simplest form** or in its **lowest terms**.

$\frac{4}{12}$ in its lowest terms is $\frac{1}{3}$.

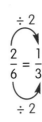

$$\div 2$$
$$\frac{2}{6} = \frac{1}{3}$$
$$\div 2$$

Example

Write $\frac{72}{80}$ in its lowest terms.

Solution

You can cancel in small steps.

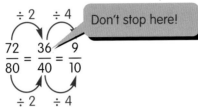

$$\div 2 \quad \div 4$$

Don't stop here!

$$\frac{72}{80} = \frac{36}{40} = \frac{9}{10}$$

$$\div 2 \quad \div 4$$

Or you can cancel in one step by dividing both numbers by 8.

$$\div 8$$
$$\frac{72}{80} = \frac{9}{10}$$
$$\div 8$$

The answer to a problem may be a fraction.
It is good practice to write that fraction in its lowest terms.

Now try these 19.1

1 Copy and complete these to show equivalent fractions.

(a) $\frac{1}{5} = \frac{2}{\square}$

(b) $\frac{3}{4} = \frac{\square}{12}$

(c) $\frac{5}{6} = \frac{10}{\square}$

(d) $\frac{1}{8} = \frac{\square}{40}$

(e) $\frac{4}{7} = \frac{\square}{21}$

(f) $\frac{7}{10} = \frac{\square}{100}$

(g) $\frac{1}{2} = \frac{15}{\square}$

(h) $\frac{6}{7} = \frac{\square}{35}$

(i) $\frac{1}{3} = \frac{\square}{24}$

(j) $\frac{3}{4} = \frac{\square}{36}$

2 Which of these fractions is the larger?

(a) $\frac{1}{2}$ or $\frac{3}{8}$

(b) $\frac{2}{3}$ or $\frac{5}{9}$

(c) $\frac{2}{3}$ or $\frac{3}{4}$

(d) $\frac{5}{6}$ or $\frac{6}{7}$

3 Write these fractions in their lowest terms.

(a) $\frac{2}{6}$

(b) $\frac{4}{8}$

(c) $\frac{6}{9}$

(d) $\frac{9}{12}$

(e) $\frac{10}{16}$

(f) $\frac{10}{25}$

(g) $\frac{4}{16}$

(h) $\frac{15}{25}$

(i) $\frac{12}{15}$

(j) $\frac{18}{20}$

(k) $\frac{18}{24}$

(l) $\frac{20}{60}$

(m) $\frac{9}{27}$

(n) $\frac{16}{40}$

(o) $\frac{30}{45}$

(p) $\frac{8}{36}$

(q) $\frac{18}{45}$

(r) $\frac{50}{100}$

(s) $\frac{28}{70}$

(t) $\frac{33}{36}$

Continued ...

For questions **4** to **6**, write your answers as fractions in their lowest terms.

4 In a class of 27 pupils, 24 had breakfast this morning.
What fraction had breakfast?

5 In a school there are 1400 pupils and 100 teachers.
What fraction of the school are teachers?

6 A group of 24 people are asked whether they liked watching football or rugby best.
These are the results.

Football	Rugby	No preference
12	8	4

(a) What fraction liked watching football best?

(b) What fraction liked watching rugby best?

(c) What fraction had no preference?

(d) You did the survey to decide where the group should go for its next outing.
Why is writing the results as fractions in their lowest terms not the best way to display the results of your survey?

19.2 Converting a decimal to a fraction

In Chapter 6 you learned that the digits to the right of the decimal point represents tenths, hundredths, thousandths, and so on.

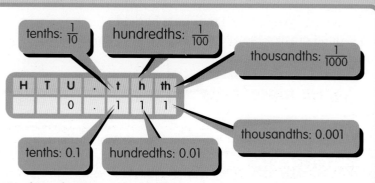

You can use a place value table to convert a decimal to a fraction.

Example

Convert these decimals to fractions in their lowest terms.

(a) 0.7   **(b)** 0.02   **(c)** 0.39

Solution

(a)

H	T	U	.	t	h	th
		0	.	7		

$0.7 = \frac{7}{10}$

Cancel down to the lowest terms

(b)

H	T	U	.	t	h	th
		0	.	0	2	

$0.02 = \frac{2}{100} = \frac{1}{50}$ so $0.02 = \frac{1}{50}$

$\div 2$

$\div 2$

Continued

(c) There are two ways to work this out.

In Chapter 1 you learnt that $39 \div 100 = 0.39$.

You also know $39 \div 100 = \frac{39}{100}$.

So $0.39 = \frac{39}{100}$.

Alternatively, you can use your knowledge of equivalent fractions.

H	T	U	.	t	h	th
		0	.	3	9	

$0.39 = \frac{3}{10} + \frac{9}{100}$

$$\frac{3}{10} \overset{\times 10}{\underset{\times 10}{=}} \frac{30}{100}$$

So $0.39 = \frac{39}{100}$.

Now try these 19.2

1 Convert these decimals to fractions in their lowest terms.

(a) 0.5	**(b)** 0.9	**(c)** 0.2	**(d)** 0.25	**(e)** 0.75	**(f)** 0.06
(g) 0.15	**(h)** 0.16	**(i)** 0.99	**(j)** 0.45	**(k)** 0.08	**(l)** 0.64
(m) 0.09	**(n)** 0.95	**(o)** 0.68	**(p)** 0.005	**(q)** 0.002	**(r)** 0.293

2 Decide whether these are true or false. Give a reason for your answer.

(a) $0.5 = \frac{3}{4}$	**(b)** $0.4 = \frac{8}{20}$	**(c)** $0.25 = \frac{2}{8}$	**(d)** $0.1 = \frac{3}{30}$	**(e)** $0.05 = \frac{1}{20}$	**(f)** $0.7 = \frac{12}{20}$
(g) $0.75 = \frac{12}{16}$	**(h)** $0.6 = \frac{40}{50}$	**(i)** $0.35 = \frac{70}{200}$	**(j)** $0.04 = \frac{6}{50}$	**(k)** $0.2 = \frac{7}{42}$	**(l)** $0.03 = \frac{3}{10}$

19.3 Adding and subtracting fractions

Look at this diagram.

In total, $\frac{3}{5}$ has been coloured.

3 out of 5 squares have been coloured.

$\frac{2}{5}$ of the rectangle has been coloured pink.

$\frac{1}{5}$ of the rectangle has been coloured blue.

This shows that $\frac{2}{5} + \frac{1}{5} = \frac{3}{5}$.

From this calculation, you know the answer to two other calculations.

$\frac{3}{5} - \frac{1}{5} = \frac{2}{5}$ — The total amount coloured take away the blue part leaves the pink part.

Continued ...

and $\frac{3}{5} - \frac{2}{5} = \frac{1}{5}$ — The total amount coloured take away the pink part leaves the blue part.

Now look at this diagram.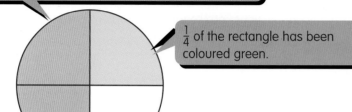

$\frac{2}{4}$ or $\frac{1}{2}$ of the circle has been coloured purple.

$\frac{1}{4}$ of the rectangle has been coloured green.

In total, $\frac{3}{4}$ has been coloured.

3 out of 4 parts have been coloured.

This shows that $\frac{1}{2} + \frac{1}{4} = \frac{3}{4}$.

From this calculation, you know the answer to two other calculations.

$\frac{3}{4} - \frac{1}{2} = \frac{1}{4}$ — The total amount coloured take away the purple part leaves the green part.

and $\frac{3}{4} - \frac{1}{4} = \frac{1}{2}$ — The total amount coloured take away the green part leaves the purple part.

If fractions have the same denominator, you say they have a **common denominator**.

To add fractions that have a common denominator
● add the numerators to get the numerator of the answer
● use the common denominator as the denominator of the answer.

Example
Work out $\frac{3}{7} + \frac{2}{7}$.

Solution
$\frac{3}{7} + \frac{2}{7} = \frac{5}{7}$ — Three sevenths + two sevenths = five sevenths.

To subtract fractions that have a common denominator
● subtract the numerators to get the numerator of the answer
● use the common denominator as the denominator of the answer.

Example
Work out $\frac{11}{12} - \frac{1}{12}$.

Solution

Eleven twelfths – one twelfth = ten twelfths.

$\frac{11}{12} - \frac{1}{12} = \frac{10}{12}$

$= \frac{5}{6}$

$\div 2$

$\frac{10}{12} = \frac{5}{6}$

$\div 2$

1 Work out these.

(a) $\frac{1}{5} + \frac{1}{5}$ (b) $\frac{3}{11} + \frac{4}{11}$ (c) $\frac{2}{9} + \frac{1}{9}$ (d) $\frac{1}{12} + \frac{5}{12} + \frac{1}{12}$

2 Work out these.

(a) $\frac{2}{5} - \frac{1}{5}$ (b) $\frac{6}{7} - \frac{2}{7}$ (c) $\frac{5}{8} - \frac{3}{8}$ (d) $\frac{7}{10} - \frac{3}{10}$

3 Work out $\frac{1}{2} + \frac{1}{8}$.

4 Work out $\frac{3}{4} - \frac{5}{8}$.

5 Brain strain

Work out $\frac{4}{5} - \frac{1}{2}$.

6 Kate has $\frac{1}{2}$ a litre of orange juice and $\frac{1}{4}$ of a litre of apple juice.

How much juice does she have altogether?

7 James has $\frac{3}{4}$ kilograms of flour.

He uses $\frac{1}{4}$ kilogram to make a cake.

How much flour does he have left?

8 Maisie has 1 litre of milk.

She drinks $\frac{1}{4}$ of a litre.

How much milk does she have left?

19.4 Multiplying a fraction by an integer

Look at this diagram.

$\frac{1}{5}$ of the rectangle is orange.

In this diagram, twice as many squares are orange.

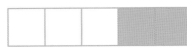

$\frac{2}{5}$ of the rectangle is orange.

This shows that $\frac{1}{5} \times 2 = \frac{2}{5}$.

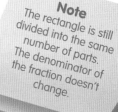

Note
The rectangle is still divided into the same number of parts. The denominator of the fraction doesn't change.

Now look at these diagrams.

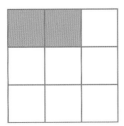 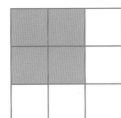

These show that $\frac{2}{9} \times 2 = \frac{4}{9}$.

To multiply a fraction by an integer

● multiply the numerator by the integer

● use the denominator of the fraction as the denominator of the answer.

Example

Work out $\frac{2}{15} \times 4$.

Solution

$2 \times 4 = 8$

$\frac{2}{15} \times 4 = \frac{8}{15}$

The denominator doesn't change.

① Work out these.

(a) $\frac{1}{7} \times 5$ (b) $\frac{1}{9} \times 7$ (c) $\frac{1}{10} \times 3$ (d) $\frac{1}{8} \times 6$

② Work out these.

(a) $\frac{3}{8} \times 2$ (b) $\frac{3}{17} \times 4$ (c) $\frac{3}{20} \times 4$ (d) $\frac{4}{25} \times 5$

③ Lee uses $\frac{1}{4}$ of a litre of paint to paint one door of a cupboard.

How much paint does he use to paint three of the doors?

④ In a relay race, a team of four runners each runs $\frac{1}{5}$ km.

How far does the team run altogether?

⑤ Sandra sends a parcel containing a Christmas present to one of her nieces.

It weighs $\frac{1}{2}$ kg.

She sends identical presents to each of her other four nieces.

How much do her parcels weigh in total?

19.5 Finding a fraction of an amount

16 sweets are shared equally between two people.

Each person will get $\frac{1}{2}$ of the sweets.

Each person will get 8 sweets.

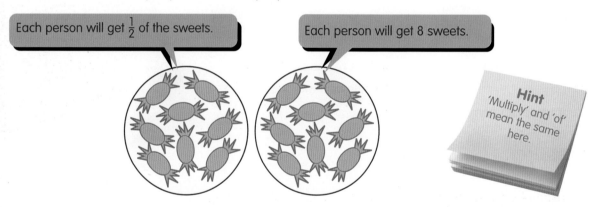

Hint
'Multiply' and 'of' mean the same here.

This shows that $\frac{1}{2}$ of 16 = 8 or $\frac{1}{2} \times 16 = 8$.
You can find $\frac{1}{2}$ of 16 by working out 16 ÷ 2.

So finding $\frac{1}{2}$ of an amount is the same as dividing by 2.

21 sweets are shared equally between three people.

Each person will get $\frac{1}{3}$ of the sweets.

Each person will get 7 sweets.

Continued ...

This shows that $\frac{1}{3}$ of 21 = 7 or $\frac{1}{3} \times 21 = 7$.

You can find $\frac{1}{3}$ of 21 by working out 21 ÷ 3.

So finding $\frac{1}{3}$ of an amount is the same as dividing by 3.

Similarly,

● finding $\frac{1}{4}$ of an amount is the same as dividing by 4

● finding $\frac{1}{5}$ of an amount is the same as dividing by 5

● and so on.

Notice that the number you divide by is the denominator of the fraction.

Example

Find $\frac{1}{8}$ of 56.

Solution

$\frac{1}{8}$ of 56 = 7.

> Finding $\frac{1}{8}$ of an amount is the same as dividing by 8.
> So 56 ÷ 8 = 7.

Example

Sam wants to buy a new pair of trainers costing £65.

His mum agrees to pay $\frac{1}{5}$ of the price.

How much does his mum give him?

Solution

$\frac{1}{5}$ of £65 = £13.

> Finding $\frac{1}{5}$ of an amount is the same as dividing by 5.
> So 65 ÷ 5 = 13.

> Don't forget to include the units.

> **Hint**
> Don't forget, it is a good idea to check your answer. You can work backwards from your answer.
> £13 × 5 = £65

All the fractions you have worked with in this section so far have had a numerator of 1.

They are called **unit fractions**.

For example, $\frac{1}{8}$ and $\frac{1}{5}$ are unit fractions.

To find, for example, $\frac{3}{5}$ of an amount, you can use the fact that $\frac{3}{5}$ is $3 \times \frac{1}{5}$.

Example

Find $\frac{3}{5} \times 45$.

Solution

$\frac{3}{5} \times 45 = 3 \times \frac{1}{5} \times 45$

> $\frac{1}{5} \times 45 = 45 ÷ 5 = 9$

$= 3 \times 9$

$= 27$

1. Work out these.

(a) $\frac{1}{3}$ of 30　　(b) $\frac{1}{6} \times 24$　　(c) $\frac{1}{5} \times 40$　　(d) $\frac{1}{10}$ of 70　　(e) $\frac{2}{3}$ of 15

(f) $\frac{3}{4}$ of 32　　(g) $\frac{3}{5} \times 35$　　(h) $20 \times \frac{1}{2}$　　(i) $\frac{7}{8} \times 64$　　(j) $28 \times \frac{3}{7}$

2. How many months are there in $\frac{2}{3}$ of a year?

3. Holly goes shopping with £48 in her purse.

   She buys things with $\frac{5}{6}$ of her money.

   How much does she spend?

4. Daisy has an MP3 player that can store 500 tracks.

   She has filled $\frac{3}{5}$ of the memory.

   How many tracks has she stored?

5. Sophie is making Christmas decorations.

   She has 2 metres of ribbon.

   Each decoration takes $\frac{1}{10}$ of the ribbon.

   What length of ribbon is used for each decoration?

6. **Brain strain**

   Alec draws an angle that is $\frac{4}{9}$ of a right angle. What angle does he draw?

Units of measurement

Coming up ...

- recognising units of length, mass, capacity and money
- reading and interpreting scales
- converting from one metric unit to another
- interpreting the answer on a calculator display

Do you remember?

- how to measure a line to the nearest millimetre
- how to multiply by 10, 100 and 1000
- how to add, subtract, multiply and divide integers and decimals

Chapter starter

The words on the cards are all connected with measuring.

Arrange the words into groups.

How many different ways can you think of to classify them?

Do some words fit into more than one category?

Do some words not fit into any of your categories?

Try to add more words to your categories.

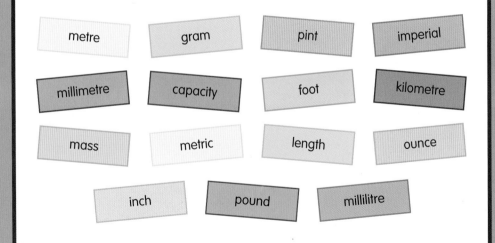

metre · gram · pint · imperial · millimetre · capacity · foot · kilometre · mass · metric · length · ounce · inch · pound · millilitre

Key words

metric	mass
imperial	gram (g)
length	kilogram (kg)
millimetre (mm)	pound (lb)
centimetre (cm)	ounce (oz)
metre (m)	capacity
kilometre (km)	millilitre (ml)
inch	centilitre (cl)
foot	litre (l)
yard	pint
mile	gallon

You are probably familiar with many units used for measuring length, mass and capacity.

There are two systems of measurements: **metric** units and **imperial** (old) units.

Mass

Mass is a measure of how heavy something is.

These are the units of mass and their abbreviations.

Metric	Imperial
gram (g)	ounce (oz)
kilogram (kg)	pound (lb)
	stone (st)

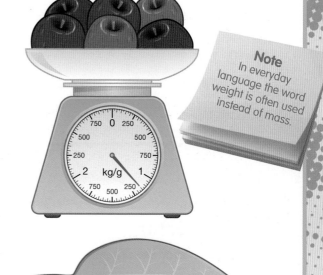

Note
In everyday language the word weight is often used instead of mass.

Length

These are the units of length and their abbreviations.

Metric	Imperial
millimetre (mm)	inch
centimetre (cm)	foot (ft)
metre (m)	yard (yd)
kilometre (km)	mile

Capacity

Capacity is a measure of the volume taken up by a liquid or gas.

These are the units of capacity and their abbreviations.

Metric	Imperial
millilitre (ml)	fluid ounces (fl oz)
litres (sometimes	pints
abbreviated to l)	gallons

① What would be suitable units to measure the following?

Give a metric unit and an imperial unit for each.

(a) Your height

(b) The mass of a packet of crisps

(c) The distance from London to Birmingham

(d) The amount of water in a full bath

(e) The thickness of a sheet of paper

(f) Your mass

② **Puzzle**

Imagine a can of lemonade.

(a) Estimate the height of the can in centimetres.

(b) Estimate the mass of the can in grams.

(c) Estimate the capacity of the can in centilitres.

Compare your answers with three other people.
Can you agree on a good estimate?
Try to find the actual answers to see how good your estimates are.

20.2 Using scales

You need to be able to read scales not only in your school subjects but also in everyday life.

As you learnt in Chapter 16 when reading graph scales, you must identify what each division of the scale represents.

Look back at the pictures in the previous section.

The leaf is 5 cm and 6 millimetres long.

You can also say it is 5.6 cm long or 56 mm long.

The apples weigh 1 kilogram and 150 grams.

You can also say they weigh 1.150 kg or 1150 g.

The jug contains approximately 750 ml of liquid.

You can't give an accurate measurement in this case.

What do these scales read?

1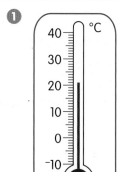

2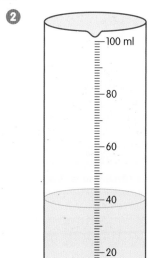

3

4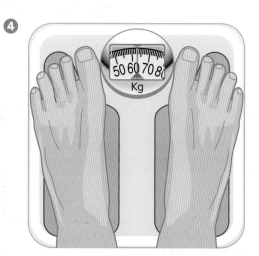

With a friend

Measure some of the objects around you.

Record your results in a table like this.

There are some suggestions in the table to get you started.

Object	Measurement	Unit
Length of my table		
Thickness of my textbook		
Mass of my textbook		
Contents of my water bottle		

Mrs Crawford asks the class what result they got when they measured their tables.

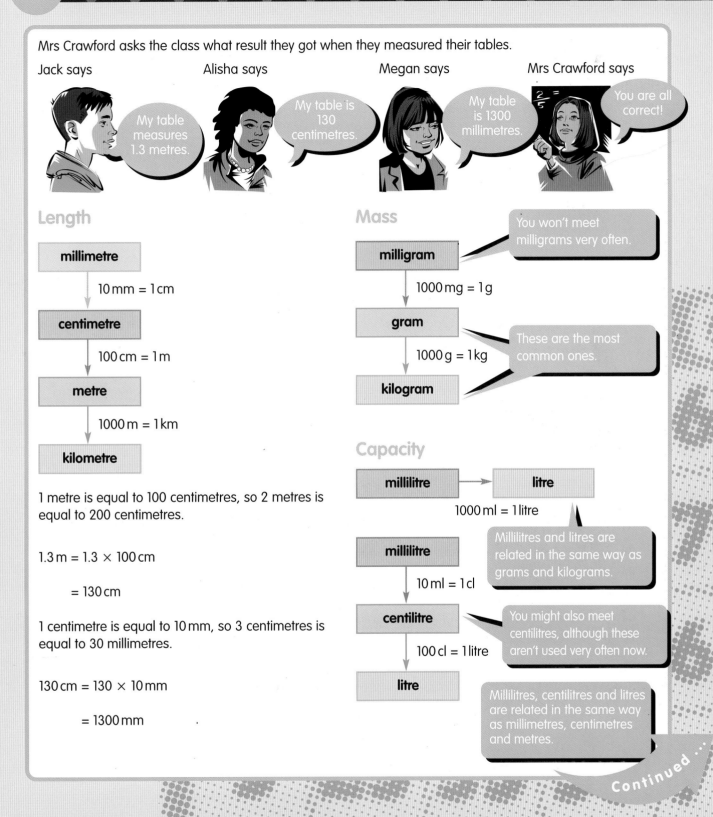

Jack says

My table measures 1.3 metres.

Alisha says

My table is 130 centimetres.

Megan says

My table is 1300 millimetres.

Mrs Crawford says

You are all correct!

Length

| millimetre |

10 mm = 1 cm

| centimetre |

100 cm = 1 m

| metre |

1000 m = 1 km

| kilometre |

1 metre is equal to 100 centimetres, so 2 metres is equal to 200 centimetres.

1.3 m = 1.3 × 100 cm

= 130 cm

1 centimetre is equal to 10 mm, so 3 centimetres is equal to 30 millimetres.

130 cm = 130 × 10 mm

= 1300 mm

Mass

| milligram |

You won't meet milligrams very often.

1000 mg = 1 g

| gram |

These are the most common ones.

1000 g = 1 kg

| kilogram |

Capacity

| millilitre | ⟶ | litre |

1000 ml = 1 litre

Millilitres and litres are related in the same way as grams and kilograms.

| millilitre |

10 ml = 1 cl

| centilitre |

You might also meet centilitres, although these aren't used very often now.

100 cl = 1 litre

| litre |

Millilitres, centilitres and litres are related in the same way as millimetres, centimetres and metres.

Continued ...

You need to be able to convert from one unit to another.

Example

(a) How many grams is 3.6 kg?

(b) Convert 900 millilitres to litres.

(c) Sam and Harry planted acorns one autumn.

They measure their trees each year.

This year Sam's tree is 2.3 m tall.

Harry's tree is 252 cm tall.

Whose tree is taller?

Solution

(a) 3.6 kg = 3.6 × 1000 g

= 3600 g

> 1 kg = 1000 g

(b) 900 ml = 900 ÷ 1000 litre

= 0.9 litre

> 1000 ml = 1 litre
> so 1 ml = (1 ÷ 1000) litre

(c) 2.3 m = 2.3 × 100 cm

= 230 cm

> To compare the measurements, they *must* be in the same units.

230 cm is less than 252 cm so Harry's tree is taller.

Now try these 20.3

Hint
Remember to include the units in your answer.

1 Convert these.

(a) 4 kilometres to metres

(b) 4 metres to centimetres

(c) 16 kilograms to grams

(d) 7 litres to millilitres

(e) 4.7 centimetres to millimetres

(f) 0.8 metres to centimetres

(g) 3.25 litres to millilitres.

(h) 1.2 metres to millimetres

2 Convert these.

(a) 6000 grams to kilograms

(b) 12 000 metres to kilometres

(c) 9000 millilitres to litres

(d) 1.8 litres to millilitres

(e) 7540 metres to kilometres

(f) 230 grams to kilograms

(g) 15 centimetres to metres

(h) 4 millimetres to centimetres

3 It is the law that children under 1.35 m tall must use a car seat up until their 12th birthday.

(a) Hannah is 10.
She is 1.5 m tall.
Must she use a car seat?
Give reasons for your answers.

(b) Sarah is 12.
She is 130 cm tall.
Must she use a car seat?

(c) Amanda is 11.
She is 134 cm tall.
Must she use a car seat?

4 Liam has a 2-litre bottle of lemonade.

He pours drinks for himself and two friends.
The glasses hold 250 ml each.
How much lemonade is left in the bottle?

5 The Smiths' cat had three kittens.

The Smith children weighed them.
Blackie weighs $\frac{1}{2}$ kg.
Tabitha weighs 386 g.
Tiger weighs 0.62 kg.
Put the kittens in order of mass, lightest first.

Continued ...

A metre square is a square with sides of 1 metre.

A centimetre square is a square with sides of 1 cm.

(a) How many centimetre squares will fit inside a metre square?

(b) How many millimetre squares will fit inside a metre square?

20.4 Units on a calculator

As well as the units in this chapter, you have also met units of money, temperature and time.

A calculator cannot tell you the units of your answer.
You have to interpret the result yourself.

Example

Use a calculator to work out the answers to these.

(a) Find the cost of 5 tickets to the cinema at £3.50 a ticket.

(b) The total mass of 4 quadruplets is 70 kg.

What is the mean mass of the quadruplets?

Give your answer in kilograms and grams.

(c) After 20 return journeys to work a teacher has travelled 350 kilometres.

How long was each return journey?

Solution

For each of the questions, the calculator display shows this.

17.5

You need to consider the units involved.
Then you need to write the answer in a suitable form.

(a) The total cost of the tickets is £17.50.

> The answer is in pounds.
> £17.5 is not a suitable written answer.
> The 5 represents 0.5 of a pound which is
> $0.5 \times 100p = 50p$.

Hint
Real amounts of money that are not whole numbers of pounds must have two decimal places.

(b) The mean mass of the quadruplets is 17 kilograms and 500 grams.

> The answer is in kilograms.
> 17.5 kg is a correct answer but you are asked to give your answer in kilograms and grams.
> $0.5 kg = 0.5 \times 1000 g = 500 g$

(c) Each return journey is 17.5 km.

> The answer is in kilometres.
> 17.5 kilometres is a suitable answer.

1 This calculator display shows the result of a calculation.

| 2.5 |

Write the result
(a) as a sum of money
(b) in metres and centimetres
(c) in kilograms and grams
(d) in litres.

2 This calculator display shows the result of a calculation.

| 48.07 |

Write the result
(a) as a sum of money
(b) in metres and centimetres
(c) in litres and millimetres.

3 This calculator display shows the result of a calculation.

| 0.75 |

(a) If the units of the result is £, write the answer in pence.
(b) If the units of the result is kilograms, write the answer in grams.
(c) If the units of the result is metres, write the answer in centimetres.

4 Steve buys four portions of burger and chips at £2.35 each.

How much does he pay?

5 Robin cuts a piece of tape that is 98 cm long into 5 equal pieces.

How long is each piece?

Give your answer in centimetres and millimetres.

6 A supermarket receives 40 packs of cereal.

The total mass is 50.4 kg.

How much does each pack weigh?

Give your answer in kilograms and grams.

Transformations

Coming up …

- reflecting shapes
- rotating shapes
- translating shapes

Do you remember?
- how to recognise reflection symmetry
- how to recognise rotation symmetry

Chapter starter

A tessellation is created when a shape is repeated over and over again without any gaps or overlaps.

Look at the tessellation drawn below on a centimetre square grid.
It is made up entirely of this shape.

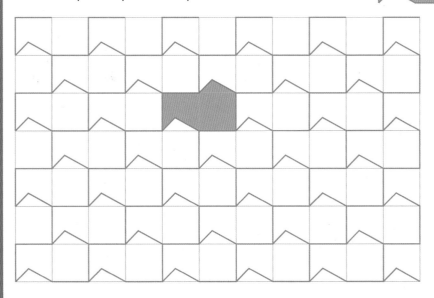

Key words

transformation
tessellation
origin
object
image
reflection
reflect
line of symmetry
axis of symmetry
mirror line
congruent
vertex (plural: vertices)
rotation
rotate
centre of rotation
translation
translate

1 Does the purple shape have reflection symmetry?

2 Does the purple shape have rotation symmetry?

3 Imagine sliding one of the shapes 3 cm to the right and 1 cm down.

It lands exactly on top of another identical shape.

In what other ways can you move one shape on top of another one?

Continued …

4 Draw your own tessellation by following these steps.

- Take a piece of squared paper and draw a simple shape on one side of one of the squares.

- Trace the shape on a piece of tracing paper and slide it to the opposite side of the square.

- Draw a simple shape on the top of the square.

- Trace the shape on a piece of tracing paper and slide it to the opposite side of the square.

- Trace the whole of the shape and slide it horizontally to the right.
  Your shapes should fit together perfectly.

- Continue moving your shape horizontally and vertically to create a tessellation as large as you like.

- You can colour your tessellation.

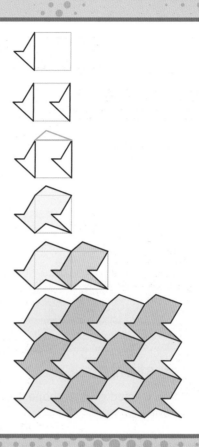

21.1 Reflecting shapes

Reflection is a type of **transformation**.

When an **object** is reflected, the reflection is called the **image**.

The image is exactly the same shape and size as the object but it has been flipped over.

When two shapes are exactly the same shape and size they are **congruent**.

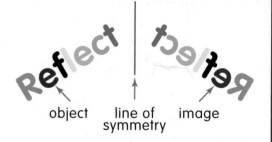

object   line of   image
symmetry

Example

Copy this diagram.

Reflect the triangle in the *y* axis.

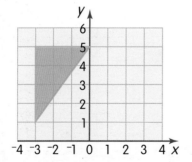

Continued ...

Solution

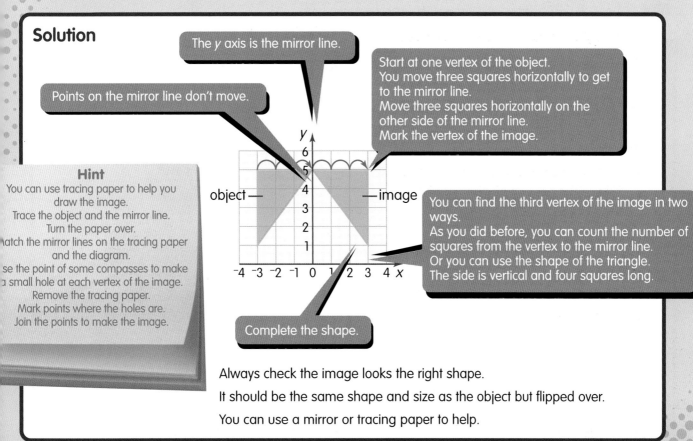

The y axis is the mirror line.

Points on the mirror line don't move.

Start at one vertex of the object.
You move three squares horizontally to get to the mirror line.
Move three squares horizontally on the other side of the mirror line.
Mark the vertex of the image.

Hint
You can use tracing paper to help you draw the image.
Trace the object and the mirror line.
Turn the paper over.
Match the mirror lines on the tracing paper and the diagram.
Use the point of some compasses to make a small hole at each vertex of the image.
Remove the tracing paper.
Mark points where the holes are.
Join the points to make the image.

You can find the third vertex of the image in two ways.
As you did before, you can count the number of squares from the vertex to the mirror line.
Or you can use the shape of the triangle.
The side is vertical and four squares long.

Complete the shape.

Always check the image looks the right shape.

It should be the same shape and size as the object but flipped over.

You can use a mirror or tracing paper to help.

Now try these 21.1

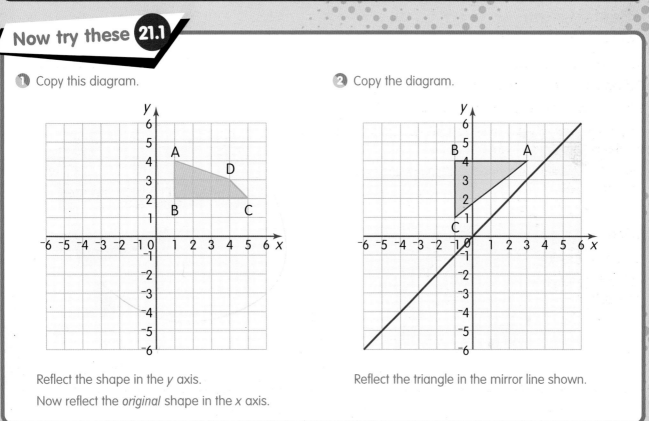

1 Copy this diagram.

2 Copy the diagram.

Reflect the shape in the y axis.

Now reflect the *original* shape in the x axis.

Reflect the triangle in the mirror line shown.

Rotation is another type of **transformation**.

When an object is rotated, it is rotated either clockwise or anticlockwise.

It can be rotated through 90°, 180° or any other angle.

The **centre of rotation** is the point it turns about.

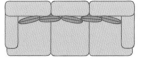

Here is a sofa.

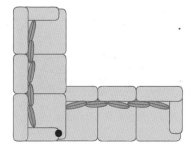

Here it is rotated 90° anticlockwise about the left armrest, at the point marked ●.

Here it is rotated through 180° about the midpoint of the back.

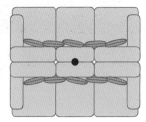

The sofa and the image of the sofa are congruent.

They are exactly the same shape but are in different positions.

Hint

When you rotate an object through 180° it is unnecessary to say whether it is rotated clockwise or anticlockwise. The image will be in the same position whether the rotation is clockwise or anticlockwise.

Example

Copy this diagram.

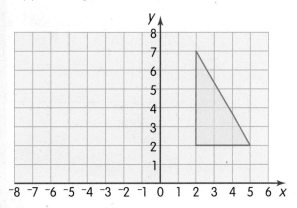

Rotate the triangle anticlockwise through 90° about the origin.

Continued ...

Solution

The origin is the centre of rotation. The centre of rotation doesn't move.

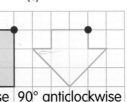

image

object

y
8
7
6
5
4
3
2
1
-8 -7 -6 -5 -4 -3 -2 -1 0 1 3 4 5 6 x

Hint
You can use tracing paper to help you draw the image.
Trace the object.
Place your pencil point or the point of some compasses on the centre of rotation.
Turn the tracing paper through a right angle in an anticlockwise direction.
Use the point of some compasses to make a small hole at each vertex of the image.
Remove the tracing paper.
Mark points where the holes are.
Join the points to make the image.

The line joining a vertex on the object to the centre of rotation is at right angles (perpendicular) to the line from the centre of rotation to the matching vertex on the image. The two lines are the same length.

**When you turn an object through 90°, all the edges of the object that are vertical will be horizontal on the image.
Similarly, all the edges that are horizontal on the object will be vertical on the image.**

Always check the image looks the right shape.

Rotate your diagram in the opposite direction to the rotation you drew.

The image should look exactly the same as the object did to start with.

The opposite of a rotation of 90° anticlockwise is a rotation of 90° clockwise.

Now try these 21.2

1 Copy these shapes and draw the rotations described.
● marks the centre of rotation.

(a)   (b)   (c)

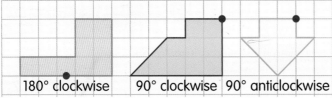

180° clockwise | 90° clockwise | 90° anticlockwise

(d)   (e)   (f)

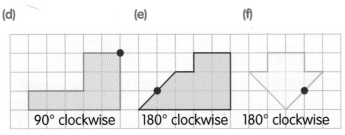

90° clockwise | 180° clockwise | 180° clockwise

2 Copy this diagram.

Rotate the triangle through 90° anticlockwise about the origin.

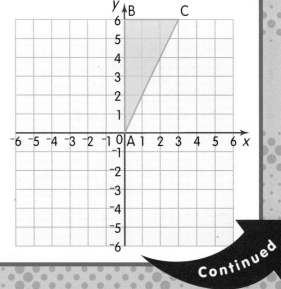

y
B   C
6
5
4
3
2
1
-6 -5 -4 -3 -2 -1 0 A 1 2 3 4 5 6 x
-1
-2
-3
-4
-5
-6

Continued ...

3 Copy the diagram.

Rotate the triangle through 90° clockwise about the origin.

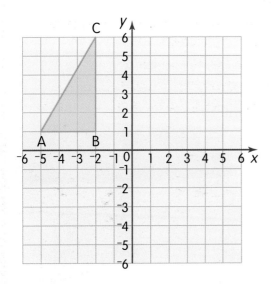

4 Copy this diagram.

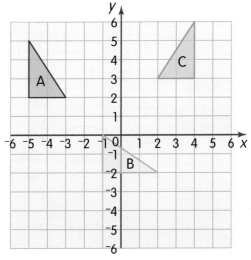

(a) Shape A has been reflected on to shape B. Draw in the mirror line.

(b) Shape B has been rotated on to shape C. Find the centre of rotation. Mark it on your diagram.

21.3 Translating shapes

Here is a tessellation.

To move shape A on to shape B, you rotate it 180° about the point marked ●.

To move shape A on to shape C, you reflect it in the red line.

To move shape A on to shape D, you slide it to the right.

To move shape A on to shape E, you slide it down.

When you slide a shape without turning it around or over, it is called a **translation**.

This is another type of transformation.

The image looks just the same as the object, but it is in a different position.

The object and image of a translation are congruent.

So A to D is a translation, A to E is a translation, A to G is a translation, ...

But A to B is not a translation, A to C is not a translation, A to H is not a translation.

Continued ...

Look at this diagram.

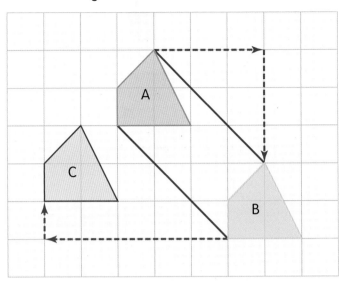

Shape A is translated on to shape B by moving three squares to the right and three squares down.

The red lines join two of the vertices of the object to the image.

They are the same length.

The translation that moves shape B on to shape C is five squares left and one square up.

Hint
You must use 'left' or 'right', not 'across' as you need to say which way you are moving.

Example

In the diagram, what translation moves

(a) shape B on to shape A?

(b) shape C on to shape A?

Solution

(a) Three squares left and three squares up.

Notice this is the opposite of the translation from A to B.

(b) Two squares right and two squares up.

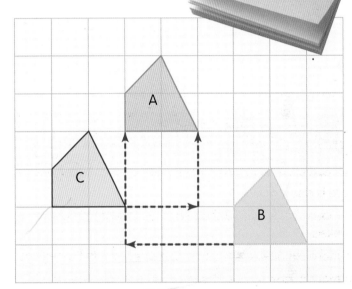

Now try these 21.3

1. In the diagram, which of the numbered shapes are translations of

   (a) shape A

   (b) shape B?

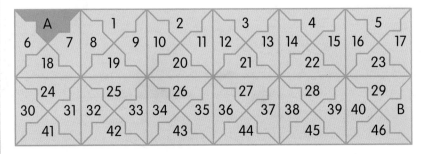

2. Copy this diagram. Translate the triangle by four squares to the right and two squares down.

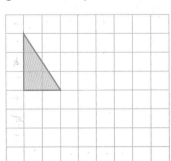

Continued ...

3 Describe the following translations:

(a) From A to D

(b) From A to C

(c) From A to E

(d) From C to E

(e) From E to A

(f) From B to D

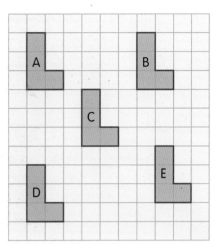

4 Brain strain

Use dotty paper or a pinboard for this question.

(a) How many different translations of the triangle are possible on this 4 by 4 grid?

(b) How many different translations are possible on a 5 by 5 grid?

(c) Investigate the number of translations that are possible on any size of grid.

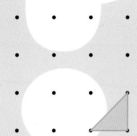

Solids

Subject links
● design and technology

Coming up ...

● identifying three-dimensional shapes
● using two-dimensional representations of three-dimensional shapes
● constructing nets of three-dimensional shapes
● finding the surface area of cubes and cuboids

Chapter starter

This shape-sorting toy is very badly designed.

A lot of the shapes can be posted through more than one hole.

1 Which of the holes can you post each of the shapes through?

2 How would you redesign the toy so that each shape can be posted through one hole only?

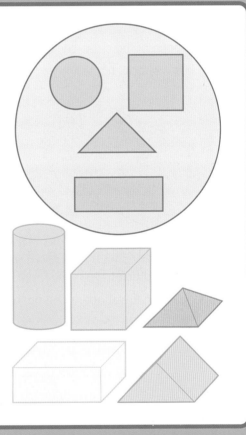

> *Do you remember?*
> ● *how to measure and draw lines*
> ● *how to construct triangles (SAS and ASA)*
> ● *how to calculate the area of a rectangle*

Key words

two-dimensional	base
three-dimensional	face
solid	edge
cube	vertex (plural: vertices)
cuboid	
prism	cross-section
cylinder	intersect
pyramid	isometric paper
tetrahedron	net
cone	surface
sphere	surface area

A **solid** is a three-dimensional shape.

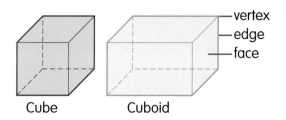

Cube   Cuboid

You will already be familiar with cubes and cuboids.
Do you know the mathematical names for different parts?

A **prism** is a solid with a uniform **cross-section**.

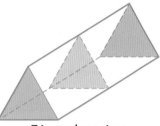

Triangular prism

The name of a prism depends on the shape of the cross-section.
A prism with a circular cross-section has a special name.

Note
Cubes and cuboids are also prisms. They have square or rectangular cross-sections.

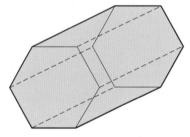   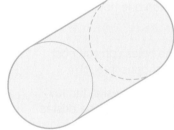

Triangular prism   Hexagonal prism   Cylinder

A **pyramid** is a solid with faces that meet at a point.

Pyramids have different names depending on the shape of the base.

A **sphere** has no straight edges.

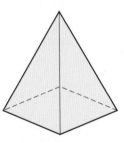   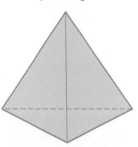      

Square-based pyramid   Tetrahedron   Cone   Sphere

Note
A tetrahedron can also be called a triangular-based pyramid

1 What are the names of these solids?

(a)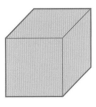

(b)

(c)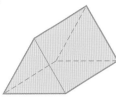

(d)

2 The Earth is, roughly, a sphere. So is a tennis ball.

Where might you see these solids in everyday life?

(a) A cube

(b) A cuboid

(c) A triangular prism

(d) A cylinder

3 Imagine a cube.

(a) What is the greatest number of faces you can see at the same time?
What is the smallest number?

(b) What is the greatest number of edges you can see at the same time?
What is the smallest number?

(c) What is the greatest number of vertices you can see at the same time?
What is the smallest number?

(d) Is it possible to see exactly six edges?

(e) Is it possible to see exactly six vertices?

4 What am I?

(a) I have six faces and they are all the same shape.

(b) I have five faces and two of them are equilateral triangles.

(c) I have six edges and four vertices.

(d) I have no flat faces.

(e) I am a pyramid with ten edges.

5 Here is a cube which has had all its corners cut off.

(a) What shape are the large faces?

(b) How many faces does the solid have?

(c) How many edges does it have?

(d) How many vertices does it have?

You can use isometric paper to draw solids.

Here is a cube drawn on isometric paper.

Its sides are 3 centimetres long.

Make sure the isometric paper is the right way round. The dots should be in vertical lines.

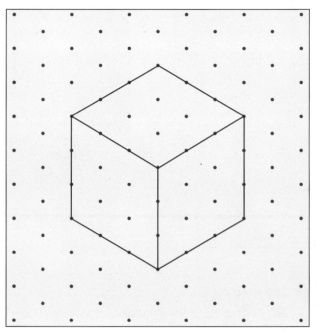

You can see that the vertical edges are vertical but the horizontal edges are drawn at angles.

This helps to make the drawing look three-dimensional.

Here is a shape made from some cubes.

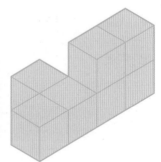

These are the two views drawn on isometric paper.

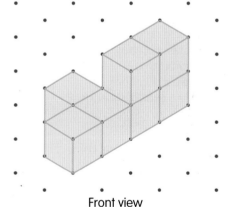

Front view

You can see seven cubes.

There might be more that you can't see.

Here is the back view of the *same* group of cubes.

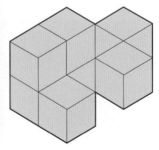

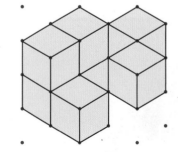

Back view

Now you can tell that there are eight cubes altogether.

1 How many cubes are there in each of these solids?

(a)

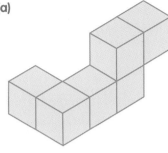

(b)

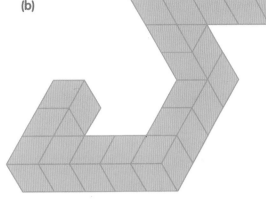

2 Ethan has tried to draw four different views of the same shape.

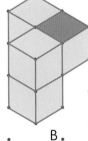

A

B

C

D

He has made a mistake.

He has drawn two different shapes.

Which drawings are of the same shape?

Make the shapes out of cubes to check.

3 Ethan sticks another cube on to each shape in question 2.

He sticks the cube on the shaded face.

Make each new shape out of cubes.

Then draw each shape on isometric paper.

4 Draw these solids on isometric paper.

(a)

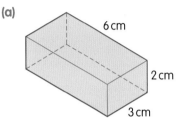

6 cm

2 cm

3 cm

(b)

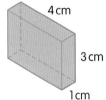

4 cm

3 cm

1 cm

(c)

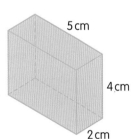

5 cm

4 cm

2 cm

(d)

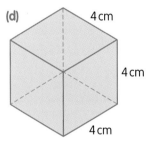

4 cm

4 cm

4 cm

(e)

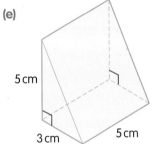

5 cm

3 cm

5 cm

22.3 Nets

A **net** is a flat shape which can be folded to make a three-dimensional shape.
Here is a net of a cube.
When it is made into a cube, the blue face is on the opposite side to the orange face.
You should be able to work out which face will be opposite the green face.
A solid can have a number of different nets.

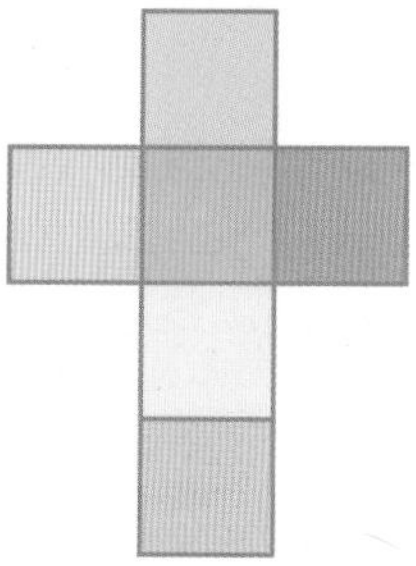

Now try these 22.3

1. Explain why each of these shapes can't be a net of a cube.

(a)

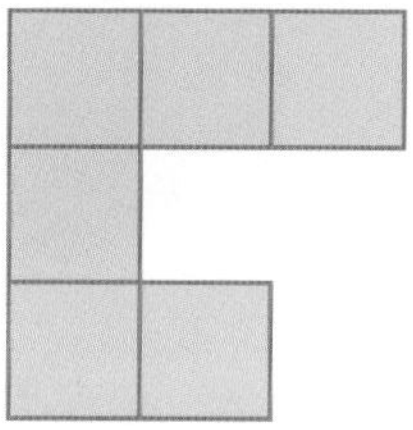

(b)

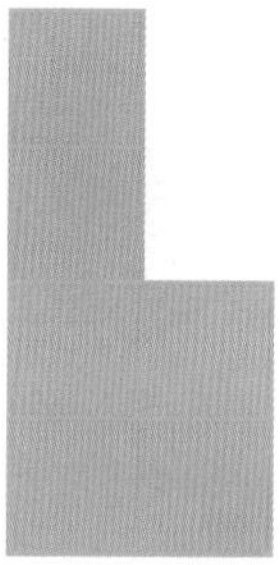

(c)

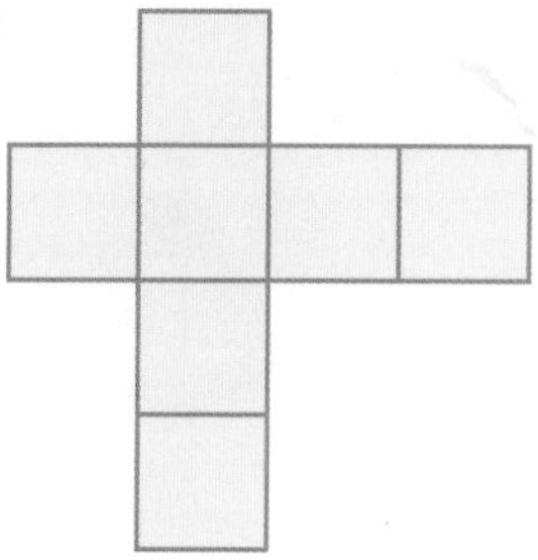

2. Pentominoes are shapes made of five squares joined edge to edge.

Here are two examples.

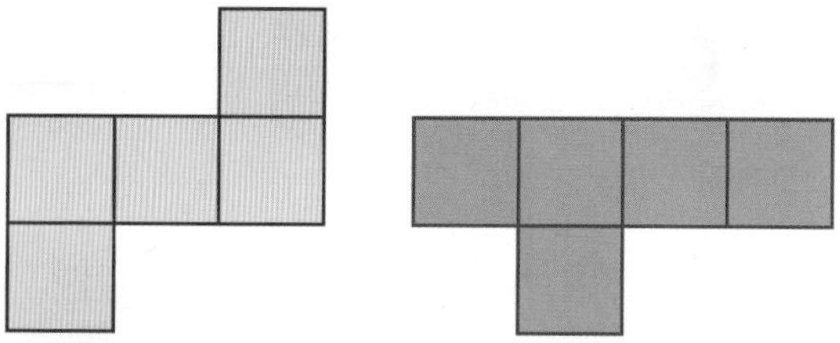

Which of the twelve possible pentominoes can be folded to make a cube without a lid?

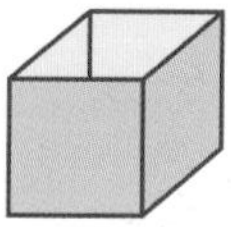

3 Puzzle

Draw three different nets of a cube.
Imagine each one is going to be made into a dice.
On your nets, write the numbers 1 to 6 on the faces.

4 Brain strain

How many different nets of a cube can you find?

5. Draw a net for each of these cuboids.

(a)

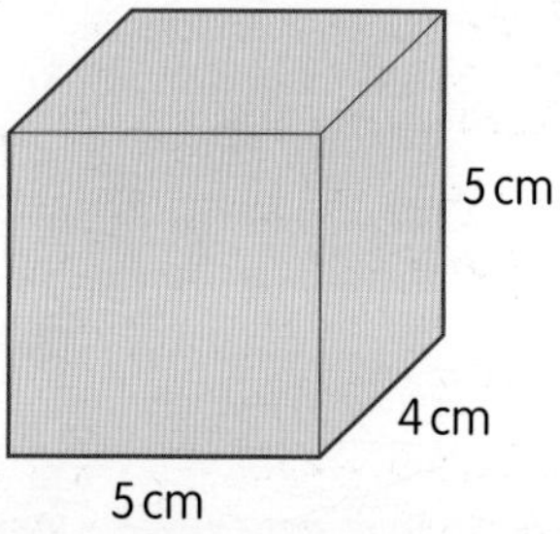
5 cm
4 cm
5 cm

(b)

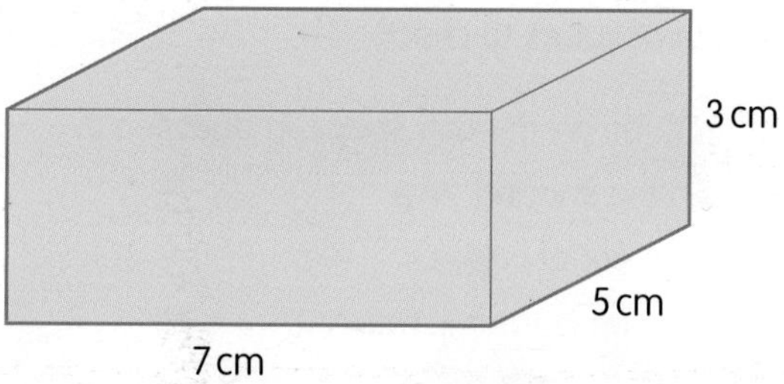
3 cm
5 cm
7 cm

Continued ...

6 A chocolate maker sells boxes of chocolates.

He wants the box to look as if there is a ribbon going all the way round the box, as in the picture.

Draw a net for the box.

Draw on the net where the 'ribbon' should be printed.

Try to make the 'ribbon' cross each edge exactly in the middle.

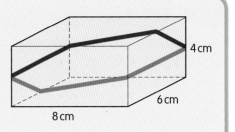

4 cm

6 cm

8 cm

7 Which of these are nets?

For those that are, name the solid they would make.

Copy them and cut them out to check.

(a)

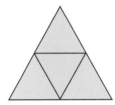

(b)

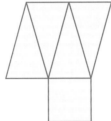

(c)

(d)

(e)

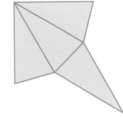

8 How can you change the shapes in question **7** that aren't nets so that they will fold to make solids?

With a friend

1 For each solid, sketch two different nets.

2 Decide who will make which net.

Use a ruler and protractor to make an accurate drawing.

3 Decide where to put the flaps.

Fold the nets to make the solids.

4 Did both nets work equally well or did one give a better result?

7 cm

60°

7 cm

Tetrahedron

All the faces are the same shape.

70°

70°

5 cm   5 cm

Square-based pyramid

All the triangular faces are the same shape.

Remember
The area of a rectangle = length × width
$A = lw$

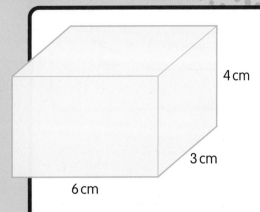

4 cm

3 cm

6 cm

Here is a cuboid.

It has six rectangular faces.

The top rectangle is 6 cm long and 3 cm wide.	Its area is 18 cm².
You can't see the bottom, but it is the same shape and size.	Its area is 18 cm².
The front is 6 cm by 4 cm.	Its area is 24 cm².
You can't see the back, but it is the same size as the front.	Its area is 24 cm².
The right-hand face is 3 cm by 4 cm.	Its area is 12 cm².
The hidden left-hand face is the same.	Its area is 12 cm².
The total surface area is	108 cm².

In the previous section you learnt about the net of a cuboid.

You can use the net to help you.

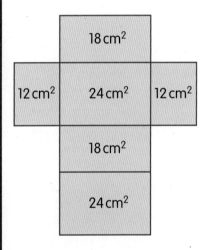

Total surface area = 18 cm² + 24 cm² + 18 cm² + 24 cm² + 12 cm² + 12 cm²
= 108 cm²

Here is another way you can use the net of the cuboid.

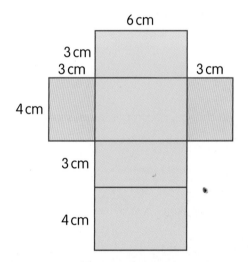

The length of the green rectangle is 3 cm + 4 cm + 3 cm + 4 cm = 14 cm.

The width is 6 cm.

Its area is 14 cm × 6 cm = 84 cm².

The end rectangles are both 3 cm × 4 cm = 12 cm².

Total surface area = 84 cm² + 12 cm² + 12 cm²
= 108 cm²

1 **(a)** On centimetre squared paper, draw a net for each of these cuboids.

(b) Find the surface area of each of the cuboids.

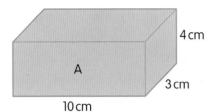

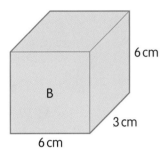

2 Look at this net of a cuboid.

(a) What are the dimensions of the cuboid the net would make?

(b) What is the surface area of the cuboid?

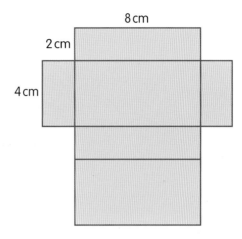

3 Design a cuboid with a surface area of 62 cm².

23 Percentages, fractions and decimals

Subject links
- science
- geography
- design and technology

Coming up …

- writing a percentage as a fraction
- writing a percentage as a decimal
- writing a fraction as a percentage
- writing a decimal as a percentage
- finding a percentage of an amount
- working with percentages using a calculator
- solving problems involving percentages

Do you remember?

- how to write one number as a fraction of another
- how to find equivalent fractions
- how to divide by 100
- how to convert a decimal to a fraction
- how to find a fraction of an amount
- how to interpret a calculator display
- how to make estimates

Chapter starter

1 In this hundred square, 50 squares are pink.

What fraction of the hundred square is pink?

Give your answer in its lowest terms.

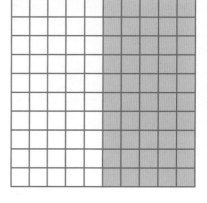

2 What fraction of this hundred square is pink?

What is this as a decimal?

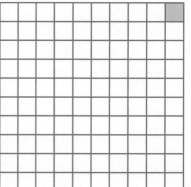

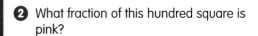

Continued …

Key words

percentage

per cent (%)

fraction

decimal

3 How many squares do you need to colour to show $\frac{1}{4}$?

What is $\frac{1}{4}$ as a decimal?

4 How many squares do you need to colour to show

(a) 0.27 (b) 0.1?

5 A children's charity explain how they spend the donations they receive.

Here's how we spend each £1 you donate.

Early childhood development	38p
Girls' education	22p
Child protection	19p
Children's health	10p
HIV and AIDS	8p
Other	3p
Total	£1.00

(a) What fraction is spent on

(i) girls' education

(ii) children's health?

Don't forget, you should give your answers in their lowest terms.

(b) Why do you think the charity don't use fractions to show how they spend the money?

Do you know of any other ways of showing these figures?

23.1 Converting percentages to fractions

Ellie's school shirt is made from a mixture of cotton and polyester.

You read % as 'per cent'.

COTTON POLYESTER MIX
80% COTTON
20% POLYESTER

Note
Cent means 100.

80% cotton means 80 parts in every 100 parts are cotton.

$80\% = \frac{80}{100}$

You learnt how to write one number as a fraction of another in Chapter 19.

20% polyester means 20 parts in every 100 parts are polyester.

$20\% = \frac{20}{100}$

Ellie's shirt is only made from cotton and polyester because

$80\% + 20\% = 100\%$

and $100\% = \frac{100}{100} = 1$ whole.

This is the label on Naomi's shirt.

PURE COTTON
100% COTTON

Her shirt is made entirely from cotton because 100% = 1 whole.

Example

In Nigeria, only 62% of women can read.

What is this as a fraction in its lowest terms?

Solution Write 62 as a fraction of 100.

$62\% = \frac{62}{100}$

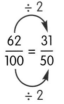

$\frac{62}{100} = \frac{31}{50}$

Cancel the fraction to its lowest terms.

$\frac{31}{50}$ of women in Nigeria can read.

1 Write these percentages as fractions in their lowest terms.

(a) 20%	**(b)** 50%	**(c)** 1%	**(d)** 12%	**(e)** 90%	**(f)** 25%
(g) 7%	**(h)** 4%	**(i)** 44%	**(j)** 60%	**(k)** 38%	**(l)** 2%
(m) 64%	**(n)** 99%	**(o)** 5%	**(p)** 14%	**(q)** 85%	**(r)** 72%

2 In a science test Nemeth scored 65%.

What fraction of the marks did he get?

3 A survey found that 18% of disabled parking bays at a supermarket were

being used by drivers who were not disabled.

What fraction is this?

4 84% of people in Britain believe that the French are better cooks than the British.

What fraction do *not* believe this?

23.2 Converting percentages to decimals

You can convert percentages to decimals by writing them as fractions then converting to decimals.

Example

Convert these percentages to decimals.

(a) 27%   **(b)** 65%   **(c)** 8%   **(d)** $32\frac{1}{2}\%$

> Write as a fraction.
> Do not cancel the fraction.
> It is easy to divide 65 by 100.
> It is not so easy to divide 13 by 20.

Solution

> Write as a fraction.

(a) $27\% = \frac{27}{100}$

> Convert to a decimal.

$= 27 \div 100$

$= 0.27$

H	T	U	.	t	h	th
	2	7	.			
		0	.	2	7	

(b) $65\% = \frac{65}{100}$

$= 65 \div 100$

> Convert to a decimal.

$= 0.65$

H	T	U	.	t	h	th
	6	5	.			
		0	.	6	5	

Continued ...

(c) $8\% = \frac{8}{100}$

$= 8 \div 100$

$= 0.08$

H	T	U	.	t	h	th
		8	.			
		0	.	0	8	

⚠ Don't forget the zero after the decimal point.
0.08 = 8%
0.8 = 80%

Write the $\frac{1}{2}$ as a decimal.

(d) $32\frac{1}{2}\% = 32.5\%$

$32.5\% = \frac{32.5}{100}$

$= 32.5 \div 100$

$= 0.325$

Write as a fraction. Don't worry about the decimal in the numerator. This is not your final answer.

H	T	U	.	t	h	th
	3	2	.	5		
		0	.	3	2	5

Now try these 23.2

❌

① Copy and complete this table.

Write the fractions in their lowest terms.

Percentage	10%	20%	30%	40%	50%	60%	70%	80%	90%	100%
Fraction										
Decimal										

② Convert these percentages to decimals.

(a) 16% **(b)** 82% **(c)** 79% **(d)** 22% **(e)** 15% **(f)** 3%

(g) 36% **(h)** 7% **(i)** 1% **(j)** 31% **(k)** 9% **(l)** 2%

(m) 17.5% **(n)** 26.8% **(o)** 6.3% **(p)** $12\frac{1}{2}\%$ **(q)** 0.1% **(r)** $3\frac{1}{2}\%$

③ If a taxpayer makes a donation to a charity, the charity can claim Gift aid from the government.

The government gives the charity 28% of the donation.

What is 28% as a decimal?

How much does the charity receive from the government when £1 is donated?

23.3 Converting fractions to percentages

You can convert fractions to percentages by writing them as equivalent fractions with a denominator of 100.

Example

(a) Convert $\frac{17}{50}$ to a percentage.

(b) Out of 600 people, 120 had sent a text message in the last hour.

What percentage had sent a text message in the last hour?

Continued …

Solution

(a)

Convert to an equivalent fraction with a denominator of 100.

$\times 2$

$$\frac{17}{50} = \frac{34}{100}$$

$\times 2$

$\frac{34}{100} = 34\%$ — 34 parts out of 100 is 34%.

(b) 120 as a fraction of 600 $= \frac{120}{600}$

$\div 6$

$$\frac{120}{600} = \frac{20}{100}$$

Convert to an equivalent fraction with a denominator of 100.

$\div 6$

$\frac{20}{100} = 20\%$ — 20 parts out of 100 is 20%.

This method will not work if the denominator can't be made into 100 by multiplying or dividing.

You can estimate percentages by converting fractions to percentages.

You will learn what to do in these cases in Year 8.

Example

Estimate how full this bottle of water is.

Give your answer as a percentage.

Solution

The bottle is about $\frac{1}{4}$ full.

$\times 25$

$$\frac{1}{4} = \frac{25}{100} = 25\%$$

$\times 25$

The bottle is about 25% full.

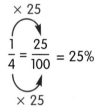

Remember
100% is 1 whole.

Example

About what percentage of the cake is left?

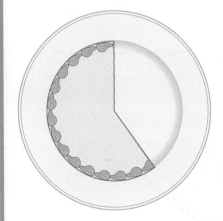

Solution

A little more than $\frac{1}{2}$ is left.

$\times 50$

$$\frac{1}{2} = \frac{50}{100} = 50\%$$

$\times 50$

About 60% of the cake is left.

You want a little more than 50%.

1. Write these fractions as percentages.

   (a) $\frac{2}{5}$ (b) $\frac{3}{10}$ (c) $\frac{1}{2}$ (d) $\frac{3}{4}$ (e) $\frac{7}{20}$

   (f) $\frac{13}{50}$ (g) $\frac{9}{25}$ (h) $\frac{90}{200}$ (i) $\frac{21}{25}$ (j) $\frac{27}{300}$

2. Estimate the percentage of these shapes that is green.

   (a) 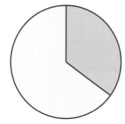   (b)   (c)

   (d) 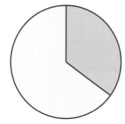   (e)   (f)

3. An advertisement for Purrfect Meals cat food claims that 8 out of 10 cats prefer their food compared to others.

   What percentage of cats prefer Purrfect Meals cat food?

4. These are Chloe's results in four assessments.

   (a) Write her results as percentages.

   (b) In which subject does Chloe do best?

Geography	18 out of 25
French	130 out of 200
ICT	41 out of 50
Mathematics	60 out of 80

5. This information appears on a 25 gram bag of crisps.

Protein	1.9 g
Carbohydrate	12.9 g
Fat	8.0 g
Fibre	1.5 g
Salt	0.7 g

   (a) Mohammed says

   32% of the crisps is fat.

   (b) Jordan says

   32% × 2 = 64%

   I've eaten two bags of these crisps. 64% of the crisps that I've eaten is fat.

   Show that Mohammed is correct.   Show that Jordan is not correct.

You can convert a decimal to a percentage by writing it as a fraction.

You may need to convert the fraction to an equivalent fraction with a denominator of 100.

Example

Write these decimals as percentages.

(a) 0.48   **(b)** 0.7   **(c)** 0.03   **(d)** 0.175

Solution

(a) $0.48 = \frac{48}{100}$ 48 hundredths

     $= 48\%$ 48 parts out of 100 is 48%.

(b) $0.7 = \frac{7}{10}$ 7 tenths

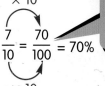

$\frac{7}{10} = \frac{70}{100} = 70\%$ Write as an equivalent fraction with a denominator of 100.

Don't write 0.7 as 7%.

(c) $0.03 = \frac{3}{100}$ 3 hundredths

     $= 3\%$

(d) $0.175 = \frac{175}{1000}$ 175 thousandths

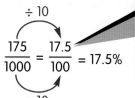

$\frac{175}{1000} = \frac{17.5}{100} = 17.5\%$ Write as an equivalent fraction with a denominator of 100. Don't worry that the numerator is a decimal.

Now try these 23.4

1 Copy and complete this table.
Write the fractions in their lowest terms.

Decimal	0.01	0.05	0.1	0.25	0.5	0.75
Fraction						
Percentage						

2 Write these decimals as percentages.

   (a) 0.13   **(b)** 0.88   **(c)** 0.2   **(d)** 0.99

   (e) 0.06   **(f)** 0.95   **(g)** 0.7   **(h)** 0.125

   (i) 0.3   **(j)** 0.356   **(k)** 0.09   **(l)** 0.375

3 Are these true or false?

   (a) $0.6 < 10\%$ **(b)** $0.85 > 79\%$ **(c)** $0.04 > 5\%$ **(d)** $24\% < 0.3$

   (e) $8\% < 0.1$ **(f)** $0.125 > 12\%$ **(g)** $99\% > 1$ **(h)** $0.005 < 1\%$

   (i) $3\% < 0.2$

One method of finding a percentage of an amount is to convert the percentage to a fraction and work out the fraction of the amount.

This is usually the best method to use if you are working without a calculator.

In section 23.1 you learnt how to write a percentage as a fraction.

It is worth remembering some simple equivalents.

$$10\% = \tfrac{1}{10} \qquad 25\% = \tfrac{1}{4} \qquad 50\% = \tfrac{1}{2} \qquad 1\% = \tfrac{1}{100}$$

Example

Work out 10% of 340.

Solution

> Change 10% to $\tfrac{1}{10}$.

10% of $340 = \tfrac{1}{10}$ of 340

$= 340 \div 10$

> To find $\tfrac{1}{10}$ of an amount you divide by 10.

$= 34$

Example

Work out 70% of 30.

> Work out 10% of 30.

> Then find 70% by multiplying by 7.

Solution

$70\% = 7 \times 10\%$

10% of $30 = \tfrac{1}{10}$ of 30

$= 30 \div 10$

$= 3$

70% of $30 = 7 \times 3$

$= 21$

Here is another way to work out 70% of 30.

$70\% = 50\% + 20\% \longrightarrow 20\% = 2 \times 10\%$

50% of $30 = \tfrac{1}{2}$ of $30 \qquad 10\%$ of $30 = \tfrac{1}{10}$ of 30

$= 30 \div 2 \qquad\qquad = 30 \div 10$

$= 15 \qquad\qquad\qquad = 3$

20% of $30 = 2 \times 3$

$= 6$

70% of $30 = 15 + 6$

$= 21$

Example

Lola gives 5% of her wages each week to charity.

She earns £90 per week.

How much does she give to charity each week?

Solution

$5\% = 10\% \div 2$

10% of £90 $=$ £90 $\div 10$

> $10\% = \tfrac{1}{10}$ so divide by 10.

$=$ £9

5% of £90 $=$ £9 $\div 2$

> $5\% = 10\% \div 2$

$=$ £4.50

> Don't forget the units.

Continued ...

Example

24 000 people attend an open air rock festival.

26% of the crowd are under 18 years old.

How many of the crowd are under 18 years old?

Solution

$$26\% = 25\% + 1\%$$

25% of 24 000 = $\frac{1}{4}$ of 24 000   1% of 24 000   = $\frac{1}{100}$ of 24 000

$$= 24\,000 \div 4$$ $$= 24\,000 \div 100$$

= (6000)   = (240)

26% of 24 000 = (6000) + (240)

$$= 6240$$

6240 people attending the festival are under 18 years old.

Now try these 23.5

① Work out these.

(a) 10% of 60   (b) 25% of 36   (c) 50% of 248   (d) 1% of 2500

(e) 20% of 120   (f) 5% of 320   (g) 75% of 24   (h) 26% of 800

(i) 40% of £75   (j) 15% of 40 g   (k) 90% of 50 m   (l) 12% of 6500 ml

② There are 1400 pupils at a school.

   51% of the pupils are girls.

   How many girls are there?

③ The price of a mobile phone is £60.

   In a sale the price is reduced by 25%.

   How much is the reduction?

④ There are 120 questions in an online music quiz.

   Each correct answer gets one point.

   Tom scores 60% and Jordan scores 65%.

   How many questions did they each answer correctly?

⑤ A magazine surveys 5000 people.

   It finds that 24% of people learn about the culture of a country before they visit it.

   How many people was this?

Continued ...

⑥ Astrid works out 35% of £280.

10% of £280 = £28
30% of £280 = 3 × £28 = £84
5% of £280 = £28 ÷ 2 = £14
35% = 30% + 5%
     = £84 + £14
     = £98

Su Ling says

I can work
the answer out with one
step fewer.

How does Su Ling work out the answer?

⑦ These are guideline daily amounts of some food types for children aged between 5 and 10 years old.

Calories	Fat	Saturates	Sugar	Fibre	Salt
1800	70 g	20 g	85 g	15 g	4 g

(a) Two slices of wholemeal bread provide 30% of the guideline daily amount of fibre.

How much fibre is in two slices of wholemeal bread?

(b) A chocolate wafer bar contains 5% of the guideline daily amount of calories.

How many calories are in the chocolate wafer bar?

(c) A bowl of whole grain cereal with semi-skimmed milk provides $12\frac{1}{2}$% of the guideline daily amount of salt.

How much salt is in the bowl of cereal with milk?

23.6 Percentages on a calculator

In the previous section, you learnt how to find a percentage of an amount without a calculator. In this section you will learn how to find the percentage of an amount using a calculator.

The example shows three different methods for finding a percentage of an amount using a calculator.

Continued ...

Example

Find 37% of £1450.

Hint
Remember it is always a good idea to make an estimate of the answer. 37% of £1450 is about $\frac{1}{3}$ of £1500.
£1500 ÷ 3 = £500

Solution

Method 1: Find 1% then find 37%

$37\% = 1\% \times 37$

1% of £1450 $= \frac{1}{100}$ of £1450

> Use your calculator to work out 1450 ÷ 100.

$= £1450 \div 100$

$= £14.50$

> Don't clear the calculator display. You can use the answer to save you keying 14.5 again.

37% of £1450 $= £14.50 \times 37$

$= £536.50$

> Use your calculator to work out 14.5 × 37.

Method 2: Writing the percentage as a fraction

37% of £1450 $= \frac{37}{100}$ of £1450

> Find $\frac{1}{100}$ of £1450 then multiply the result by 37 to find $\frac{37}{100}$.
> Use your calculator to work out 1450 ÷ 100 × 37.

$= £1450 \div 100 \times 37$

$= £536.50$

Method 3: Writing the percentage as a decimal

$37\% = 0.37$

> 'of' means 'multiply' here. Use your calculator to work out 0.37 × 1450

37% of £1450 $= 0.37 \times £1450$

$= £536.50$

Remember to interpret the calculator display. Money must have exactly two digits to the right of the decimal point if it is not a whole number of pounds.

1 Work out these.

(a) 72% of 250   (b) 45% of 80   (c) 16% of 575   (d) 93% of 4500

(e) 8% of 225   (f) 38% of 75   (g) 3% of 220   (h) 70% of 138

(i) 6% of 52   (j) 17.5% of 80   (k) $2\frac{1}{2}$% of 640   (l) 0.3% of 32 000

2 A top is 77% wool, 19% polyester and 4% lycra.

The mass of the top is 890 grams.

What mass is lycra?

3 A drink is made by mixing orange cordial and water.

The drink is 15% cordial and 85% water.

(a) Lauren makes a 240-millilitre glass of the drink.

How much water does she use?

(b) Joshua makes a 5-litre jug of the drink.

How much cordial does he use?

(c) Harry wants to make a weaker drink.

He makes 350 millilitres using 91% water.

How much cordial does he use?

4 64% of Year 7 pupils in a school say they eat the recommended five portions of fruit and vegetables every day.

(a) There are 250 pupils in Year 7.

How many pupils eat five portions of fruit and vegetables every day?

(b) 17.5% of these pupils were not telling the truth.

How many pupils do actually eat five portions of fruit and vegetables every day?

24 Proportion and ratio

Subject links
- geography
- design and technology
- art

$$\frac{1}{2} \qquad \frac{2}{14}$$

$$\frac{1}{3} \qquad \frac{5}{6}$$

Coming up …

- using proportion
- using ratio notation
- the difference between ratio and proportion
- finding equivalent ratios
- writing a ratio in its simplest form
- dividing a quantity in a given ratio
- solving problems involving proportion and ratio

Do you remember?

- how to find equivalent fractions
- how to write a fraction in its lowest terms
- how to convert a fraction to a percentage

Chapter starter

$$\frac{3}{6} \qquad \frac{2}{6} \qquad \frac{15}{18} \qquad \frac{2}{4}$$

$$\frac{1}{7} \qquad \frac{1}{2} \qquad \frac{10}{12} \qquad \frac{2}{14}$$

$$\frac{3}{9} \qquad \frac{1}{3} \qquad \frac{5}{15} \qquad \frac{5}{6}$$

$$\frac{3}{21} \qquad \frac{5}{10}$$

Match up the equivalent fractions.

Key words

part
whole
quantity
proportion
ratio (:)
equivalent ratio
simplest form

Dan does a pilot survey.

He asks five people to vote for their favourite pizza topping.

Pepperoni

Vegetarian

Hawaiian

Pepperoni

Margherita

The **proportion** who voted for pepperoni is 2 out of 5
or $\frac{2}{5}$ or 0.4 or 40%.

The proportion who did not vote for pepperoni is 3 out of 5
or $\frac{3}{5}$ or 0.6 or 60%.

> **Hint**
> You can describe a proportion using words, fractions, decimals or percentages.

Here is a diagram to show the proportion of people who
voted for pepperoni in the pilot survey.

In the actual survey, Dan asks 20 people.

Here is a diagram to show the proportion of people who voted for pepperoni in the actual survey.

⬤⬤○○○
⬤⬤○○○
⬤⬤○○○
⬤⬤○○○

The proportion who voted for pepperoni is

8 out of 20   or $\frac{8}{20} = \frac{2}{5}$.

> Remember you should always give a fraction in its lowest terms.

The proportion of people who voted for pepperoni is the same as in his pilot survey.

You can use proportion to solve problems.

Example

Blushing Pink paint is
made by mixing 7 litres of
red paint with 3 litres of
white paint.

BLUSHING PINK

Continued ...

Shocking Pink paint is made by mixing 3 litres of red paint with 1 litre of white paint.

Which shade of pink has the greater proportion of red paint?

Solution

Blushing Pink

7 litres out of 10 litres is red.

The proportion of red paint is $\frac{7}{10}$ = 70%.

Shocking Pink

3 litres out of 4 litres is red.

The proportion of red paint is $\frac{3}{4}$ = 75%.

> Write 7 as a fraction of 10.
> Then convert to a percentage because it is easier to compare percentages than fractions with different denominators.

Shocking Pink has the greater proportion of red.

> 75% is greater than 70%.

Example

David and Victoria travel to the USA.

At the time, £1 is worth $1.9.

How many dollars is £1000 worth?

Solution

£1	is worth	$1.9.
× 1000 ↓		↓ × 1000
£1000	is worth	$1900.

> 1000 times as many pounds.

Example

Here is a recipe for egg foo yung.

(a) How much butter is needed to make egg foo yung for 12 people?

(b) How many eggs are needed to make egg foo yung for 2 people?

Egg foo yung
For 4 people

8 eggs
50 g butter
250 g beansprouts
2 tablespoons soy sauce
100 g ham

Solution

(a) For 4 people,   50 g of butter is needed.

   × 3 ↓   ↓ × 3

> There are three times as many people.

   For 12 people,   150 g of butter is needed.

> 3 × 50 g = 150 g

(b) For 4 people,   8 eggs are needed.

   ÷ 2 ↓   ↓ ÷ 2

> There are half as many people.

   For 2 people,   4 eggs are needed.

1. Karen has two packets of biscuits.

   Packet A has 12 chocolate biscuits and 8 plain ones.

   Packet B has 28 chocolate biscuits and 22 plain ones.

   Which packet has the greater proportion of chocolate biscuits?

2. Amir makes a drink by mixing 50 ml of orange juice with 200 ml of lemonade.

   Billy makes a drink by mixing 40 ml of orange juice with 120 ml of pineapple juice.

   Whose drink has the greater proportion of orange juice?

3. Callum spends £9 on a T-shirt and £21 on a pair of trainers.

   Sophie spends £24 on a T-shirt and £36 on a pair of trainers.

   Who spent the smaller proportion of their money on trainers?

4. £1 is worth 1.6 euros.

   How much is £100 worth?

5. Four packets of jelly beans cost £1.60.

   Find the cost of

   (a) eight packets

   (b) two packets.

6. Six exercise books cost £2.40.

   Find the cost of

   (a) 1 exercise book

   (b) 24 exercise books.

7. Here is a recipe for garlic mayonnaise.

   > **Garlic Mayonnaise**
   > Serves 2
   >
   > 2 cloves of garlic
   > 1 teaspoon of lemon juice
   > 1 egg yolk
   > 120 ml of olive oil
   > $\frac{1}{8}$ teaspoon of salt

   (a) How many cloves of garlic are needed to make enough for six people?

   (b) How much olive oil is needed to make enough for eight people?

   (c) A chef needs to make enough for 16 people.

   How much salt will he need?

8. Here are the ingredients to make 1 litre of Tropical Delight.

   > 400 ml pineapple juice
   > 250 ml mango juice
   > 200 ml orange juice
   > 150 ml grapefruit juice

   (a) George makes half a litre of Tropical Delight.

   How much pineapple juice does he need?

   (b) Michael makes a 5-litre jug of Tropical Delight.

   Show that he needs 1 litre of orange juice.

   (c) Lauren has 600 ml of pineapple juice.

   She uses it to make some Tropical Delight.

   How much mango juice, orange juice and grapefruit juice does she need?

9. Eight pencils cost £4. Find the cost of 14 pencils.

There are 11 finalists in 'The Z Factor'.

There are five female singers and six male singers.

To compare the number of females to the number of males you can use a **ratio**.

The ratio of females to males is 5 to 6.

You can write this as females : males = 5 : 6.

> The symbol : is used for ratios.

The order you write a ratio is important.

The ratio of males to females is 6 : 5.

> If you change the order of the words you must change the order of the numbers to match.

It is important to understand the difference between ratio and proportion.

The proportion of the shape that is green is $\frac{7}{10}$ or 70%.

The proportion of the shape that is yellow is $\frac{3}{10}$ or 30%.

The ratio of green parts to yellow parts is 7 : 3.

The ratio of yellow parts to green parts is 3 : 7.

Now try these 24.2

1 Look at this shape.

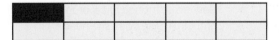

(a) What is the ratio of red parts to yellow parts?

(b) What is the ratio of yellow parts to red parts?

(c) What proportion of the shape is yellow?

2 Su Ling has three 20p coins and two 50p coins.

(a) What proportion of the coins are 50p coins?

(b) Su Ling says

> The ratio of 20p coins to 50p coins is 2 to 3.

Explain why she is wrong.

Continued ..

3 Luke and William are playing snooker.

At the start of a game there are 15 red balls and 7 balls that are not red.

(a) What is the ratio of red balls to balls that are not red?

Later in the game there are three fewer red balls on the table.

(b) What is the ratio of red balls to balls that are not red now?

4 In a classroom there are 16 girls and 14 boys.

Three girls leave the room and two boys enter the room.

What is the ratio of boys to girls now?

24.3 Equivalent ratios

There are 10 men and 15 women on a bus.

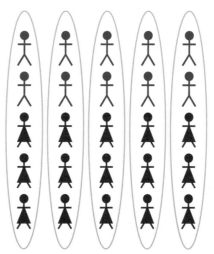

The ratio of men to women is 10 : 15.

The people can be divided into five equal groups.

Each group has two men and three women.

For every two men on the bus there are three women.

The ratio of men to women is 2 : 3.

The ratios 10 : 15 and 2 : 3 both represent the ratio of men to women on the bus.

2 : 3 is the ratio in its **simplest form**.

Example

Write 27 : 12 in its simplest form.

Solution

$$
\begin{array}{ccc}
27 & : & 12 \\
\div 3 \downarrow & & \downarrow \div 3 \\
9 & : & 4
\end{array}
$$

Note

Writing a ratio in its simplest form is similar to writing a fraction in its lowest terms. You learnt how to do that in Chapter 19.

For example, $\frac{10}{15} = \frac{2}{3}$.

Continued ...

Example

Craig divides his DVD collection into music, comedy and films.

He has 20 music DVDs, 8 comedy DVDs and 28 film DVDs.

Write the ratio of music DVDs to comedy DVDs to film DVDs in its simplest form.

Solution

music : comedy : film = 20 : 8 : 28

20   :   8   :   28
÷ 4↓   ↓ ÷ 4   ↓ ÷ 4
5   :   2   7

> There are three parts to his collection so there are three parts to the ratio.

As with cancelling fractions, you can simplify the ratio in stages.

20   :   8   :   28
÷ 2↓   ↓ ÷ 2   ↓ ÷ 2
10   :   4   :   14
÷ 2↓   ↓ ÷ 2   ↓ ÷ 2
5   :   2   :   7

In some problems you will need to use multiplication to make equivalent ratios.

Example

The ratio of pupils in Year 7 who go swimming regularly to those who do not go swimming regularly is 2 : 5.

60 pupils go swimming regularly.

How many do not go swimming regularly?

Solution

2   :   5
× 30↓   ↓ × 30
60   :   150

> You need to find a ratio equivalent to 2 : 5.
> Match up the numbers you have. 60 pupils go swimming so the ratio you want is 60 : something.

150 Year 7 pupils do not go swimming regularly.

> Remember to answer the question.

Now try these 24.3

1 Write these ratios in their simplest form.

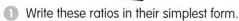

(a) 6 : 2	**(b)** 10 : 15	**(c)** 9 : 12	**(d)** 14 : 7	**(e)** 20 : 16
(f) 12 : 18	**(g)** 40 : 30	**(h)** 15 : 25	**(i)** 50 : 35	**(j)** 35 : 42
(k) 24 : 30	**(l)** 45 : 18	**(m)** 100 : 25	**(n)** 36 : 30	**(o)** 72 : 45
(p) 4 : 8 : 6	**(q)** 10 : 20 : 40	**(r)** 15 : 6 : 12	**(s)** 32 : 20 : 8	**(t)** 21 : 28 : 14

Continued

2 Copy and complete these equivalent ratios.

(a) 2 : 3 = ☐ : 6

(b) 4 : 1 = 12 : ☐

(c) ☐ : 8 = 3 : 2

(d) 20 : ☐ = 5 : 6

(e) 6 : 7 = ☐ : 35

(f) 4 : 3 = 32 : ☐

3 A factory makes different shades of green paint by mixing different amounts of blue and yellow paint.

They make 100 litres of each shade of green.

The amounts of blue and yellow paint used are shown.

Shade of paint	Amount of blue paint (litres)	Amount of yellow paint (litres)
Gorgeous green	60	40
Meadow green	65	35
Rich green	76	24
Hint of green	18	82

Work out the ratio of blue paint to yellow paint for each shade.

Give your answers in their simplest form.

4 The ratio of texts to calls made by Yasmin and Imogen on their mobile phones is 6 : 5.

(a) Yasmin made 24 texts.

How many calls did she make?

(b) Imogen made 35 calls.

How many texts did she send?

24.4 Dividing in a given ratio

In the problems in this section you are given the ratio and the number making up the whole.

You have to find the numbers making up one or more of the parts.

Example

To make squash you mix water and cordial in the ratio 5 : 1.

Megan makes 240 ml of squash.

How much water does she use?

Continued …

Solution

The squash has 5 parts water and 1 part cordial.

> **Add to find the total number of parts in the whole.**
>
> 5 + 1 = 6 parts altogether
>
> **Divide the whole quantity by the total number of parts.**
>
> 240 ml ÷ 6 = 40 ml
>
> **Multiply the quantity in one part by the number of parts you want.**
>
> 5 parts water = 5 × 40 ml
> = 200 ml of water
>
> **Check your answer by adding the quantities making up the whole.**
>
> 1 part is cordial: 40 ml of cordial
> 5 parts are water: 200 ml of water
> 200 ml + 40 ml = 240 ml which is the amount of squash made. ✓
>
> **Give your answer.**

Megan uses 200 ml of water.

Example

Hannah and Lucy share £56 in the ratio 3 : 5.

How much does each receive?

Solution

> **Add to find the total number of parts in the whole.**
>
> 3 + 5 = 8 parts altogether
>
> **Divide the whole quantity by the total number of parts.**
>
> £56 ÷ 8 = £7
>
> **Multiply the quantity in one part by the number of parts you want.**
>
> 3 parts = 3 × £7 = £21
> 5 parts = 5 × £7 = £35
>
> **Check your answer by adding the quantities making up the whole.**
>
> £21 + £35 = £56 ✓
>
> **Give your answer.**

Hannah receives £21 and Lucy receives £35.

1. Share £24 in these ratios.

   (a) 1 : 3   **(b)** 5 : 3   **(c)** 7 : 5

2. Divide 200 in these ratios.

   (a) 3 : 7   **(b)** 4 : 1   **(c)** 23 : 27

3. Oliver has a party and invites 18 friends.

   The ratio of girls to boys is 2 : 7.

   How many boys does he invite?

4. The ratio of home fans to away fans at a football match is 19 : 1.

   The attendance is 40 000.

   How many away fans are there?

5. The ratio of vegetarians to non-vegetarians at a restaurant is 2 : 23.

   (a) There are 50 people at the restaurant.

   How many are not vegetarian?

   (b) The restaurant expects the ratio of vegetarians to non-vegetarians to be roughly the same each night.

   They expect about 200 customers at the weekend.

   About how many vegetarian meals should they make?

Substitution and formulae

Subject links
- science
- design and technology

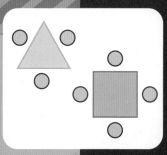

Coming up …

- using formulae expressed in symbols
- substituting numbers into a formula
- writing formulae using words or symbols

Chapter starter

New tables are needed for the school canteen.

Here are some seating arrangements.

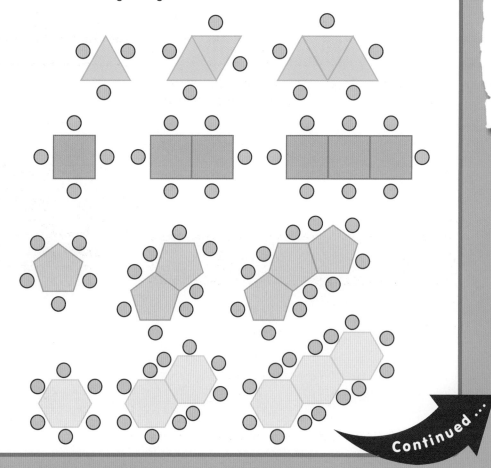

Continued …

Do you remember?

- about the order of operations
- how to use algebraic notation
- how to substitute a number into an expression

Key words

formula (plural: formulae)

substitute

substitution

symbols

variable

Alisha wants to work out how many people can be seated when 20 tables are joined together.

She has found some rules.

To work out the number of people who can be seated you ...

... multiply the number of tables by 2 and then add 2.

... multiply the number of tables by 4 and then add 2.

... multiply the number of tables by 3 and then add 2.

... add 2 to the number of tables.

① Match together each of Alisha's rules with the correct table shape.

② Find your own rules for heptagonal (seven sides) and octagonal (eight sides) tables.

③ Investigate further.

25.1 Using formulae expressed in symbols

A **formula** is a rule for working something out. It can be written in words or symbols.
Replacing the words or symbols in a formula with numbers is called **substitution**.

Five Stars Cinema uses this formula to work out how much to charge its customers.

| Price = 8 × number of adults + 5 × number of children |

This can be written using symbols.

| $P = 8a + 5c$ |

Remember you don't need to write the '×' signs.
5c means 5 × c or 5 lots of c.

Five Stars
☆☆☆☆☆
Adult £8
Child £5

where P stands for price in pounds,

  a stands for number of adults,

and c stands for number of children.

P, a and c are called **variables**.

This means they represent numbers which can take on different values (they can vary).

For example, the price, P, varies because it depends on how many people are going to the cinema.

Continued ...

The more people, the higher the price.

Example

Work out the cost of two adults and four children seeing a film at Five Stars Cinema.

Solution

$a = 2$ and $c = 4$

$P = 8a + 5c$ — Substitute into the formula.

$P = 8 \times 2 + 5 \times 4$ — Don't forget to write in the '×' signs now.

$= 16 + 20$

$= 36$

The cost is £36.

Now try these 25.1

① This is the formula for the perimeter, P, of a square.

$P = 4s$

where s is the length of one side of the square.

Work out the perimeter, P, of these squares.

(a) 5 cm

(b) 7 cm

s

② This is the formula to convert number of litres, L, to number of millilitres, M.

$$M = 1000L$$

How many millilitres do each of these containers hold?

(a) 2 litres (b) 0.5 litres (c) 5.25 litres

③ An electricity supplier uses this formula to work out an electricity bill.

$$C = 15d + 10n$$

where
C = cost in pence
d = number of daytime units of electricity used
n = number of night time units of electricity used.

Peter has used 300 daytime units and 200 night time units.

Find his total bill in

(a) pence
(b) pounds.

Continued …

4 A car hire company uses this formula to work out the hire cost.

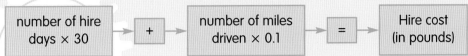

number of hire days × 30 + number of miles driven × 0.1 = Hire cost (in pounds)

(a) Work out how much each of these customers are charged for hiring a car.

(i) Peter hires a car for 4 days and drives 100 miles.

(ii) Tilly hires a car for 7 days and drives 500 miles.

(iii) Hayden hires a car for 10 days and drives 1040 miles.

(b) How much does the company charge for

(i) each day of car hire

(ii) each mile driven?

5 Look at this pattern of five triangles.

This is the formula for the number of matchsticks used.

$$m = 2t + 1$$

where m = number of matchsticks used
and t = number of triangles made.

Work out how many matchsticks are needed to make

(a) three triangles
(b) six triangles
(c) nine triangles.

6 Brain strain

Super Savers Bank uses this formula to work out how much interest a customer earns in a year.

$$I = PR \div 100$$

where I is the amount of interest earned
P is the amount of money invested
R is the percentage interest rate.

Work out how much interest the following customers should earn in one year.

(a) Catherine invests £500 at an interest rate of 5%.

(b) Kirsty invests £1000 at an interest rate of 6%.

(c) Jamie invests £250 at an interest rate of 4%.

7 This is the formula for the **area**, A, of a triangle.

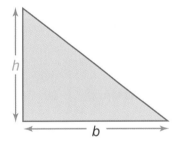

$$A = \frac{1}{2}bh$$

Work out the area of these triangles.

(a)
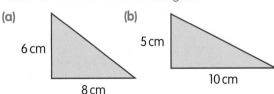
6 cm
8 cm

(b)
5 cm
10 cm

You can write formulae using words or symbols as in this example.

Example

At a boating lake this sign is displayed.

Write a formula for the cost of hiring a rowing boat in

(a) words   **(b)** symbols.

> **Boating Lake**
>
> Rowing boats   £5 deposit
>
> plus   £4 per hour

Solution

(a) Cost = 5 + 4 × number of hours

| the deposit | the cost per hour |

(b) $C = 5 + 4h$ *You don't need the '×' sign.*

| the deposit | the cost per hour |

where C = cost in pounds

and h = number of hours the boat is hired for.

Now try these 25.2

① This sign is displayed at a zoo.

> **ZOO**
>
> Adults   £15
> Children   £8

(a) Write down how to work out the cost for a group of four adults and three children to go to the zoo.

(b) Use these algebra cards to write a formula for the price in pounds, P, for a adults and c children to go to the zoo.

+	8	a
×	15	c
=		P

② Sophie is going mountain biking.

(a) Write down how to work out how much it costs Sophie to hire a mountain bike for 6 hours.

(b) Fill in the boxes to complete the formula for the cost (in pounds), C, of hiring a mountain bike for h hours.

> **Mountain bikes for hire**
>
> £10 deposit plus
> £3 per hour

$$C = \boxed{} + 3 \triangle$$

Continued ...

3 A video game awards bonus points for collecting gold coins and stars.

○	Gold coins	10 points
☆	Stars	25 points

(a) Write down how to work out the bonus points awarded for collecting 5 gold coins and 8 stars.

(b) Fill in the boxes to complete the formula for the number of bonus points, P, when g gold coins and s stars are collected.

$$P = 10 \triangle + \diamond s$$

4 Boxes of raisins cost r pence each.

Bottles of water cost w pence each.

Write down formulae for the price, P, of each of these.

(a) 4 bottles of water

(b) 1 bottle of water and 1 box of raisins

(c) 4 bottles of water and 3 boxes of raisins

5 Look at this fence.

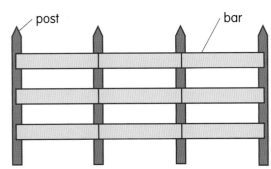

post   bar

The diagram shows three sections of fencing.

(a) Copy and complete this table.

(b) Fill in the boxes to complete this formula for the number of posts, p, needed for s sections.

$$p = \square + \diamond$$

Number of sections	Number of posts	Number of bars
1		
2		
3		

(c) Fill in the boxes to complete this formula for the number of bars, b, needed for s sections.

$$b = \triangle \square$$

(d) Harry wants to build a fence with ten sections.

Use your formulae to work out how many posts and how many bars he needs.

Continued...

6 Brain strain

Look at these polygons.

The diagonals from *one* vertex (corner) are shown in blue.

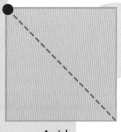
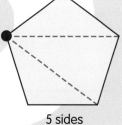
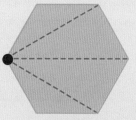

4 sides   5 sides   6 sides

(a) Copy and complete this table.

(b) Find a formula for the number of diagonals, *d*, for a polygon with *n* sides.

(c) Use your formula to work out how many diagonals there are from one vertex of a polygon with 20 sides.

(d) Explain why your rule works.

Number of sides	Number of diagonals from one vertex
4	
5	
6	

Equations

Coming up …

- solving equations with an unknown on one side
- constructing equations to solve problems
- checking the solution to equations

Do you remember?
- how to use algebraic notation
- about inverse operations
- how to simplify algebraic expressions
- that the sum of the angles in a triangle is 180°
- how to find the perimeter of a rectangle

Chapter starter

1 Solve these clues to find the mystery numbers.

(a) When you double ★ the answer is 246.

(b) When you add 7 to ◆ the answer is 123.

(c) ◊ is even

and ◊ is a prime number.

(d) ● is odd

and ● has two digits

and ● is less than 40

and ● is a square number.

(e) ■ has two digits

and ■ is a square number

and ■ is a cube number.

(f) When you double ☺ the answer is more than 20.

When you add 10 to ☺ the answer is less than 30.

☺ is a triangular number.

2 Choose your own mystery number.

Make up some clues and give them to a friend to solve.

Key words

equation

balance

unknown

solve

solution

Look at these scales.

The scales balance.

The mass on the left-hand side is the same as the mass on the right-hand side.

You do not know the value of *x* so it is called an unknown.

You can write an equation for the scales.

$2x + 1 = 5$

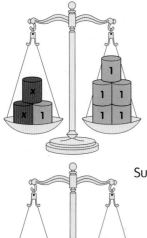

When you add or subtract the same amount to *both sides* of the scales they stay balanced.

When you multiply or divide *both sides* of the scales by the same amount they stay balanced.

You can use these facts to find the value of *x*.

$$2x + 1 = 5$$

Subtract 1   Subtract 1

$$2x = 4$$

Divide by 2   Divide by 2

$$x = 2$$

You have solved the equation $2x + 1 = 5$.

The solution is $x = 2$.

You can check your answer by substituting back into the original equation.

$$2x + 1 = 5$$

Check when $x = 2$: $2 \times 2 + 1 = 5$ ✓

For each of the balance problems in questions **1** to **8**,

(a) write down an equation for the problem

(b) draw scales and write out a new equation for each stage of your solution

(c) check your solution.

①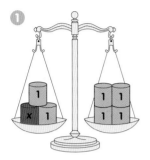
②
③
④

⑤
⑥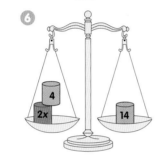
⑦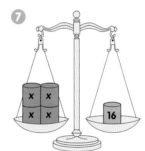
⑧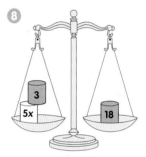

⑨ Solve these equations.

Show each step of your working.

Check each of your solutions.

(a) $a + 4 = 7$ **(b)** $b + 8 = 12$ **(c)** $c + 9 = 21$ **(d)** $3d = 21$

(e) $5e = 10$ **(f)** $8f = 24$ **(g)** $3g + 1 = 10$ **(h)** $4h + 2 = 22$

(i) $7i + 2 = 9$ **(j)** $4 + 10j = 64$ **(k)** $4k + 4 = 20$ **(l)** $2 + 5l = 7$

26.2 Solving problems using equations

I think of a number. When I multiply it by 9 and subtract 11 the answer is 52. What is my number?

Mohammed

You can write down an equation and solve it to find Mohammed's number.

Continued ...

Let n represent his number.

$n \times 9 - 11 = 52$

You should write this using correct algebraic notation.

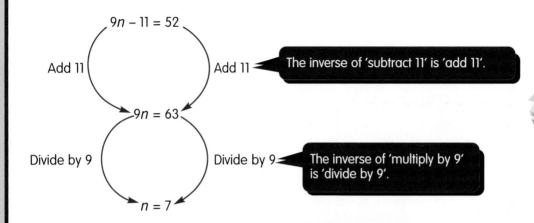

9n − 11 = 52

Add 11   Add 11 ◄ The inverse of 'subtract 11' is 'add 11'.

9n = 63

Divide by 9   Divide by 9 ◄ The inverse of 'multiply by 9' is 'divide by 9'.

n = 7

Hint
Remember to do the same thing to both sides of the equation so it balances.

Check: $9 \times 7 - 11 = 63 - 11 = 52$ ✓ ◄ Always check your work.

Example

In this algebra wall, two numbers are added to find the number in the box above.

Find the missing value.

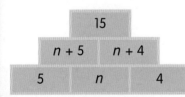

15	
n + 5	n + 4
5	n	4

Solution

The two middle bricks have to add to give 15.

So $n + 5 + n + 4 = 15$

Simplifying: $n + n$ is 2 lots of n or $2 \times n$ which is written as $2n$. And $5 + 4 = 9$.

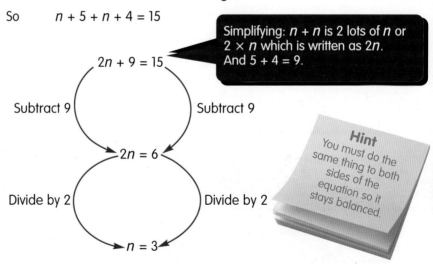

2n + 9 = 15

Subtract 9   Subtract 9

2n = 6

Divide by 2   Divide by 2

n = 3

Hint
You must do the same thing to both sides of the equation so it stays balanced.

Substitute $n = 3$ into the expressions.

15	
8	7
5	3	4

Check: $5 + 3 = 8$

$3 + 4 = 7$

$8 + 7 = 15$ ✓

1 Solve these equations. Show all your working:

    (a) $x + 2 = 12$ **(b)** $x - 5 = 6$ **(c)** $x + 7 = 10$ **(d)** $x - 8 = 7$

    (e) $2x = 18$ **(f)** $10x = 15$ **(g)** $5x + 3 = 23$ **(h)** $2x + 1 = 13$

    (i) $2x - 1 = 7$ **(j)** $3x + 2 = 17$ **(k)** $4x - 1 = 23$ **(l)** $2x + 5 = 11$

    (m) $8 + 3x = 20$ **(n)** $3x + 6 = 15$ **(o)** $7x - 5 = 2$ **(p)** $7x - 1 = 20$

    (q) $13x - 11 = 54$ **(r)** $2x + 7 = 1$ **(s)** $12x - 15 = 93$ **(t)** $5x + 19 = 4$

    (u) $x + 6.2 = 11$ **(v)** $7.1 + 3y = 9.5$

2 Look at how Oliver solves the equation $3x + 6 = 21$.

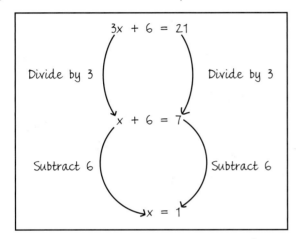

Oliver has made a mistake.

    (a) How can you show Oliver that he has the wrong answer without solving the equation?

    (b) What is Oliver's mistake?

    (c) Solve the equation correctly.

3 Both of these rectangles have a perimeter of 30 cm.
   Find the length and width of each rectangle.

    (a)

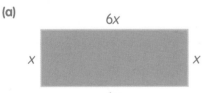

    (b)

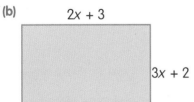

Continued ...

❹ Brain strain

For each of these triangles,

(i) write down an equation for the sum of the angles in the triangle

(ii) solve your equation

(iii) find the size of each angle in the triangle.

(a)

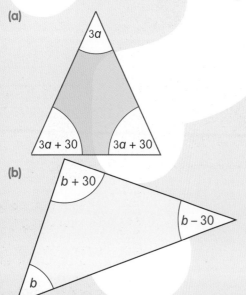

(b)

❺ Brain strain

Use equations to solve these puzzles.

(a) There are 156 tracks altogether on David's and Myra's MP3 players.

David has 26 fewer tracks on his MP3 player than Myra has on hers.

How many tracks are there on each MP3 player?

(b) A video game awards twice as many points for catching a dragon as it does for catching a unicorn.

Mark gets 150 points for catching three dragons and four unicorns.

How many points are awarded for catching a dragon?

(c) Freya's little sister, Paige, is 7 years younger than her.

The sum of their ages is 25.

How old is Paige?

(d) Three brothers share £150 between them.

The oldest gets twice as much as the youngest.

The middle brother gets £10 more than the youngest.

How much money do they each get?

Graphs

Subject links
- geography
- science

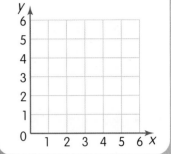

Coming up ...

- drawing a straight-line graph for a line with an equation such as $y = x + 2$
- drawing and interpreting graphs representing real-life situations

Chapter starter

Here are the rules for coordinate four-in-a-line.

1 Make a copy of this coordinate grid.

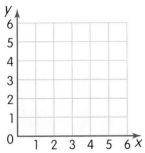

2 Choose to mark coordinates with a × or a •.

Take it in turns to choose a point.

You must say the coordinates of the point before you plot it.

3 The winner is the first person who makes a line of four points.

The line can be horizontal, vertical or diagonal.

4 Write down the coordinates of the winning line.

(Keep them safe because you will need them again later.)

5 What patterns can you see in the coordinates of the winning lines?

Play a game of coordinate four-in-a-line with a friend.

Do you remember?

- how to plot and read coordinates in all four quadrants
- how to substitute a number into an expression

Key words

coordinates

horizontal

vertical

parallel

equation

x coordinate

y coordinate

axis (plural: axes)

x axis

y axis

graph

conversion graph

Look at your winning lines from the Chapter starter.

Are any of the lines parallel to the axes?

What patterns can you see in the coordinates of those lines?

Look at these lines.

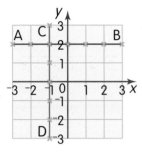

The line AB is parallel to the *x* axis.

The points marked have these coordinates.

(⁻3, 2)

(⁻2, 2)

(⁻1, 2)

(0, 2)

(1, 2)

(2, 2)

(3, 2)

> The *y* coordinate is always 2.

The **equation of the line** AB is $y = 2$.

The equation of a **horizontal** line is always $y = $ a number.

The line CD is parallel to the *y* axis.

The points marked have these coordinates.

(⁻1, 3)

(⁻1, 2)

(⁻1, 1)

(⁻1, 0)

(⁻1, ⁻1)

(⁻1, ⁻2)

(⁻1, ⁻3)

> The *x* coordinate is always ⁻1.

The equation of the line CD is $x = ⁻1$.

The equation of a **vertical** line is always $x = $ a number.

Now try these 27.1

❶ Write down the coordinates of four points on each of these lines.

Find the equation of each line.

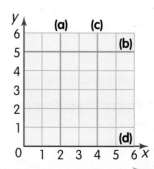

Continued ...

2 Draw a pair of axes and number them from ⁻4 to 4.

Plot these lines on the same axes.

(a) $y = 1$ **(b)** $x = 3$ **(c)** $y = ⁻2$ **(d)** $x = ⁻3$

3 Look at this graph.

(a) What are the equations of these lines?

(i) line AB   **(ii)** line AD

(b) Without drawing, write down the equations of the lines BC and DC so that shape ABCD is a rectangle.

(c) Copy the diagram.

Draw lines BC and DC to check your answer to part **(b)**.

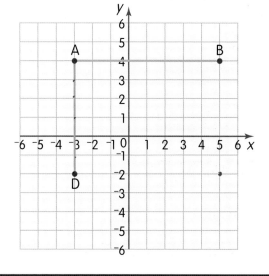

27.2 Straight-line graphs

Look at your winning lines from the Chapter starter again.

Are any of the lines sloping?

What patterns can you see in the coordinates of those lines?

Look at this line.

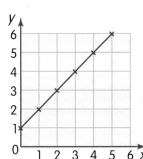

The points marked have these coordinates.

(0, 1)

(1, 2)

(2, 3)

(3, 4)

(4, 5)

(5, 6)

The y coordinates are equal to the x coordinates add 1.

All the points on the line follow this rule.

The equation of the line is $y = x + 1$.

Continued ...

Example

(a) Make a table of values for the equation $y = 2x$.

(b) Plot the points on a coordinate grid.

Draw the line $y = 2x$.

Solution

(a)

x	0	1	2	3	4	5
y = 2x	0	2	4	6	8	10
coordinates	(0, 0)	(1, 2)	(2, 4)	(3, 6)	(4, 8)	(5, 10)

Find the y coordinate by substituting the value of the x coordinate into the equation of the line.
For example, $2 \times 5 = 10$

(b)

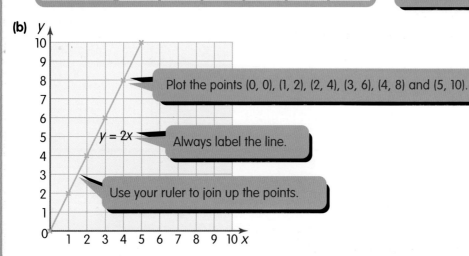

Plot the points (0, 0), (1, 2), (2, 4), (3, 6), (4, 8) and (5, 10).

$y = 2x$

Always label the line.

Use your ruler to join up the points.

Now try these 27.2

1 (a) Copy and complete these tables of values.

x	0	1	2	3	4	5
y = x + 2	2			5		
coordinates	(0, 2)			(3, 5)		

x	0	1	2	3	4	5
y = x + 3	3					8
coordinates	(0, 3)					(5, 8)

x	0	1	2	3	4	5
y = x + 4					8	
coordinates					(4, 8)	

(b) Draw a pair of axes and number them from 0 to 10.

Plot the points from the first table on the grid.

Use your ruler to join the points with a straight line

Label the line.

Now draw the other two lines.

(c) What do you notice about the three lines?

Continued ...

2 (a) Copy and complete this table of values for the equation $y = x + 5$.

x	0	1	2	3	4	5
y = x + 5	5					
coordinates	(0, 5)					

(b) Draw a pair of axes and number the x axis from 0 to 10 and the y axis from 0 to 15.

Use your table of values to help you draw the line $y = x + 5$.

Extend your line as far as you can.

(c) Choose a point on the line that isn't in the table of values.

Write down the coordinates of the point.

Does it follow the rule $y = x + 5$?

(d) Check that other points on the line follow the same rule.

3 (a) Copy and complete this table of values for the equation $y = 10 - x$.

x	0	1	2	3	4	5
y = 10 − x	10				6	
coordinates	(0, 10)				(4, 6)	

When $x = 4$ then $y = 10 - x = 10 - 4 = 6$.

(b) Draw a pair of axes and number them from 0 to 10.

Use your table of values to help you draw the line $y = 10 - x$.

Extend your line until it meets the x axis.

(c) Choose a point on the line that isn't in the table of values.

Write down the coordinates of the point.

Does it follow the rule $y = 10 - x$?

(d) Check that other points on the line follow the same rule.

Some real-life situations can be represented by straight-line graphs.

Example

(a) Use the table below to draw a temperature conversion graph.

Temperature in Celsius (°C)	0	30	40
Temperature in Fahrenheit (°F)	32	86	104
coordinates	(0, 32)	(30, 86)	(40, 104)

Hint

You only need two points to draw a straight-line graph but it is good practice to use at least three. You can draw a straight line between any two points. You use the third point to check that you have drawn the line correctly.

(b) Use the conversion graph to convert

(i) 25° Celsius to Fahrenheit

(ii) 100° Fahrenheit to Celsius.

Solution

(a)

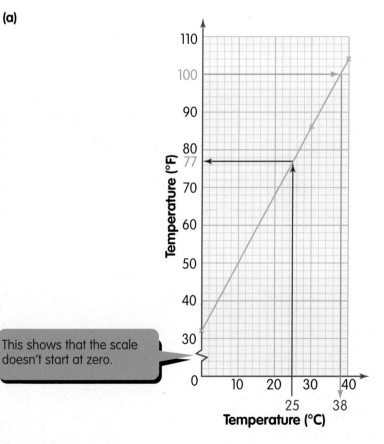

This shows that the scale doesn't start at zero.

(b) (i) 25°C = 77°F

(ii) 100°F = 38°C

Rob is planning a family holiday to Egypt.

1 Rob looks up the average monthly temperatures in Egypt.

Month	Jan	Feb	Mar	Apr	May	Jun	Jul	Aug	Sept	Oct	Nov	Dec
Temperature (°C)		20		28	33	35		35	30		25	
Temperature (°F)	59		77	82	91		104			86		68

(a) Use the conversion graph in the example on page 222 to complete Rob's table.

(b) Rob wants to go on holiday when the average temperature is less than 30°C.
Which months should Rob avoid?

2 A phone company uses the following graph to work out how much to charge customers for calling from Egypt.

(a) How much will Rob be charged for making a 20-minute phone call?

(b) Rob wants to spend no more than £10 on phone calls.
How many minutes can Rob spend on the phone for £10?

(c) Copy and complete this sentence with words from the box.

As the length of a phone call ...., the cost of the call ....

| increases | decreases | stays the same |

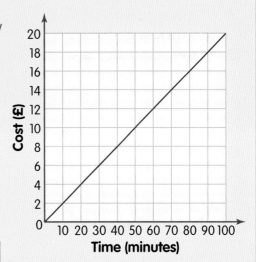

3 Rob wants to take a conversion graph between miles and kilometres on holiday.

Number of miles	0	50	100
Number of kilometres	0	80	160
coordinates			

(a) Follow these steps to draw a conversion graph between miles and kilometres.
● Copy the table and insert the coordinates.
● Draw a pair of axes on graph paper.
● Number the horizontal axis from 0 to 100 in steps of 10.
● Number the vertical axis from 0 to 160 in steps of 10.
● Label the horizontal axis 'Number of miles'.
● Label the vertical axis 'Number of kilometres'.
● Plot the points (0, 0), (50, 80) and (100, 160).
Use a ruler to join the points.

(b) Use your graph to convert the following distances to miles.

(i) Cairo to Ismailia: 144 km

(ii) Cairo to Barrages: 32 km

28 Probability

Subject links
- PHSE
- geography
- science

Coming up …

- the probability scale
- finding possible outcomes
- working out theoretical probabilities
- estimating probabilities
- comparing theoretical and experimental probabilities
- solving problems involving probability

Chapter starter

There are 52 cards in a pack of cards.
There are 13 hearts, 13 diamonds, 13 spades and 13 clubs.
Each group of 13 cards is called a suit. Within each suit there are the same type of cards: Ace (1), 2, 3, 4, 5, 6, 7, 8, 9, 10, Jack, Queen, King.

1 How many fours are there in a pack of cards?

2 How many spades are there in a pack of cards?

3 How many Kings are there?

Do you remember?
- how to write one number as a fraction of another
- how to simplify fractions
- how to convert between fractions, decimals and percentages
- how to use a tally chart

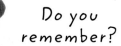

Key words

probability	certain
outcome	possible
experiment	random
event	estimate
impossible	trial
unlikely	fair
even chance	biased
likely	

An **outcome** is the result of an experiment involving probability.

For example, if you toss a coin there are two possible outcomes: heads and tails.
Similarly, if you roll a dice there are six possible outcomes: 1, 2, 3, 4, 5 and 6.

An **event** is one or more outcomes of an experiment involving probability.

An event can be a single outcome, such as the number 6, or a combination of outcomes, such as a number less than 4.

The **probability** of an event tells you how likely or unlikely that event is to happen.

A probability scale can be used to show probabilities.

| Impossible | Very unlikely | Unlikely | Even chance | Likely | Very likely | Certain |

Now try these 28.1

1 For each of the words, choose the correct definition.

If you are not sure use a dictionary to look up the word.

Word	Definition
(a) Certain	could happen
(b) Impossible	will probably happen
(c) Likely	will probably not happen
(d) Possible	will definitely happen
(e) Unlikely	could not happen

2 For each of these events say whether it is certain, impossible, likely, unlikely or there is an even chance that it will happen.

(a) It will snow somewhere in the United Kingdom next winter.

(b) The next car you see will have pink stripes.

(c) You will roll an even number with an ordinary dice.

(d) There will be 30 days in November next year.

(e) You will watch television this evening.

3 These two spinners are used in a game.

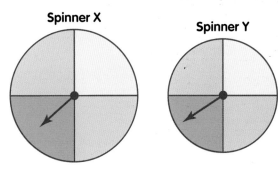

Spinner X   Spinner Y

Are these statements true or false?

(a) There is a greater chance of getting red on spinner X than on spinner Y because the area of red is bigger on spinner X.

(b) The chance of getting red is the same on spinner X and spinner Y because a quarter of the circle is red on both spinners.

4 At the start of a football match the referee tosses a coin to decide which team will kick off.

Explain why this is a fair way to decide which team will kick off.

28.2 Theoretical probability

An event that is impossible or cannot happen has a probability of 0.

An event that is certain to happen has a probability of 1.

All other probabilities are between 0 and 1.

> Probabilities can be written as fractions, decimals or percentages. For example $\frac{1}{2}$ or 0.5 or 50%.

> 1 in 2, 1 out of 2 and 1 : 2 are not probabilities, because they are not fractions, decimals or percentages.

0     $\frac{1}{2}$ 1

Impossible   Even chance   Certain

When you roll a dice, each of the outcomes is **equally likely**.

In cases like this, you can work out a numerical value for the probability of the event.

The probability of an event = $\dfrac{\text{the number of ways the event can happen}}{\text{the total number of possible outcomes}}$

Example

(a) What is the probability of getting a number less than five when you roll an ordinary dice?

(b) You roll the dice 30 times.

How many times do you expect to get a number less than five?

Solution

(a) There are four ways of getting a number less than five: 1, 2, 3 and 4.

There are six possible outcomes: 1, 2, 3, 4, 5 and 6.

The probability of an event = $\dfrac{\text{the number of ways the event can happen}}{\text{the total number of possible outcomes}}$

The probability of getting a number less than five = $\dfrac{4}{6}$.

> The number of ways you can get a number less than 5.

$= \dfrac{2}{3}$

> The total number of possible outcomes.

> The probability that you get a number less than five is $\frac{2}{3}$.

(b) You expect to get a number less than five $\frac{2}{3}$ of the 30 times.

$\frac{2}{3}$ of 30 = 30 ÷ 3 × 2

$= 20$

In 30 rolls you expect to get a number less than five 20 times.

1 There are ten packets of crisps in a multi-pack bag.

Five are ready salted, three are cheese and onion and two are salt and vinegar.

Gino takes a packet at random.

What is the probability that the crisps are

(a) ready salted

(b) cheese and onion

(c) salt and vinegar?

2 Mississippi is a state in the USA.

Each of the letters in the name is written on a card and put into a hat.

A letter is taken at random from the hat. What is the probability that the letter is

(a) M   **(b)** I   **(c)** S   **(d)** P   **(e)** A?

3 The national lottery uses balls numbered from 1 to 49.

What is the probability that the first ball picked is

(a) even   **(b)** odd?

4 This spinner has eight equal sectors.

You spin the spinner once.

What is the probability of getting

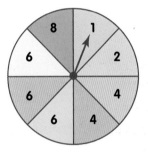

(a) an odd number   **(b)** an even number

(c) a number less than 10   **(d)** a multiple of 4

(e) a multiple of 5   **(f)** a factor of 16

(g) a square number   **(h)** a prime number?

5 **(a)** Copy this spinner.

Write numbers on your spinner so that the probability of getting an even number is $\frac{1}{3}$.

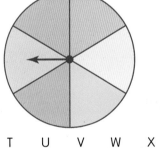

(b) What is the probability of getting an odd number?

6 A fair dice is rolled.

Each letter on the probability scale represents one of the following events.

Match the events to the letters.

(a) A 6 is rolled.   **(b)** A number that is not 6 is rolled.

(c) A 10 is rolled.   **(d)** A multiple of 2 is rolled.

(e) A factor of 60 is rolled.   **(f)** A 3 or a 6 is rolled.

(g) A number greater than 2 is rolled.

7 Dan says that a rugby match can have three outcomes: win, lose or draw. He says that since there are three outcomes, the probability that one team wins is $\frac{1}{3}$. Is he correct? Why?

Continued ...

8 (a) There are two red counters and one blue counter in a bag.

Emily takes a counter without looking.

What is the probability that the counter is blue?

(b) Emily puts the counter back in the bag and adds some more blue counters.

The probability that she picks a blue counter is now $\frac{2}{3}$.

How many blue counters are there in the bag?

9 There are 12 sweets in a jar.

Some are orange flavoured and some are lemon flavoured.

The probability that a sweet taken at random from the bag is orange flavoured is 50%.

(a) Eva takes a sweet at random and eats it.

What is the probability that the sweet is lemon flavoured?

(b) The sweet Eva ate was orange flavoured.

Eva takes another sweet.

What is the probability that it is

(i) orange flavoured   **(ii)** lemon flavoured?

---

10 Puzzle

Eight cards each have a number from 1 to 10 on one side.

The probability that a card taken at random is
- an even number is 0.5
- a prime number is 0.25.

Write down one example of eight numbers that could be on the cards.

Research

In 1654, a Frenchman called the Chevalier de Méré wanted help to find out his chances of winning in dice games.
He asked two French mathematicians, Pierre Fermat and Blaise Pascal, for advice.
The work that these two mathematicians did is thought to have been the beginning of the branch of mathematics called probability.

Find out about the work they did.

Pierre Fermat
1601–1665

Blaise Pascal
1623–1662

When each of the possible outcomes are not equal, you can't find the probability of an event using the formula in the previous section.

In these cases you can only **estimate** the probability.

You can do this by doing an experiment or by looking at data already collected. Therefore, a probability found in this way is called an experimental probability.

You then use this formula.

Experimental probability of an event = $\dfrac{\text{the number of times the event happens}}{\text{the number of trials}}$

If you are finding the probability of getting a head when you toss a coin, a **trial** is one toss of the coin.

A **fair** coin is equally likely to show heads or tails.

A **biased** coin is more likely to show heads than tails, or the reverse.

Similarly, a biased dice is more likely to show one number than the other numbers.

You can do experiments to test if coins or dice are fair or biased.

With a friend

1 What is the probability of getting heads when you toss a fair coin?

2 What is the probability of getting tails when you toss a fair coin?

3 You toss a coin ten times.
   (a) How many heads do you expect?
   (b) How many tails do you expect?

4 Copy this frequency table.
   Toss a coin ten times and record the results in your table.
   Did you get the number of heads and tails you expected?

	Tally	Frequency
Heads		
Tails		

5 Compare your results with a friend's.
   Do you think the coins you are using are fair?

6 Repeat parts **3**, **4** and **5** for 20 tosses of a coin.
   You can do this by adding another ten results to your frequency table.

7 Continue increasing the number of times you toss the coin.
   Do you need to get exactly the same number of heads and tails to know that your coin is fair?
   Explain your answer.

8 Would you expect to get exactly the same results if you did this experiment again?
   Explain your answer.

① Working in groups, roll a dice 50 times and record your results. The theoretical probability of throwing a six is $\frac{1}{6}$.

(a) Find the experimental probability of throwing a 6.

(b) How can you improve the accuracy of the experimental probability?

② Jack is playing a game with this fair spinner.

Jack says

The last spin was an odd number, so the next spin is very likely to be an even number.

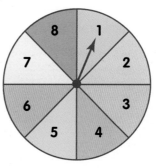

Is Jack right?

Give a reason for your answer.

③ When seeds are planted, some grow and some do not.

David plants 40 tomato seeds and 36 grow.

April plants 20 of the same seeds in the same conditions.

(a) One of David's seeds was chosen at random. What is the probability that it grew?

(b) If April has the same success rate as David with her seeds, how many of April's seeds are likely to grow?

(c) Will April's seeds definitely have the same success rate as David's? Give a reason for your answer.

Representing data

Coming up ...

- drawing bar charts
- drawing pie charts

Chapter starter

Mr Simpson has a doughnut stall.

He sells five types of doughnut: chocolate, cream, iced, jam and plain.

He decides to draw a chart to show the doughnut sales each day.

Remember the different types of chart you met in Chapter 16.

1 What type of chart do you think Mr Simpson should use to show the sales of doughnuts each day?

2 What are the advantages and disadvantages of each type of graph for showing this information?

Do you remember?
- how to interpret tables, charts and graphs
- how to plot points on a graph
- that the angles around a point add up to 360°
- how to find an equivalent ratio
- how to find a fraction of an amount
- how to draw angles

Key words

bar chart

bar-line chart

frequency

axes

key

pie chart

sector

You learnt how to find information from bar charts in Chapter 16.

These are some important things to remember when you draw a bar chart.

● A hand-drawn bar chart should be drawn on squared paper or graph paper.

● You should leave spaces between the bars.

● You need to include a title and labels on both the horizontal and vertical axes.

● You need to choose a suitable scale.

● You may also need to include a key.

● The numbers on the frequency axis mark the lines not the spaces.

> The numbers are wrongly marked in the spaces rather than on the line.

● The numbers on the frequency axis go up in equal steps.

> The numbers do not go up in equal steps.

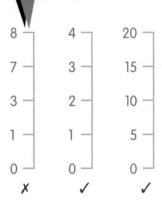

Example

Bethany did a survey of 60 pupils to find out their lunchtime arrangements.

These are her results.

> 25 had a school lunch.
> 21 had a packed lunch.
> 11 had lunch at home.
> 3 had no lunch.

Draw a bar chart to show this information.

Continued ...

Solution

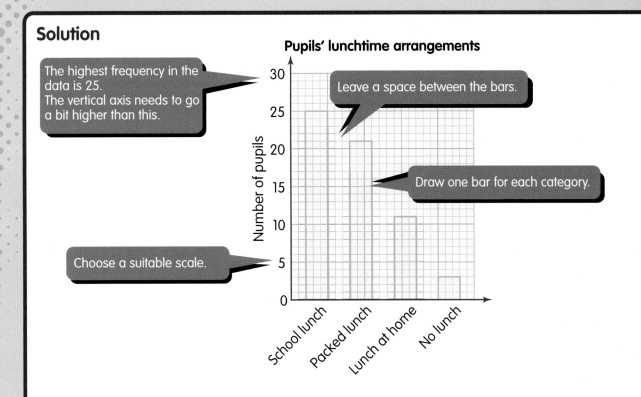

Pupils' lunchtime arrangements

The highest frequency in the data is 25.
The vertical axis needs to go a bit higher than this.

Leave a space between the bars.

Draw one bar for each category.

Choose a suitable scale.

In Chapter 16 you met different types of bar chart.

You draw them in a similar way to the simple bar chart in the example above.

This is a bar-line graph showing the same information as in the example above.

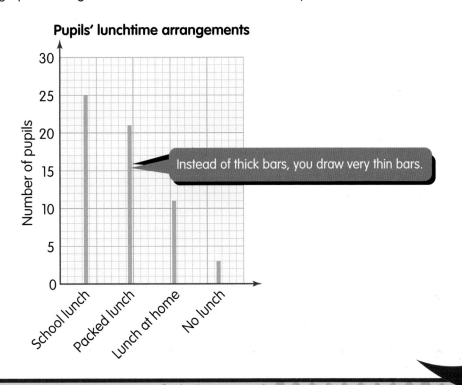

Pupils' lunchtime arrangements

Instead of thick bars, you draw very thin bars.

Continued ...

Bethany's original data about pupils' lunchtime arrangements was divided into boys and girls.

This is her original data.

Lunchtime arrangement	Number of boys	Number of girls
School lunch	15	10
Packed lunch	7	14
Lunch at home	6	5
No lunch	2	1

Here are two ways she could show this information.

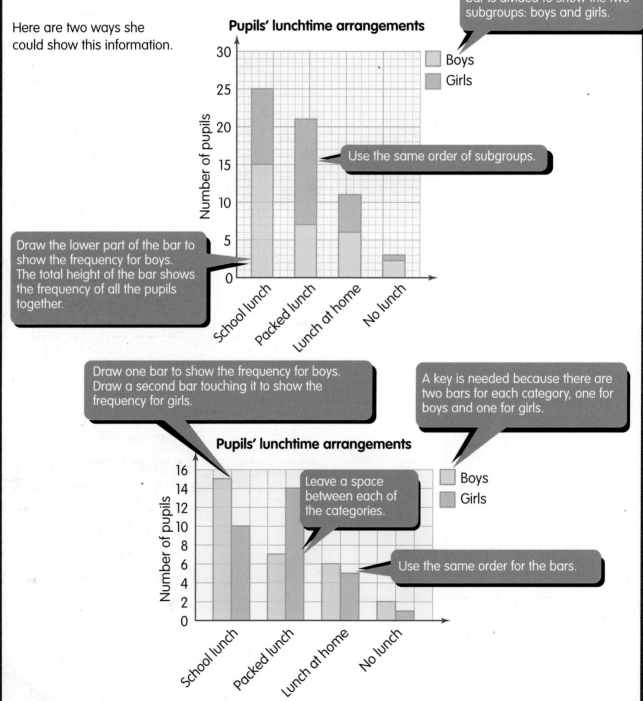

A key is needed because each bar is divided to show the two subgroups: boys and girls.

Use the same order of subgroups.

Draw the lower part of the bar to show the frequency for boys. The total height of the bar shows the frequency of all the pupils together.

Draw one bar to show the frequency for boys. Draw a second bar touching it to show the frequency for girls.

A key is needed because there are two bars for each category, one for boys and one for girls.

Leave a space between each of the categories.

Use the same order for the bars.

1 The table shows how the money you pay for a jar of coffee is spent.

Draw a bar chart to show this information.

Process	Approximate percentage of cost
Roasting	30%
Selling	30%
Processing	20%
Transporting	10%
Growing	10%

2 The table shows the amount of sugar in 330 millilitres of some drinks.

Draw a bar chart to show this information.

Drink	Amount of sugar (grams)
Blackcurrant drink	45
Cola	35
Energy drink	55
Fruit juice drink	40
Water	0

3 Sound is measured in decibels.

Sounds over 80 decibels can damage your hearing.

The table shows how loud some sounds are.

Draw a bar chart to show this information.

Sound	Sound level (decibels)
Rustling leaf	10
Normal speech	60
Vacuum cleaner	70
Busy road	80
Disco speaker	100
Personal music player (loud)	105
Jet aircraft (50 m away)	140

4 The table shows the number of goals scored by a school team in 20 hockey matches.

Draw a bar-line graph to show this information.

Number of goals scored	0	1	2	3	4
Number of matches	2	6	5	4	3

5 In 1810 over 5000 members of the Royal Navy died.

The table shows the causes of death.

Copy and complete the percentage bar to show the information from the table.

Remember to include a key.

Cause of death	Approximate percentage of deaths
Disease	50
Accident	30
Shipwreck	10
War	10

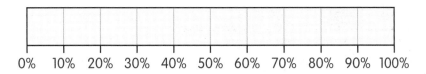

Continued ...

(6) The table shows the results of a maths test taken by a group of pupils.

Copy and complete these bar charts to show two ways to display this information.

Mark	1–10	11–20	21–30	31–40	41–50
Boys	1	1	8	12	8
Girls	0	3	6	15	6

(a)

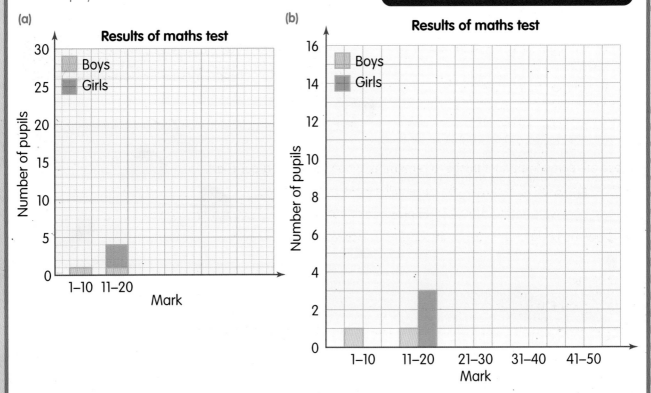

(b)

(7) This table shows the number of portions of fruit and vegetables eaten by a group of 12-year-olds one day.

Number of portions	0	1	2	3	4	5	6
Number of boys	2	4	7	5	2	0	0
Number of girls	1	2	7	3	6	0	1

Draw a bar graph to show this information.

Draw separate bars for the boys and the girls.

Remember to include a key.

(8) In a triathlon event competitors swim 1500 metres, then cycle 40 kilometres, then run 10 kilometres.

Kulsam, Alicia, Bernie and Jasmine take part in a triathlon event.

The table shows the percentage of their total time spent on each activity.

Draw a bar chart to show this information.

Draw one bar for each competitor.

Remember to include a key.

	Kulsam	Alicia	Bernie	Jasmine
Swimming	10	15	20	25
Cycling	60	55	45	50
Running	30	30	35	25

You learnt how to find information from pie charts in Chapter 16.

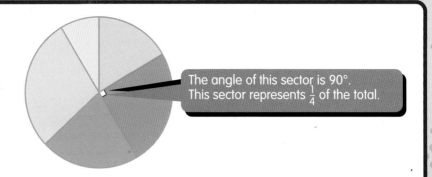

The angle of this sector is 90°. This sector represents $\frac{1}{4}$ of the total.

In a pie chart the circle is divided up into **sectors**.

The size of the angle of the sector depends on what fraction of the whole the sector represents.

These are some important things to remember when you draw a bar chart.

- The angles at the centre of the circle will always add up to 360°.
- You must write what each sector represents or colour the pie chart and draw a key.
- Draw the circle and measure the angles as accurately as you can.

Example

Jane is given £10 for her birthday.

She buy sweets costing £1, a DVD costing £4, a book costing £3 and saves £2.

Show this information in a pie chart.

Solution

Here are two methods for finding the angles for the sectors.

Method 1

There are 360° in a full circle.

The pie chart represents £10 altogether.

> **Hint**
> This method uses equivalent ratios. You learnt about these in Chapter 24.

360° represents £10.
÷10 ↓   ↓ ÷10
36° represents £1

> You need to find how many degrees are needed for £1.

Item	Amount	Angle
Sweets	£1	$1 \times 36° = 36°$
DVD	£4	$4 \times 36° = 144°$
Book	£3	$3 \times 36° = 108°$
Save	£2	$2 \times 36° = 72°$
Total	£10	360°

> Check the angles add up to 360°.

Continued …

Method 2

£1 as a fraction of £10 is $\frac{1}{10}$.

The pie chart represents £10 altogether.

There are 360° in a full turn.

$\frac{1}{10}$ of 360° represents £1.

Don't cancel the fractions.

To find $\frac{1}{10}$ of an amount, divide by 10.

Item	Amount	Fraction	Angle
Sweets	£1	$\frac{1}{10}$	360° ÷ 10 = 36°
DVD	£4	$\frac{4}{10}$	360° ÷ 10 × 4 = 144°
Book	£3	$\frac{3}{10}$	360° ÷ 10 × 3 = 108°
Save	£2	$\frac{2}{10}$	360° ÷ 10 × 2 = 72°
Total	£10	$\frac{10}{10}$ = 1	360°

To find $\frac{4}{10}$ of an amount, find $\frac{1}{10}$ of the amount, then multiply by 4. You have already worked out $\frac{1}{10}$ of the amount.

Check the angles add up to 360°.

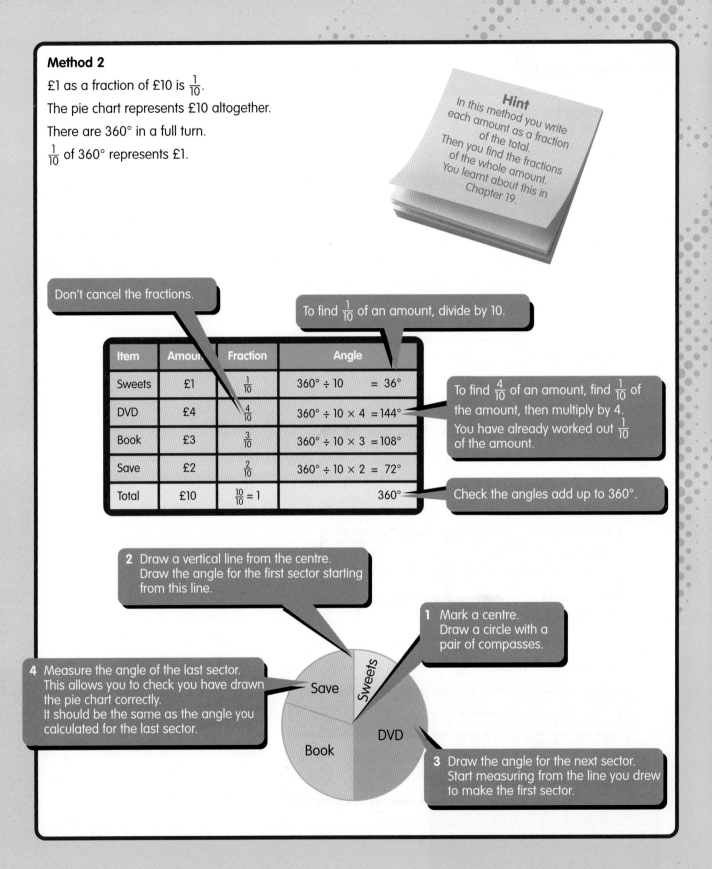

2 Draw a vertical line from the centre. Draw the angle for the first sector starting from this line.

1 Mark a centre. Draw a circle with a pair of compasses.

4 Measure the angle of the last sector. This allows you to check you have drawn the pie chart correctly. It should be the same as the angle you calculated for the last sector.

3 Draw the angle for the next sector. Start measuring from the line you drew to make the first sector.

1 Half of the people watching a football match are men.

A quarter of the people are women.

The rest are children.

Draw and label a pie chart to show this information.

2 An egg is about three-quarters water, one-eighth fat and one-eighth protein.

Draw and label a pie chart to show this information.

3 Mr McGregor plants vegetables in his garden.

He plants three rows of cabbages, four rows of carrots and five rows of potatoes.

(a) How many rows of vegetables does Mr McGregor plant altogether?

(b) Copy and complete this sentence.

> The number of degrees for one row of vegetables is 360° ÷ ☐ = ☐.

(c) Copy and complete this table.

Vegetable	Number of rows	Angle
Cabbages	3	3 × ☐ = ☐
Carrots	4	4 × ☐ = ☐
Potatoes	5	5 × ☐ = ☐
Total		

(d) Draw and label a pie chart to show this information.

4 The table shows how the pupils in a class voted in a mock election.

Party	Number of votes	Angle
Labour	8	
Conservative	8	
Liberal Democrats	4	
Other	10	
Total		

(a) How many pupils voted in the mock election?

(b) In a pie chart, how many degrees will represent one pupil?

(c) Copy and complete the table.

(d) Draw and label a pie chart to show this information.

Hint
What fraction of the total number of rows is one row?

Continued …

⑤ The table shows the number of pupils in Year 7 who received awards for swimming.

Award	Number of pupils	Angle
Bronze	10	
Silver	7	
Gold	3	
Total		

(a) Copy and complete the table.

(b) Draw and label a pie chart to show this information.

⑥ Amir carried out a survey to find out the favourite sports of his friends.

These are his results.

football	rugby	football	football	cricket	football
basketball	football	rugby	rugby	football	cricket
football	basketball	cricket	football	rugby	rugby

Draw a pie chart to show this information.

Investigation

Carry out a statistical investigation of your own.

Investigate what Year 7 pupils like to do in their spare time.

❶ Begin by writing some statements you want to check are correct or not.

❷ Write some questions to find out whether your statements are true or false.

❸ Collect the data you need.

❹ Draw some charts to show your data.

❺ Write a report explaining what you have done and what you have found out.